TRIGGER™
The mental health & wellbeing publisher

www.triggerpublishing.com

Theinspirationalseries™
Overcoming adversity and thriving

Love, Interrupted
Navigating Grief One Day at a Time

BY SIMON THOMAS

We are proud to introduce The**inspirational**series™. Part of the Trigger family of innovative mental health books, The**inspirational**series™ tells the stories of the people who have battled and beaten mental health issues. For more information visit: www.triggerpublishing.com

THE AUTHOR

Simon Thomas was loved and admired by a generation of children – and their parents – as presenter on the iconic children's magazine series, *Blue Peter*. He tried to get the job twice before his persistence paid off and he was awarded the cherished role in 1999. He made the move to *Sky Sports News* in 2005, and became the lead presenter of Sky's Football League coverage in 2010. He got his dream job – presenting live Premier League matches for Sky – in 2016.

In November 2017, Simon's life was thrown into turmoil. His wife, Gemma, died suddenly from acute myeloid leukaemia (AML). Left to care for their young son, Ethan, on his own, he resigned from Sky Sports, and put all his efforts into helping them both through the most difficult year of their lives.

Simon is a keen fundraiser, and is the President of the Bloodwise charity where he helps raise awareness of AML and other blood cancers. He also established the Gemma Thomas Fund to raise money that will help fund important research into AML.

First published in Great Britain 2019 by Trigger

Trigger is a trading style of Shaw Callaghan Ltd & Shaw Callaghan 23 USA, INC.

The Foundation Centre

Navigation House, 48 Millgate, Newark

Nottinghamshire NG24 4TS UK

www.triggerpublishing.com

Copyright © Simon Thomas 2019

British Library Cataloguing in Publication Data

A CIP catalogue record for this book is available upon request
from the British Library

ISBN: 978-1-78956-104-3

This book is also available in the following e-Book and Audio formats:

AUDIO: 978-1-78956-030-5

MOBI: 978-1-78956-029-9

ePUB: 978-1-78956-027-5

Simon Thomas has asserted his right under the Copyright,
Design and Patents Act 1988 to be identified as the author of this work

Cover and back cover images by Vicki Sharp Photography

Cover design and typeset by Fusion Graphic Design Ltd

Printed and bound in Great Britain by Clays Ltd, Elcograf S.p.A

Paper from responsible sources

TRIGGER™

The mental health & wellbeing publisher

www.triggerpublishing.com

Thank you for purchasing this book.
You are making an incredible difference.

Proceeds from all Trigger books go directly to
The Shaw Mind Foundation, a global charity that focuses
entirely on mental health. To find out more about
The Shaw Mind Foundation visit,
www.shawmindfoundation.org

MISSION STATEMENT

Our goal is to make help and support available for every
single person in society, from all walks of life.
We will never stop offering hope. These are our promises.

Trigger and The Shaw Mind Foundation

the *Shaw* **mind**
FOUNDATION

Creating hope for children,
adults and families

Bloodwise
The **blood cancer** charity

About Bloodwise

Blood cancer is the UK's third biggest cancer killer, claiming 15,000 lives each year.

We're here to put an end to that.

We're a community of supporters, researchers, nurses, volunteers and campaigners, working together to transform the lives of people affected by blood cancer. By funding ground-breaking research. By campaigning to improve care and access to treatment. And by giving people information and support when they need it most.

Since starting out in 1960, our research has saved thousands of lives. It's also led to improved treatments that have reduced the devastating long-term effects for survivors.

But there's still so much more to do.

With your help, we believe we can cure blood cancer in this lifetime.

Join us at **bloodwise.org.uk**

Bloodwise support line service:
0808 2080 888 (freephone)

For Gemma – loving, compassionate, missed.

INTRODUCTION

Dan Walker

Loss is something we don't really talk about. It's the sort of thing that wakes you up in the middle of the night. Loss is something that has changed Simon's life forever.

I remember when I met him for the first time. We were both playing for different teams in a football tournament in London. Simon had just left *Blue Peter* and was working for Sky.

I grabbed a quick word while he was surrounded by a few autograph hunters, and he was kind and generous. We have stayed in contact ever since.

When I first heard the news about Gemma I felt numb. When I listened to Simon explain how he told their son Ethan that his mum would not be coming back, I was driving on the M6 with tears running down my face. He has made me cry a lot over the past few months.

On the anniversary of Gemma's death I interviewed Simon for the BBC. We spoke for what seemed like hours. We are both Christians and faith was one of the main topics of that conversation. It was more of a discussion than an interview.

Where do faith and grief meet? How is faith affected when you lose someone you can't feel complete without? Simon has made me think about all sorts of issues over the past 18 months – things we all need to consider. That's why I feel this book is so important.

Simon addresses everything you're about to read with a breathtaking honesty. The vivid description of his mental health struggles feels incredibly relevant and he explores his feelings and failings in a way that demands respect.

Dealing with grief is such a personal thing but I feel all of us can learn something from this book. I found myself asking 'What would I do?' or 'How would I react?' at the bottom of virtually every page.

In recent months I have found myself getting exasperated by a few individuals on social media who feel they have some ownership over Simon's public grief and have judged him for the way he has dealt with his wife's death. If you are feeling a bit "judgey" now, then please put this down and come back to it another time.

One of the great encouragements from this book is the kindness of friends and strangers that shines through the pages.

Despite that ... be prepared. What you're about to read is a pretty brutal account of loss. Be careful where you open it. It will take you through the full range of human emotion and examine all the struggles and pitfalls along the way. But, and this is important, there is hope and peace in here – a peace "that passes understanding".

Simon, Ethan and the rest of Gemma's family and close friends – just like many people we all know – have had to deal with something truly awful. This book highlights the lows but also shows you that there is a narrow way out the other side. Things can, and will, get better.

THE LONGEST DAY OF MY LIFE

At a quarter to six on a bright, cold November evening, after what had felt like the longest day of my life, my world fell apart.

After hours of listening to a horrible, relentless rattle in her throat, as she struggled for breath, the sound suddenly stopped. With two gentle breaths that you could barely hear, she fell silent. Her face looked almost angelic. In that one moment, Gemma, the mother, the daughter, the sister and friend, the mother of my boy, and the woman I had loved for 16 years, was gone.

In that moment of peace, when the lights finally dimmed and faded, our future changed forever. I was gripped by a sick feeling in my stomach, like nothing I had ever felt before.

How on earth had this happened so fast? How had life been turned upside down in the space of just three days? Even now, I still struggle to comprehend how something can strike you down so quickly.

Sadly, inevitably, nearly all of us will be touched by cancer at some stage in our lives, whether directly or indirectly. We all know just how devastating the disease is for countless people. But I'd always thought that cancer at least afforded you some time ... Time to try to get your head around it, to talk about what it is going to mean for you as a family, to try to eke out whatever time in life is left; time to steel yourself to say the final goodbye.

We never had that chance. She was gone in a moment.

Just three weeks before, everything had felt so normal. There was still some late autumn warmth in the sun, our beloved boy, Ethan, was enjoying the first term of a new school year, and family life felt as happy, and as good, as it ever had been.

It was a Monday morning at the end of October. I was at home enjoying my morning coffee and reading the sports pages, and Gemma was on the school run. But when she arrived back home, she didn't look in a good way at all. She hobbled through the front door, wincing in pain with every step she took. I asked her what on earth was wrong. It turned out that while walking Ethan from the car to the school gate, she had tripped up the kerb and landed badly on her foot. I did question how on earth she had managed to trip up a kerb, but unsurprisingly, this question didn't go down too well!

As she took off her shoe to reveal her foot, I could see that it was already quite swollen, and a nasty bruise was developing. Up until that point, my experience of foot injuries was based on little more than the outpouring of national concern when David Beckham injured his metatarsal ahead of the 2002 World Cup. But I didn't need to be a medical genius to tell that this was more than just a bit of bruising. An hour or so later we were in the A&E department in Henley, and later that morning it was confirmed that Gemma had broken a bone in her foot. At the time, it felt like a huge blow. She knew she wouldn't be able to drive for the next six weeks and she was going to have to wear a great big boot that looked like part of Darth Vader's outfit. As her tears of frustration flowed, she said, 'Why does this kind of stuff always happen to me?'

Ever since Ethan had been born in 2009, Gemma had struggled with insomnia. She had long periods where she would regularly endure nights when she didn't sleep at all. I lost count of the mornings where I would ask how she slept, and through tired eyes, and with a resigned tone in her voice, she would reply, 'I haven't.' I never understood how she managed to function. She had every right to feel sorry for herself, she had every right to say 'You, do the school run so I can get some rest,' but every single time, she dragged herself out of bed and got on with the job of being Ethan's mum.

A month before, while I'd been away working, she had sent me this text message, which really encapsulates the impact that her lack of sleep had on her emotionally:

Darl I'm so sorry – I'm trying hard not to let this sleep issue impact you and Ethan too much, but it's difficult as I'm feeling rotten most of the time at the moment, either due to my severe lack of sleep or the amount of medication I'm taking – or both probably. I really hate this situation and I'm doing my best – I'm sure it's temporary and I'll be back on track soon. I know it's not great for you either – I'm sorry for that. I love you both so very, very, much xxxx.

The morning she broke her foot came in the midst of a really bad period of insomnia. She had also been having headaches that had gone from a few a week, to an almost daily occurrence. To me, a broken foot didn't seem much more than an irritating inconvenience; to her, it felt like the final straw. She had had enough.

With Gemma out of action, I got used to my new life of doing the school run. I had always enjoyed doing it when Gemma couldn't, but I wasn't used to experiencing the incessant chatter of the school gate every day. (Unless you're a seasoned school runner, it can feel like a bizarre world that takes you outside of your comfort zone as you struggle to fit in.)

Meanwhile, Gemma was trying to get used to life with her Darth Vader boot. Like so many other times over the course of our marriage, she adapted brilliantly, and without ever complaining. But I could see that the headaches and the feeling of tiredness were growing steadily worse. Every time she complained of another headache, I would urge her to go to the doctors. All too often, my concerned advice was met with Gemma's trademark roll of the eyes. She might not have been worried, but I was beginning to worry very much ...

A few years earlier, I had suffered quite badly with depression, and slowly, but surely, I had begun to feel it creeping back into our lives. Only this time, it came with an unwanted bedfellow: anxiety. I was worried about Gemma, but I didn't know to what extent my worries were being affected by the depression.

The depressive feelings had been slowly wearing me down, and the doctor had signed me off work, and prescribed antidepressants. I was due to go back for a follow-up appointment a couple of weeks after Gemma's disagreement with the kerb. The night before the appointment, she sent a message to her close friend, Esther, that gives a glimpse into how she was really feeling:

I'm in bed. Had some tea and then started feeling horrendous – feel like I'm totally done in at the moment . . . permanent banging headache, mouth ulcers, exhausted and about two hours sleep last night . . . Know it will get better but it feels tough right now.

I had little idea of how bad she actually was, but I asked if we could have a joint appointment. At the very least, I wanted to find out if there really was anything to worry about.

Mid-morning, we sat down with a doctor we had always liked, and always got on with ... although we'd half joked that if you needed a prescription for anything quickly – he'd be your man.

Gemma told him she'd been having reoccurring headaches for the past few weeks, and how she'd been feeling so very tired most of the time. The doctor knew about Gemma's long-term struggles with insomnia, and, understandably, felt the tiredness was linked to it. But then he asked about her headaches; specifically, how stressed she was feeling about *me*.

I knew Gemma must have been worried; why wouldn't she be? To see your other half struggling with mental illness is horrible. And deeply unsettling. You want to do anything you can to help make it better, but you feel helpless.

Between the lack of sleep and the stress of seeing me hit so hard by depression, it wasn't surprising Gemma's headaches were so bad. We left with a prescription of Codeine for her, and more depression pills for me. For a time, the Codeine did its job of easing the pain; but Gemma's tiredness was becoming markedly worse.

Some of it, I could see for myself. Some of it, I found out later. Her friend Liz told me just how hard Gemma had found a shopping trip to Reading later that week. When it had come to hobbling back to the car park in her big old boot, Gemma told Liz she didn't have the energy to get there; she said she felt physically weak, and had to sit down. Eventually, Gemma being Gemma, she got up, carried on, and made it back to the car. Had I known about it at the time, it would have set off an alarm bell in my head.

But the next morning, the alarm bells were definitely ringing. As I took up her cup of tea on Thursday morning, I noticed the big bruise on her thigh. As I asked her where the bruise had come from, she replied in a very matter-of-fact way, that it was from when she had fallen. I thought it was weird that it was still there, three weeks after the accident, but Gemma seemed unconcerned and that was the end of the conversation. We never talked about it again.

Knowing what I know now about blood cancers, a bruise like that can be a tell-tale sign that something serious is at work. But back then, we thought nothing more of it.

By the Friday morning it was becoming ever clearer that this wasn't just headaches mixed in with another dose of insomnia, Gemma was getting ill. Really ill.

When I got back from the morning school run, she was still in bed. So many times down the years, she had managed to function, even when she'd felt as rough as sandpaper. This time was different. She told me she had no energy to do anything, and needed to spend the morning in bed. But even as I told her to rest, she immediately started worrying about the weekend. Our friends, Michael and Angellica and their family were coming to stay; it had been in the diary for weeks. Gemma had booked a lovely table in an outside igloo, at a restaurant in the nearby village of Sonning, and she didn't want to let them down.

I had known Angellica and Michael since our CBBC days. I had lost touch with so many of the presenters I worked with during those heady days at Television Centre, but Angellica and Michael had stayed close friends with us both. The weekend they were due to come was in the weeks following Angellica winning the BBC's *Celebrity MasterChef*. Gemma had always loved cooking and had religiously followed Angellica's amazing journey to the final. During and after every episode she would text Angellica with her excited commentary. And when the final episode was broadcast that saw her crowned champion, Gemma sent her this text:

Never in doubt. Brilliant Angellica – so proud! Well done!!!!! xxxx

Part of Gemma's excitement about seeing Angellica was to talk about a book idea they'd shared. It would be Angellica's book but Gemma was going to help her write it, and was already bubbling away with lots of ideas. They'd been swapping texts for most of the week, and on that Friday, Gemma texted her to say how rubbish she was feeling:

Hi Hun ... I'm so sorry and fed up about this but I've been in bed since yesterday with a pounding horrible headache that I just can't shift – actually had headache for about 10 days and it's got a lot worse and I've totally lost my appetite too – hardly eaten for 3 days. Waiting to speak to doctor – been taking Codeine which I think is making it worse. Just wanted to warn you but am so hoping I feel better tmrw – even if we just get a takeaway tmrw eve. Can I let you know in the morning? So sorry xxx

Gemma got a last-minute doctor's appointment later that day. I rushed back from dropping Ethan at a party to join her, with a sick feeling growing in my stomach. Much as my mind was trying to tell me it was nothing serious, the steady but now increasing deterioration in Gemma's health was starting to inject the fear into my mind that this could be something more sinister.

For the second time in three days, we were back in the surgery, except this time we were seeing a different doctor. Once again, we talked about the headache she couldn't shift. We talked about how her health had deteriorated since Wednesday – the increased fatigue, the fact she was struggling to get out of bed (which was so unusual for Gemma) and her loss of appetite. If the doctor *was* concerned, it never showed. He spent some time looking into her eyes with his ophthalmoscope, asking various questions about whether she had been suffering any blurred vision – she hadn't. And a few minutes later he uttered the words that will stay with me forever.

'Having looked at your general wellbeing and your vital signs, I'm satisfied there is nothing seriously wrong with you. If things get worse over the weekend, come back on Monday.'

And that was it; we got up and left the surgery. Gemma was the worst I'd ever seen her in the 16 years we'd been together, yet the doctor seemed unconcerned.

Every time I thought back to that appointment in the weeks to come, I was furious. I hated myself for not being more assertive with him. Why did I just accept what he'd said, shrug my shoulders, and leave? Why hadn't I insisted that she should, at the very least, have a blood test? Why hadn't he told us to drive to A&E, just to get it checked out? Just to be sure!

Why hadn't I screamed at him to do more?!

They say hindsight is a wonderful thing. For me, it's been a curse. Looking back at those weeks now, through the eyes of someone who has become all too aware of the plethora of symptoms a blood cancer can present, I can see exactly why everything that was happening to Gemma *was* happening.

Her white blood cell count was going through the roof, her blood was thickening with every hour, and her heart was struggling to push the thick blood through her body. No wonder she was beyond exhausted. Poor, poor Gems.

As soon as we got home, Gemma returned to bed. Ethan ran through the front door a little later, asking 'How's Mummy?' I told him he could tiptoe upstairs to see her, and a few minutes later I walked into our bedroom to see him cuddled up to Gemma in our bed. It was a sight I had seen so many times before – but this time, for some reason, it felt so different. The eyes of an eight-year-old see things so differently to the eyes of an adult. Ethan knew his mum wasn't well, but he didn't have any of the growing worries that were crowding my mind. He looked up at her pale, exhausted face and said, 'I love you, Mummy, you'll be better soon.' With that, he was off, and minutes later I could hear him pouring yet another huge box of Lego all over his bedroom floor.

At about half ten that Friday night Gemma texted Angellica again:

I really don't want to cancel!! Saw the doctor earlier – still feeling rough but don't want to let the kids down .... Let's go ahead. Hopefully will feel bit better tmrw. X

We never did get to see Angellica and Michael that weekend. And Gemma didn't feel any better the next day. The growing fatigue, the bruising, the loss of appetite and those horrible bloody headaches would never relent. Unbeknown to her, and all of us, Gemma was already in the final week of her life.

THE QUIET WHISPER OF FEAR

As Saturday passed into Sunday, there was no sign of an improvement. If anything, Gemma was getting steadily worse, hour by hour. In all the years I'd known her, I had never seen her so incapacitated: bed-bound, in constant pain, and utterly exhausted. It was almost too much for her to get out of bed and walk the three steps to our ensuite bathroom. She wasn't eating much either, just the occasional bite of toast and a few sips of tea.

Whenever I re-live that week in my mind, the sadness is just as acute. The guilt is always there, nagging away at me. And I'm still asking myself those same questions:

Why the hell didn't you do something?

Why didn't you pick her up, carry her to the car and take her straight to A&E?

Why ...?

In part, I think I wasn't seeing things with the same clarity because of the anxiety and the depression, but I also think it had something to do with Gemma ... A lot of us men (I'm trying to pretend I'm not one of them) are not exactly impressive when it comes to being ill. Even a common cold can turn a man into a gibbering wreck of self-pity while over dosing on Lemsip and Nurofen under the duvet.

But for so many women, like Gemma, their care for others, and in particular their family, almost overrides their need to care for themselves. In all the time we had been married, when Gemma had been ill, she always managed to carry on. She was always there for us, even when she felt like death warmed up. This illness was markedly different. But she continued to tell me that I didn't need to worry.

I wonder now if there's another truth to this – whenever we feel ill in a way that is different to anything we've felt before, it comes with a quiet whisper of fear. It's the fear that stops us trying to discover what's wrong, or even lets us admit to feeling scared. In our minds, we try and rationalise it. We tell ourselves it's probably nothing serious. Rather than confront the fear of what might be wrong, we bury our heads in the sand and hope that it will soon pass. Ignorance, as they say, is bliss. Maybe there was a sense of that in Gemma's reluctance to seek help, and to hold back from screaming at the doctor that she wasn't "just tired" – she felt hideous.

Gemma was continually worrying about Ethan, and what we could do to keep the weekend as normal as possible for him. She told me that Ethan really wanted to watch *Paddington 2* again, so she had booked two tickets, so I could take him to a showing, that afternoon, in Reading. Even though she was feeling, in her words, "horrendous", and finding the briefest of physical movements exhausting, that didn't stop her thinking of her darling boy. I didn't want to leave her, but she insisted.

So for the second time in eight days we went to see the brilliant *Paddington 2*, except this time it was just me and the boy – a foretaste of things to come.

As Ethan munched merrily on his popcorn, and the endless trailers played, my mind drifted back to the weekend before, when the three of us had sat in almost the same row of seats. Back then, when the film reached its heart-warming finale and Paddington rushed up to his precious Aunt Lucy, embraced her, and wished her a happy birthday, Ethan began to cry. But they weren't tears of sadness, they were tears of joy. An eight-year-old boy had been profoundly moved by the reunion of two family members whose bond of love had remained unbroken despite many miles and months apart. I remember so clearly turning to Gemma as Ethan's tears flowed and seeing the tears welling up in her eyes too. As we lay in bed that night, she told me she'd been crying tears of pride and joy for her boy, at seeing him being able to express his emotions in front of us, and feel totally at ease in doing so. In so many ways, that bond between Paddington and Aunt Lucy represented so much of the bond between Gemma and Ethan. Precious, strong, and unconditional.

As we enjoyed *Paddington 2* again, Gemma was still trying to keep her friends up to speed on how she was doing:

Feeling worse ... haven't got out of bed today apart from to have a shower – then nearly threw up ... :(Not eaten since Thursday, back to doc tmrw hopefully x

I wonder how I'd have felt if I'd known – as we lay there that Sunday night – that it was the last time Gemma would ever sleep in our bed? Never again would I get to enjoy the normal, unappreciated act of falling asleep with my wife – my rock – lying beside me. Before I turned off the light, we agreed that, first thing in the morning, we would ring the surgery to get another appointment. As I lay there, my mind was a whirlpool of fears as I began to worry ever more that this might – just might – be something more than stress; something altogether more serious.

By the time I returned from the now routine school run that Monday morning, Gemma had managed to get an appointment at the surgery for 9.30am – exactly the same time as I had an appointment with the counsellor I'd been seeing for my depression and anxiety. As I arrived home, Gemma had somehow mustered the strength to get dressed and haul herself downstairs. She said she wanted me to go to my counsellor, but she felt too ill to wait in the surgery until I'd finished, so she was trying to find someone to pick her up and take her home. I could barely believe what I was hearing – why on earth would I go to my counsellor when my wife was so very ill? Why did it even merit a discussion?

I understood her deep desire to see me get better, to see me back at work; for normality to reign again; but right then, at that moment, she was my only priority. 'I need to come with you, Darl,' I kept saying. But no matter how much I protested she was having none of it. 'Darl, you must go,' she told me tenderly. 'You need to get better.' Despite feeling sicker than she had ever felt before, she was still putting me before herself. It didn't matter what I said. Her mind was made up. With a heavy heart, I did what she asked.

To this day – and probably for the rest of my life – I will always regret that moment.

I would do anything now to be able to go back and carry her into that doctor's room. My illness could have waited, hers could not. I should have been there with her, impressing on our doctor just how bad she'd been over the weekend. But I wasn't.

An hour later, I returned home to find her back in bed. Nothing had changed. I asked her what the doctor had said. It had been five days since he'd seen her; surely he would have seen the deterioration. Surely, he would have seen the desperation to get better in her eyes? Incredibly, he hadn't.

In the hour or so after that final appointment, Gemma's friend, Catherine, texted her to confirm arrangements for a day out they'd planned.

Hi babes how are you feeling today? We're "booked in" for our date night at IKEA tomorrow but I'm guessing you're not up for it yet ... shall I cancel and we'll try and get a date in next month? XX

Gemma's reply gives a chilling insight into something of what happened in the surgery that morning:

Oh sorry – had completely forgotten about that, can we postpone? Been in bed since Thursday – still no appetite :-(Seen doctor again – he still thinks its stress-related ... I'm not so sure. Xx

It pains me to read that text again, never knowing exactly what was said between Gemma and our doctor that Monday morning. And, in the early weeks after she went, my anger and resentment towards him became, at times, unbearable.

When I re-read that text to Catherine now, some of that anger bubbles back to the surface. For weeks, I wrestled with this one simple question – if Gemma was the most poorly I had ever seen her, how the hell did he not see it?

We didn't know then, that her blood had become thick with the explosion of white blood cells caused by acute myeloid leukaemia. The damage to the blood vessels in her brain that would kill her just days later was already underway. By that Monday, it was probably already too late.

TIME TO FIGHT

By the Monday afternoon, Gemma's condition had taken a more sinister turn – she started being sick for the first time. Any lingering hope that this was just some stress-related illness disappeared. Gemma's mum, Wendy, expressed our growing pain and confusion:

My mind was working overtime ... The thought began to grow ... Was there something really terribly wrong? A brain tumour ... something else? I couldn't get her out of my thoughts. I prayed: was there anything I could do; anything I had to do? I hated interfering, I didn't want to be the interfering mother-in-law. But the answer to that prayer came back ... I had to contact Gemma and Simon's close friends, Dave and Debs. I needed to speak to someone with medical qualifications, and I knew Dave's sister, Meg, was an eye surgeon, and he said she'd be happy to contact Gems. I hated going behind Simon's back, but just felt I had to do something. I felt so helpless.

When I found out, I was angry. It felt like she didn't trust me, she didn't think her son-in-law was capable of understanding just how ill her daughter was. But as I've reflected on this, I've realised Wendy was right. And I'm glad she went behind my back. Time was no longer on our side.

Meg rang later that evening. Gently, but firmly, she told me that we needed to get help, then insisted that she speak to Gemma. In the silence after Gemma hung up, I asked what Meg had said. With a resigned tone to her voice, she said Meg wanted her to go to A&E – straightaway.

Gemma didn't want to go. But seeing her so ill, so defeated, brought me to my senses. I told her we didn't have a choice – we had to.

After calls to Wendy, and to Dave and Debs, we decided I should stay home to keep things as "normal" as possible for Ethan, while Debs took Gemma to the Royal Berkshire Hospital in Reading. Ethan was fast asleep by this time, blissfully unaware of what was unfolding, but neither of us wanted him waking up to discover that we were both gone. Reluctantly, Gemma walked out of our bedroom, down the stairs, and out of the front door to Debs' car.

Little did any of us know that she had left our house for the last time. That she would never again kiss her precious boy good night again in our home. Or lie next to me in our bed. When she left, it changed our home forever.

*

As Gemma sat in A&E, I tried to wait patiently at home, but the minutes felt like hours. I couldn't settle; I couldn't rest – all I could do was wait, and wonder what was happening.

Debs was with her:

Even though Gemma was clearly not well, she still wasn't sure she should be at A&E. Especially that night, as there had just been a report on the BBC News about how busy the Royal Berkshire's A&E department was, and how overstretched the doctors were. As we watched more and more people coming in, she said, 'Gosh, some of these people are really sick,' implying she wasn't – even though she was having hot flushes and feeling nauseous.

Gemma was very appreciative of me taking her and sorry that it was so late (we got there around 10.00 pm and waited more than an hour to be seen) In spite of the pain she was in, she still kept trying to make me laugh though – at one point she was looking at her leg poking out from her pyjama bottoms and commented on her "winter coat" (non-waxed legs). She also pointed out an "out of the ordinary" small blood blister on her leg – innocuous at the time, but possibly a sign of what was happening in her body that she was completely unaware of.

*

For the second time in 12 hours, I felt guilty that I wasn't with Gemma. I should have been by her side. But when I thought about our precious boy asleep, upstairs, I knew that I needed to be at home for him. As the clock ticked past midnight Gemma texted:

Darl, I think I'm going to be here for a while – I need you to be with me. Debs is going to head back in a bit and has offered to sleep at ours. I love you xx

At about 12.45am that Tuesday morning, Debs returned home, and we swapped places. She told me that Gemma had finally been seen, and at long last, her blood was being tested, but there was no telling how long it would be before the results came back. As I arrived at the hospital, the sick feeling in the pit of my stomach intensified. I had no idea what was about to come, but I couldn't escape the uneasy feeling: this wasn't going to be a night that would end well.

I was led into the room where seven or eight other patients lay. They pulled the curtain back, and there she was, with a drip in her arm, almost asleep. I can't put into words the love I felt for her as I saw her there. All I could do was gently embrace her and whisper into her ear that it was going to be okay. But while my heart was trying to tell me one thing, my head feared something far, far worse.

I lost count of the times the doctor and nurses visited her bedside in the small hours, but every time they did, I saw a look on their faces that didn't sit well. It felt like they knew something; something neither of us would want to hear. I tried my best to supress those fears; Gemma needed me to stay strong for her.

At just after four o'clock on that dark, winter morning, it felt like the clock stopped, and time stood still. The doctor came to Gemma's bedside and delivered the words that will stay with me forever: 'We've sent your blood to our haematology department and they've done lots of different tests ... and I'm really sorry to have to tell you that your blood is deranged ...'

In that moment, all the fear and apprehension flooded out, and I shouted out 'No!' I didn't want her to go on speaking. The last words I remember hearing were: 'I'm afraid it's a blood cancer.'

My next recollection was waking up on a hospital bed. A nurse was watching over me, encouraging me to drink sugary tea. I looked up and saw Gemma, still lying there, across the ward. I realised that as the doctor had delivered the news, and the shock waves hit, I had fainted and fallen.

My head swam, and the shock waves gathered again – only this time, something changed. It felt like a switch in my head had been flicked. This was Gemma's darkest hour; I had to be her light. As the strength returned to my legs and I got up from the bed, I knew that it was time to fight. All those times down the years she had been a rock for me, now it was my turn to be strong for her. But being a rock wasn't enough; I had to be her mountain. Whatever the next few hours, days and weeks might hold, I just had to be there for her.

I held her, and told her again and again how much I loved her. I told her we would get through this. I promised her that I would give everything I had to get her through it. I felt new strength coursing through my veins.

In the weeks and months since that morning, I have reflected on that moment again and again. It came at a time in my life like no other, when the depression and anxiety I'd been feeling had taken so great a hold; when the panic attacks had become so regular and so debilitating that I had been unable to work for a month.

If there was ever a moment for another panic attack, that was it. But it never came. Something had changed. This was the ultimate fight or flight moment, and it was time to fight. The mental illness that had gripped me for the past weeks loosened its grip and seemed to fall away, to be replaced by a surge of strength that I couldn't completely explain.

As I held her hand, and looked upon her face, etched with fear, I said to Gemma, 'Can I pray for you?' There are many parts of that night that I can't fully recollect, but the prayer that I prayed has stayed with me. I simply prayed:

'Jesus, I love this woman beyond words. I thank you for bringing her into my life. I thank you that her love for me is beyond measure. I thank you that she has brought the gift of Ethan into our lives. I thank you that we are so blessed. I'm sorry for the times I haven't shown this; but right now, Jesus, I ask that whatever it is that Gemma has, that you would take it away. I ask you right now to comfort her. I pray that you would give us both strength, and I pray that despite our fears you would give us peace, a peace that passes all understanding. Amen.'

As Gemma joined me in saying "amen" I looked again into those deep brown eyes and waited with her as she fell into a light sleep. I left her then to go and ring her mum. As I walked out of the hospital into the darkness, the winter chill hit my arms and I began to make the hardest of calls to Wendy. A call I can never forget. In among the tears, her shouts of 'No … no … no …' reverberated in my ear. We were both numb.

Wendy called Gem's sister Rebecca and told her the devastating news, while I rang Debs. This is how she remembers that call:

I was woken by my phone ringing – it was Simon, distraught. Through tears and sobs he told me, 'She has cancer – blood cancer.' He said they weren't sure what sort but were doing more tests. I can still feel the shock of that news and the realisation of what I thought it would mean for Gems – months or years of treatment with the hope of a good prognosis.

Just before 6.00am, Rebecca arrived. By this point, Gemma had been moved onto the haematology ward and the nurse who headed up that department was already with Gemma. She was such a lovely woman. In the midst of what felt like such a hopeless situation, she just radiated a wonderful positivity. She told us that her business was making people like Gemma better again. I held on to her every word. But as her team busied themselves trying to make Gemma more comfortable, our thoughts turned to Ethan ...

In less than an hour, Ethan would be up. He had gone to bed saying good night to Mummy and Daddy, like he always did. But as things stood, he would be waking up with neither of us there. Gemma insisted that Rebecca and I went back. I didn't want to leave her side; but as she had been, so many times during our 16 years together, she was right. I had to head home. I had to be there for our boy.

50-50

As I walked back through the front door, it all felt horribly surreal. In just a few short hours everything had changed. Debs was waiting for us in the hallway, and all we could do was hug each other as the tears began to flow.

My eyes glanced up the stairs – there he was – my darling boy, looking down at us, perplexed, fearful and wondering where Mummy was.

The whole way home, I had thought about how I was going to explain what was happening, and why Mummy wasn't in our bed, waiting for her morning cuddle from him, and a cup of tea from me. As he came down the stairs, I ran up to grab him. Of all the countless hugs I have given him over the years, this was the tightest and most intense. I wanted to tell him everything was okay. I wanted it to be just a normal Tuesday morning like all the others. But it wasn't. There was nothing remotely normal about that morning. However tempted I was to dress it up and play down what was happening, I couldn't. Ethan already knew his mum was very ill. I didn't use the dreaded "C" word, I just told him that Mummy was still not very well, and that she needed to stay in hospital to make her better. He didn't need to know any more because *we* didn't know any more, and we all believed she'd be okay. They *would* make her better.

After giving him breakfast and getting him ready for school, I asked him if he wanted to record Mummy a little video message. Without hesitation he stood in the corner of our kitchen, looking cute and smart in his uniform, and with that childish innocence simply said, 'Hello Mummy, I hope you get well really soon. I'll be coming to see you soon after school. I love you so much.' (Kisses the camera lens.) 'You're the best. Bye!' (Blows her a kiss).

As I walked him up to the school gate, everything was grating. Every conversation, every laugh, every bit of school gate tittle-tattle jarred. We had just been launched into a nightmare; but all around us, everything was just like it always was. In time, I would learn in a much more profound and painful way, that life must, and indeed, does, just carry on around you.

As I waved Ethan goodbye my phone began to ring. It was Gary, my boss from Sky Sports. By this point I had been off work for over a month and while he was putting absolutely no pressure on me to come back, he simply wanted to see how I was doing, and work out together whether I'd be well enough to return to work when the busy festive football period kicked into gear. I couldn't hold back the tears and blurted out, 'Gemma's got cancer.' He was stunned. I can still hear the total disbelief in his voice. In the space of just a few weeks, he had seen me go from being seemingly fit and healthy, and presenting Sky Sports' *Premier League Football*, to being virtually paralysed by anxiety, and now finding out my wife had leukaemia. As I told him I had to get back to the hospital, he said Sky was there for us both, for as long as it would take. He told me to go and give everything I had to helping Gemma get better.

In the chaos of that morning, his words were hugely reassuring. The one thing you don't want to worry about when you go through something like this, is work. Gaz's words took those fears away. I only wish the same reassurances could be given to other people who have to go through something similar. Facing financial worries on top of coping with a gravely ill family member must be absolutely crippling. Sky's unstinting support meant everything to me.

As Rebecca and I headed back to the hospital, we felt a bizarre sense of calm about what was happening. Of course, we were massively scared, but part of the calm came from the reassurance of knowing that leukaemia is something a lot of people get better from. We were desperately hoping and praying that Gemma would be one of those people too ... But then my phone beeped with a text from Gemma, and whatever sense of calm we'd felt was shattered:

Darl where are you? You need to get here quick, I'm being transferred in an ambulance to Oxford. They're getting me ready to leave now xx

My blood ran cold. Why on earth was *this* happening?

We were about half a mile from the hospital, but the traffic was predictably awful. In desperation, I swung the car onto the pavement, told Rebecca to take the car home, and ran as fast as my tired legs would allow back to the hospital.

The room where I'd left her just a few hours before was now a hive of activity as the nurses got Gemma ready to leave. I spoke to the nurse I had chatted with earlier who told me that the rapid increase in Gemma's white blood cell count had to be brought down as quickly as possible. Her blood was thickening, and her heart was struggling to push it around her body. They needed to put her on an apheresis machine that would filter out as many of the excess cells from Gemma's blood as possible. There are only a handful of these machines in the country and Oxford was the nearest. As we left the ward the nurse said, 'I'll see you soon, Gemma. When you come back, we'll get you better.'

They gently pushed her bed up the ramp into the ambulance, and I felt like I was having an out-of-body experience. There was my darling Gemma, her face drained of its usual radiance, eyes shut, holding the oxygen mask to her mouth.

As the ambulance thundered up the A4074 with the blue lights flashing and the sirens warding off the oncoming traffic, I chatted to the paramedic looking after Gemma and commented on the driving skills of his colleague in the front. I even recorded a video

– I thought it might be something "fun" to look back on in years to come when Gemma had come through this. In my mind, I was still utterly convinced that she was going to be okay. While she slept, I was bizarrely rather enjoying travelling at 90 miles an hour along a road I had crawled down so many times on the way home from work. I was in a total state of shock, and the shock somehow masked the gravity of the situation we were in.

Gemma was admitted to the haematology ward at the Churchill Hospital in Oxford. She was hooked up to the apheresis machine, and over four long hours, it took her entire blood supply out of her body twice, and ended up filling two large bags with orange looking liquid – red blood tainted with an excess of white blood cells.

Rebecca arrived and we kept vigil by Gemma's bedside. So much had happened so quickly, but we still knew very little about *why* it was happening. The pace of events had pulled us along with a frightening momentum. But now, as Gemma slept, we talked about what was to come. We knew there would be more blood tests, and then, perhaps, we would find out the reality of Gemma's condition and discover what kind of leukaemia she had.

Whatever news Dr Andy Peniket and his team were going to give us later, we knew we had to remain strong. Whatever we were feeling inside, we had to exhibit calm for Gemma. If she could sense that we were panicking, she was going to feel even more frightened. I wasn't going to let myself think of worst-case scenarios, and I made the decision to not look anything up online. Later I suggested Gemma's mum made the same decision. I'm so glad I did. Had I discovered then what I know now about the dreadful, devastating disease coursing through her body, those three short days would have had a totally different complexion. Instead of feeling a shared sense of strength and peace, we would have been lost in a maelstrom of fear that would have crippled us. We wouldn't have been able to support Gemma in the way she needed. It was already impossibly hard for her; she didn't need us collectively losing the plot.

As Gemma woke, and we held her hands, she looked exhausted. But at least some of the colour had begun to return to her cheeks. We told her again how much we loved her, and I asked her a question I could never have foreseen ever having to ask at that stage in our life together: 'Darl, when Dr Andy comes back in later to tell us what's happening and what's wrong ... How far do you want me to go with the questions? How much do you want to know? Do you want me to ask what your survival chances are?' She was too tired to really speak, but just nodded with an almost resigned motion.

When Dr Andy returned to the room, the look on his face was the same look I'd seen on the doctors' faces in the Royal Berks a few hours earlier. He told us that in a normal healthy adult, the white blood cell count should be up to ten – Gemma's count was over 450! In his words, it had turned Gemma's blood into a thick sludge. It was no wonder her body had been so horribly tired. He told us that the leukapheresis exchange had worked and brought the count down to about a hundred – and that meant they could begin an intense course of chemotherapy that night.

But – we still didn't know what was actually wrong with her. What kind of leukaemia had led to this brutal decline in her health? And that's when he told us, 'I'm afraid to say Gemma has acute myeloid leukaemia.'

We were silent. We'd never heard of it. We didn't know what that diagnosis meant.

He told us there are only around 3,100 new cases of this type of blood cancer in the UK every year; that it accounts for around just one per cent of all new cancer cases. And cases are highest amongst people aged 85 to 89 years. Gemma had been unlucky. Incredibly, tragically, unlucky.

I wanted to know how long ... how long had it been exploding in her bloodstream? He told me the reason it's called "acute" is because of the speed at which it develops ... in all likelihood, she would only have had it for three, maybe four weeks! I thought cancer gave you time – this strain gives you nothing.

Dr Andy told me about the intense chemotherapy treatment that would attack and kill the leukaemia cells. I heard him say there was a ten per cent chance she could die in the first 30 days, due to the severity of the treatment ... but it didn't quite sink in. I was too preoccupied with the question we all wanted answered – what were her chances of surviving this?

'Fifty-fifty' came the reply.

A fifty per cent chance my wife was going to die ... That she would not live to see her precious boy grow up.

I'll never know what was going through Gemma's mind in this moment, but somehow, she maintained her unflustered peace. There were no tears, no sense of panic, just a remarkable sense of calm. I have no doubt that however scared I was, she must have been feeling a hundred times worse. But she never let it show. And, slowly, very slowly, as I felt her calm spreading though me, I started to hope ... And I started to hold on to the fifty per cent chance that she would make it.

I sat looking into Gemma's tired, but beautiful brown eyes, then gripped her hand and told her, 'We're going to beat this. You're young, you're incredibly strong, you've got so much to live for. We are going to beat this and if I have to sleep by your side in this room for the next six months, I will do it. Darl, we're going to beat this.'

A GLIMMER OF HOPE

Over the next three nights, I never left her side. On the first night I slept in the armchair next to where her head lay. But in truth, neither of us really slept. The night was punctuated by a constant flow of visits from the night team, yet more blood tests, and a number of trips to the loo with Gemma. As she shuffled the six or so steps from her bed to the bathroom I followed nervously behind, pushing the drip machine and helping her through. A thin tube of bright, red liquid ran into her right arm – the process of trying to kill off the leukaemia was underway.

When you say those vows on your wedding day and promise your wife or husband that you will stand by them in sickness and in health, you don't want to think about what that might actually look like. You'd rather think about it in terms of a bout of flu, when you can stand by them with a cup of Lemsip and a good dose of love and sympathy. When you get hit by something like this, the worry is that it will turn you into a quivering wreck, making you incapable of providing the practical support your other half needs. I didn't feel like that. I just wanted to take her pain away. If I could have swapped places with her and had that drip running into my arm instead, I would have done. I couldn't bear to see her like that. All I could do was hold her, talk to her, pray with her, and support her in any way I could. So often my heart would fill with an enormous sense of helplessness, but despite that, there was never any doubt in my mind that if she had to spend the next six months or more in that room, I would stay with her. I would have never left her side, except to spend time with our boy.

The next morning, Dr Andy gave us an update on how Gemma's body was reacting to the leukapheresis treatment. Although he was never any more than cautiously optimistic, the news sounded mildly encouraging. Initially, her white blood cell count had fallen from 450 to around 100; but such is the ferocity at which the bone marrow produces the overflow of white blood cells, it had shot back up to 220 within the next six to seven hours, as expected. Overnight, following her first round of chemotherapy, the count had dropped to 200, and the hope was that it would continue to fall. When things are so bleak, you crave any hope at all, and on that morning, as the crisp November sunshine bathed the Churchill Hospital, we all felt a tiny sliver of hope. For that moment at least, it was enough. All our fears and worries could find another room and another moment to be expressed.

Meanwhile, Gemma was desperate to see Ethan. Part of me didn't want him to see his mummy looking like that, wired up to a machine that let out a relentless beep every minute; but I knew it meant everything to Gemma. What she needed, more than anything else in the world, was the reassuring comfort of an Ethan huggle.

As I walked out of the hospital, I glanced at the shops that lined the main reception. There was a WHSmith newsagent, a clothes shop, and a wig shop! I knew Ethan would immediately clock WHSmith, but I hoped he wouldn't spot the wig shop and want to know why there was a shop in the hospital selling fake hair ...

We drove back to Oxford later that afternoon, with Ethan in good spirits. His face didn't portray the strangeness of the past 48 hours as he chatted away and selected some of his favourite songs from our playlist. As my mind raced away with thoughts of how Gemma was doing, and how long the road that lay ahead would be in terms of her treatment, our boy listened to Olly Murs, and played merrily with his Lego. But that's kids – although they can understand some of what's going on, the deeper fears don't last long. I have no doubt that in the quiet of his bedroom, the fears may have crept back, but children are able to jump out of that moment of worry and occupy themselves with something else. Those fears never leave adults alone for more than a blessed moment.

As predicted, he clocked WHSmith immediately: 'Oooo, can we go in and look at the magazines?' It's a request Gemma and I had heard countless times. Minutes later, we walked out of the shop with yet another magazine full of tacky plastic toys, and walked past the wig shop! I tried to quicken our stride and distract him with a bit of magazine small talk, but he spotted it straight away: 'Daddy, why is there a shop selling wigs?' I'm not always the best at it, but 20 years of doing live TV has trained me to think on my feet – fast. Without breaking stride, I said, 'Ethan. You know people come into hospital when they're not feeling very well?' 'Yes,' he replied. 'Well often, people in hospital need a bit of cheering up because they're feeling sad, so sometimes people go into that shop to buy a silly wig and wear it to make those people laugh and feel happy.' As Ethan chuckled he said: 'Daddy that's so silly – can we buy one?' I told him maybe we could, another day, and I felt a certain sense of self-congratulation for steering him away from an altogether more difficult answer with my silly wig tale! But I was already thinking about our possible future ... wondering if we *would* have to go into that shop with Gemma, and chose a wig. In the end, I'd have given anything to have reached that far ... we never even got close.

As Ethan and I walked down the long corridor to the haematology ward I stopped, crouched down so my eyes were level with his and said, 'Now you know Mummy's not very well ...' he nodded with his innocent eyes locked onto mine. 'Well, because the doctors and nurses are trying to make Mummy better so that she can come home, there are some funny machines and tubes going into her arms. It's nothing to worry about, but I didn't want you to be upset when you see her.' With that child-like simplicity he said 'okay,' and we headed into the ward.

As I opened the door to her room, all the worries about how he might react dissipated as he cried *'Mummy,'* and nearly took out the drip machine as he ran to her bed. They embraced and covered each other with kisses while we gently tried to stop him inadvertently pulling one of the tubes out of her arms. As Gemma found the energy to pepper him with the usual questions about his day at school, I just looked on. Everything about that moment felt so totally normal. Yet the sight of the two of them chatting away on the bed was anything but normal. None of us knew what was coming, but there was a real sense of poignancy about that moment. (Like so many of these special "moments" with children, it wasn't long before he had hopped off the bed and was busying himself with his magazine.

A couple of hours later it was time to get him home for bed. We couldn't have known, as Gemma kissed him goodnight in those unfamiliar surroundings, and he left with Grannie and Auntie Rebecca, that Ethan had seen his mummy awake for the very last time. Ethan would never get to hear his precious Mummy's voice in his ears ever again.

AFTER ALL HOPE WAS GONE

Over the next 24 hours, Gemma's condition continued to give us cause for genuine hope. As the chemotherapy continued, her white blood cell count continued to fall. By the Thursday morning it was down to 37 – a world away from the 450 of three days before.

Despite everything she was going through, Gemma still found the energy to make an online order for a new sweatshirt for Ethan, and a new coat for herself. Normally something like that would have seemed so insignificant – all part of ordinary life, but looking back on it, I think it points to something more significant – Gemma, like us, believed she *would* get well.

Like me, Gemma was a Christian. Our faith and all that it meant to us was the foundation stone for our marriage. When we had hit tough times with infertility issues, it was the one thing that kept us from falling apart. A text to her friend Liz from our church that Wednesday says so much about the trust she had in God:

Feel incredibly well loved and supported and also fairly peaceful today. Read James 5 in the Bible today – was Dad's special verse when he first got ill with cancer and was healed. Treatment in full swing – had white blood cell transfer, several chemotherapy treatments and a blood transfusion – full-on but I'm doing OK. Everyone, especially Simon, amazing. Feeling for you guys too.

Of all my memories of that week and the various text messages I have looked back on, it strikes me that Gemma must have had so many fears coursing through her mind, but they never showed. At times, there was almost a serene peace about her. Even when her arm was being pierced again and again with those endless needles, she barelyflinched. There was an amazing calmness, strength, and bravery about her that I'm not sure I'd have had if it had been me in that bed.

I felt an incredible closeness between us – there were moments when it felt like the early days when we'd just met. We spent time reading the Bible with each other, praying, and listening to some of our favourite songs – we felt so totally together; a team.

CS Lewis's *A Grief Observed*, in which he vividly portrays the agony of grief after the loss of his wife, Joy, to cancer became a very important book to me in the weeks that followed. On the precious times he had with her as she neared the end, he wrote: "It's incredible how much happiness, even how much gaiety, we sometimes had together after all hope was gone."

It felt to me as if life was at its most delicate balance. Our hope hadn't gone, but I could recognise those special times of happiness were shaped by desperate circumstances. I kept thinking that, however long it took, whether it was weeks or months, I would never leave her side. I'd even begun to think how we'd do Christmas if Gemma was still in hospital and how we could still manage to make it special for Ethan. Whatever it took we were both determined to beat this – we would win this battle together ...

On that Thursday evening, our friends David (the vicar of our church,) his wife Liz, and our close friends, Dave and Debs, came to see us, and pray for Gemma. I remember feeling a real sense of optimism that night. As I brought them into her room, she was sitting on the end of her bed – for the first time that week. They knew how fast things had happened, and they'd expected to see Gemma horizontal, and in pain. Instead they saw a woman who, despite her pain, radiated a sense of hope as she beamed a smile at them. It was a moment that stayed with them both:

Debs: *Gems was tired, but feeling better than she had the day before. We prayed for her, and David gave her a small wooden cross to hold onto. He told her that in those small hours of the night, when her fears were at their worst, she should hold it and remember that in the same way she was holding the cross, God would be holding her. The lads left the room for a bit, and Liz and I asked Gemma how she was feeling about the cancer. She had already got her head around the upcoming treatment as we discussed her getting a wig and the fabulous shop downstairs! We asked how she was feeling, and she told us the medication had sent her system up the spout – what she really needed was a good poo! We laughed about that, but we did pray that she had a comfortable night and a movement! Looking back, if I'd known that would be the last time I would see Gems awake, there would have been so many other things I would have wanted to say. But we were all blissfully unaware and there was an amazing sense of peace and hope as we left her room that night.*

Liz: *She talked to us both about how full-on the treatment had been, but in spite of it all, she still seemed so hopeful and courageous. Looking back if she had known what was coming and what it would mean for Simon and Ethan – that would have totally broken her heart.*

As they kissed Gemma goodbye and I accompanied them out of the hospital into the night chill, we all felt that sense of hope and peace. Yes, we were scared, and there were plenty of questions about Gemma still to be answered, but we all felt a sense that one day, however long it would take, Gemma would eventually leave that place too and begin the long road to recovery.

I returned to the room, got Gemma comfortable, and unfolded my chair-bed, hoping for a relatively uneventful night. But as the early morning hours ticked past, Gemma started to get more and more restless. For the first time since Tuesday, she began to, once again, complain of a headache. Something was changing in Gemma, but I had no idea what. As the night wore on, her headache grew in intensity, her discomfort became ever more pronounced and her cries for relief more disquieting. No matter how hard they tried, the nigh team seemed helpless to ease her pain. With every visit to that dimly lit room, their faces portrayed an ever-growing look of concern.

So many memories of that night have become less vivid as the weeks and months have passed, maybe it's the mind's way of protecting you from some of the pain, but one memory does stand out above all the others ... As the headache worsened, Gemma sounded like she was becoming more and more muddled. The cheerful Gemma that had greeted our friends just a few hours before had suddenly disappeared. There was no cogency to what she was saying. As I held her hand and tried to muster the words to comfort her; her replies became ever more bizarre and incoherent. I tried to convince myself that it must be the side effects of the treatment, but deep down, that sick feeling in my stomach was growing once again.

At just after five o'clock on that Friday morning, Gemma needed the loo, and I began the now ingrained routine of helping her to her feet and guiding her to the bathroom with drip in tow. With one hand, I pulled the drip stand behind us, with the other I gripped her shoulder. Her walk had become little more than an unsteady shuffle. She looked like she would fall at any moment. I kept on encouraging her and telling her that we were nearly there, but her responses amounted to little more than barely comprehensible mutterings. As I eventually lay her back on the bed and helped her head onto the pillow I looked into those deep, hazelnut brown tired eyes, and said 'Darl, get some sleep.' I watched her eyes close, the eyes that I remembered seeing for the first time 16 summers ago, not knowing that they were closing for the last time.

Back in Reading, a group of guys from our church had arranged to meet early that morning to pray for Gemma. At just after seven o'clock, as arranged, I rang Dave, and through the speaker on his phone, relayed the events of the past few hours. As they sat, in silence, I told them I wasn't really sure what was going on, but felt a real sense of disquiet. As I finished the call and they turned to praying in earnest for Gemma, Dr Andy came into the room, a look of grave concern on his face, that only served to intensify my anxiety. He examined Gemma and told me she wasn't sleeping at all; she was unconscious. And he was worried that there could be some bleeding in the brain. I texted the guys in Reading:

It's potentially looking quite serious. Dr worried could be bleeding in brain. All very scary and Gemma not really with it.

Over the next couple of hours everything felt like it was cartwheeling out of control. A mobile X-Ray machine was brought in to see if there were any fluids collecting on her lungs. Then, before I could begin to comprehend what was happening, I found myself accompanying Gemma's bed down through the maze of hospital corridors to the CT scanner, where they scanned her head to try and discover what was causing this new deterioration.

When we got her back to her room, the frenzied activity of that Friday morning came to a momentary pause. As she lay unconscious with her breathing beginning to sound more laboured, I gripped her left hand, lay my head alongside hers and whispered, 'Darl, I love you so much. I don't know what's happening to you, but please hang in there. You're so strong, you're so special, you're going to be okay. I know you are.'

I whispered a simple, desperate prayer: 'Lord, I don't know what's happening to my dear Gemma; but please, if there is bleeding in her head, stop it right now. Please Lord, don't take her from us. Amen.'

As I stood up, I remembered the small wooden cross David had given Gemma. I picked it up from her bedside table, gently opened her clenched left hand, placed it into her palm and closed her fingers. That wooden cross would never leave her grip.

I watched her lying there, her eyes shut, and her breathing sounding more and more difficult … I needed to step outside, just for a moment. Opposite her door was the ward reception, and around the desk, Andy and his team were pouring over notes and X-Ray images. As the door closed behind me, they looked up and their faces betrayed a new level of seriousness. My blood ran cold. I retreated back into the room and took Gemma's hand in mine. A few moments later, Dr Andy came back into the room and asked if he could have a word ...

Despite my hopeless attempts to convince myself otherwise, I knew what was coming. As he showed me into the family and relatives' room, which I would later refer to as the "room of doom," I sat down on the sofa with my hands tightly clasped and steeled myself for whatever news he was about to reveal.

His words were calm and measured, but the situation didn't feel real. I felt like I was having an out of body experience, and his words were coming to me from somewhere else. He told me the CT scan had revealed that Gemma had 15 to 20 separate bleeds inside her brain, and he was going to need to speak to the head neurosurgeon at the hospital to see if there was anything they could do to stop them. Neither his eyes, nor his tone of voice gave the impression he had much hope. And then he said the words that will never leave me – 'I'm very sorry to have to tell you that Gemma is critically ill and there's a very real possibility she may not get better.'

Despite the shock, I barely flinched. Whilst my heart felt overburdened with fear and pain, my mind remained oddly calm. I asked him what I should do now, and what I should do about Ethan. I admired many things about Andy – not just his medical skills and his passion to help people get better; I admired his wisdom. He asked again how old Ethan was, and then said that, in his experience, however dire the circumstances, it would be better for me to bring Ethan in to see his mummy. While Ethan didn't need to know everything, he suggested that, bringing him in would be something he would probably thank me for later in life.

As Andy left to call the neurosurgeon, I sat in stunned silence. My mind could barely compute what was going on. Everything had happened so fast; but the last 12 hours had been like a tornado. One moment Gemma had been sitting on the end of her bed chatting with friends like she always did, now she was in a fight to stay alive.

*

Back at home, Ethan, Rebecca and Wendy were waking up, oblivious to the developments of the last few hours. Rebecca's reflections on the innocence of our eight-year old boy breaks my heart:

On the Wednesday and Thursday morning, I had come down the stairs from the spare room on the top floor to find Ethan playing quietly on his own on the landing. He clearly knew something wasn't quite right. He was so used to running into mummy and daddy's bedroom in the morning and jumping all over them. But that morning, Mummy and Daddy weren't there.

After telling Gem and Si about it, we all decided it would be better for him if I slept in their bed so there would be someone familiar for him to come and see in the morning. Gems and Si wanted to make it as "normal" for him as possible.

He was so sweet that Friday morning. He came creeping in at 7.00am and gently got into the bed beside me and said quietly: 'Is this Auntie Becs?' I said, 'of course it is,' and then just snuggled up to me and started chatting about all sorts of random stuff. It was so lovely and special. Little did either of us know what was to come later that day.

YOU ALWAYS WILL BE ...

The memories of those next few precious hours are ones that, in many ways, I would love to forget, but in so many other ways, I never want to. No matter how painful they are to remember.

Despite the turmoil of that Friday morning, I was still experiencing that same strange sense of calm. Partly it was shock, but partly it was something else ... In the Bible (Philippians Chapter 4 verse 7) it talks about the peace of God that passes all understanding. For so many years as a Christian, I had never really understood what these words actually meant. I just thought it was some kind of peace that you might find on a beautiful beach on a sun-soaked island, or one of those brief feelings of overall calm that come along once in a while. The bit about peace transcending all understanding had always passed me by. But this was the moment I understood for the very first time what that really meant. Here I was, on my own, in the room of doom, in a place I didn't know, with the news my wife could be gone in just a few hours. I should have been screaming, I should have been punching the walls and pleading with Andy to do something; tears of desperation should have been pouring out of my eyes. And yet, somehow, I felt a sense of peace that passed all understanding. A peace that could only be explained by my faith. In the midst of the chaos, it was a peace that found me and held me.

I got to my feet and left that room. I walked into the corridor and rang home to let Rebecca and Wendy know what was happening. It was a horrid call to make. I had to hold on to that glimmer of hope that Andy had given me that the bleeding could stop, while having to tell them the devastating news that their sister and daughter was in a critical state and might not make it.

The sense of panic in their voices was horrible to hear, but they knew from the urgency in my voice that there was no time to lose. I tried to ring our vicar, David, who had been with Gemma a few hours before. It went straight to voicemail. I tried again, and left a muddled message asking him to ring me as soon as he could. I rang Gemma's dad, David, who lived in the south of France with his wife Anne-Catherine. Yet again I was put through to voicemail. I rang Anne-Catherine; same story. Then the panic, anger, and frustration welled up inside me. Why was no one answering their phone, on this of all days?!

I thought of Ethan in his classroom, doing all the things a normal Friday morning would bring, while blissfully unaware of the nightmare unfolding 40 miles away. I rang Debs to ask if she could get him and bring him to Oxford:

Simon called and I was anticipating a positive update on Gems. But his voice was agitated and emotional – he was frustrated that no one was picking up their phones. He explained that Gemma had taken a turn for the worse in the night, and she'd been in and out of consciousness since the early hours.

He asked if I could contact our vicar, David, and ask him to come to the hospital, and then collect Ethan. As I got in the car, I put some worship songs on really loud and shouted the words out to God, with tears streaming down my cheeks. I hammered my fists on the dashboard and prayed all the way to Ethan's school that God would give me the strength and wisdom to know what to say to Ethan and help him in this moment.

He was very quiet on the way there – he said he had a headache and seemed very tired. It turned out that he was also incubating tonsillitis so wasn't feeling his best. But he put his head back and we listened to music all the way there. It was a beautiful sunny winter's day and the view over the Chiltern Hills was amazing, so we tried to focus on that.

I met Rebecca in reception, who told me that Wendy couldn't come in; she just couldn't face hearing what she feared she was going to be told. She was planning on going to Maggie's Centre next to the hospital – a beautiful haven of peace and comfort for patients and their families. But I was having none of it. Impossibly hard though it was for her, she had to be with her daughter. Gemma needed us.

I found Wendy walking from the car park; her face contorted with fear. As I embraced her and held her, it felt like she would fall to the floor at any moment. The strength in her legs had gone. It was all just too overwhelming. I told her that however hard it was for her, she had to come with me into the hospital and hear what was happening from Dr Andy. Wendy described me as frog-marching her into the hospital. I'm not sure I was quite that heavy handed, but I did know that time was no longer our friend, and we had to go and face the music, no matter how horrid the song.

Dr Andy met the three of us in the room of doom and talked us through the events of the last few hours. I held Wendy tightly. Every parent's worst nightmare is to see their children die before them; life isn't meant to go that way. But as Andy delivered the crushing news that, barring a miracle, her daughter only had a few hours left to live, that nightmare suddenly became very real. As the devastating news sank in, and the tears fell, we knew it was time to go and be with Gemma. To be with her, in her final hours.

In the short time that had passed, her breathing had become even more laboured. But now, there was a disconcerting rattle in her throat. It was horrible to listen to. I wanted to help her, I wanted to ease her pain but there was nothing anyone could do now to stop this desperate chain of events. All I could do was tell her over and over again how much I loved her. And I prayed for her.

For the next few hours I prayed out loud over my wife. Again and again, as my right hand rested on her head, I pleaded with God to stop the bleeding. As the nurses came in and out over the course of that morning to tend to her, I barely noticed them as I repeatedly prayed out loud – 'Father in the name of Jesus, as you told us when you were here on earth to go forth and heal the sick, I ask now that you would stop the bleeding in Gemma's head now. Please God stop this bleeding.'

Some Christians have argued, unhelpfully, over the years that the reason we don't see more people being healed is that people don't have enough faith. This simplistic approach to healing is both damaging and deeply hurtful. I can honestly say that in my 44 years as a Christian, I had never prayed with as much faith as I prayed that day. Maybe it was simply borne out of a denial of what was really happening; perhaps it was just pure desperation, but in my heart I genuinely believed that God would intervene, that he would save the day for Gemma. He didn't.

As I continued to petition God, the news came through that Debs had arrived with Ethan. I was about to be reunited with my boy, who was going to see his dear mum for the final time. And as I realised that, a huge, painful sadness gripped me. As I walked down the corridor, I had to fight back the tears. I wanted to fall to the ground and just weep, but I knew that for his sake, I had to be strong.

The maelstrom of emotions of those next few minutes was so intense that I can't recall what even happened, but Debs remembers with a clarity I cannot:

When Simon saw Ethan, he gave him a big hug and said he just wanted to have a chat with him before they went in to see Mummy. Simon was very composed and took Ethan into the family room. As I sat with them and Dr Andy, Simon explained that Mummy was very, very sick and the doctors were doing everything they could, but that she might not get better. Ethan started crying and Simon hugged him. Then Ethan sobbed, and Simon was crying too. The Macmillan nurse joined them, and I left – I was getting upset and probably not helping.

They were more composed when they came out, and Simon explained that Mummy might look like she was sleeping, but she could still hear him, so he could say whatever he wanted to say to her. Simon sent me ahead to warn Rebecca and Wendy that Ethan was coming in and for them to be "composed" – he didn't want Ethan to see them really upset. While they went in, Rebecca came out, and we hugged and cried. Just the day before, we had said, 'God couldn't take Gemma from us.'

I'll never know where I found the strength from in those next few moments, but as we approached the room, I picked Ethan up into my arms and whispered in his ear that I loved him so much. And so did Mummy. As we walked in, I could see Wendy struggling to put a brave face on for the sake of her grandson.

I was cradling Ethan like he was a baby again, and lifted him towards his mummy's left ear to let him speak. As he whispered in her ear how much he loved her, my heart was exploding with pain. The boy who had enjoyed the most special of relationships with his mum, was seeing her in her final moments.

How the hell could this be happening?

We hadn't been able to give him what we had all longed for – a brother or sister, and now he was about to lose his mum. The injustice of what was happening was boiling up inside me. I wanted to rage and scream and smash the walls with my fist; but all I could do was channel it into staying strong and composed for Ethan.

I never told him she was actually dying; I just couldn't bring myself to say those words. This was already beyond anything an eight-year-old child should have to endure, and I still had that possibly misguided faith that God was going to rescue Gemma.

When Liz and David arrived, Liz and Debs offered to take Ethan to Maggie's Centre and look after him there, while we waited for my sister, Becky, to arrive with his cousins. As the three of them walked over to Maggie's, Debs remembers how he was:

When Ethan came out of Gemma's room he wasn't upset or anything – he was very matter-of-fact as we went over to Maggie's to wait for his cousins, Thomas, Olivia, and Holly.

While we waited, we spent the afternoon drawing pictures of imaginary superheroes that had unusual superpowers. We created a scoring system so we could play "Top Trumps". Ethan's drawings were easily the most imaginative! We set up and played the Playmobil Zoo – one of Ethan's favourites as he was growing up. Liz created a scenario where one of the little boys kept getting lost or ending up in strange places – Ethan got really involved and found it very funny. At any quiet moment he would ask, 'When is Thomas going to be here?' There was much relief for all of us when he finally arrived.

That was the story of the next few hours – the gathering of close family and friends around us. Our friend, Dan, who was vicar of a church in Oxford, had planned to pop in to see Gemma that day, but ended up staying with us all until the very end. It felt like we had a fortress of friends surrounding us. No friend should ever have to endure watching a dear friend lose their life, but each and everyone of them stood shoulder to shoulder with us during our darkest hours. Despite the undoubted agony they were feeling, their love and strength was incredible.

At about one o'clock that afternoon, my mindset began to shift. And I found myself beginning to accept that, however much I prayed for Gemma to be healed, and with however much faith I had, it wasn't going to happen. I knew that, with whatever time we had left, it was time to prepare to say goodbye.

I didn't know it then, but later I found out that one o'clock had been a significant point for Dr Andy too. It signalled the point where any hope that the bleeding would stop ended. If Gemma had somehow survived after that, she would have been so severely brain damaged that she would have been unrecognisable from the Gemma we knew. Maybe I'm reading too much into this, maybe it was just coincidence; but at that point in the day, when unbeknown to us there was no longer any hope of getting the old Gemma back, my mindset had altered.

Over the next four and three-quarter hours I rinsed out what little time I had left with her. I never stopped telling her, over and over again, how much I loved her. I recounted the story of when we first met, and how I had fallen in love with her. I whispered my memories of our wedding day and told her how she had made me the happiest man alive. I said sorry for the times I had let her down. I reminded her again and again just what an amazing mum she had been for our beautiful boy. In between, I played one of her favourite songs close to her ear. It's by a band called Bright City that is part of a church in Brighton called St Peter's. Although it is a song of worship to God, the words in the second verse encapsulated so much of what Gemma meant to me:

When I am lost
You're always near
And You covered me despite my frailty
My hiding place
You are my strength
You have always been and You will always be.

(Bright City – 'I Will Rest'. Label – Bright City Collective Ltd)

So much of that final afternoon is a haze now, but I do vividly remember Rebecca curled up in a ball on the bed by Gemma's feet, holding and kissing her sister's hand. The same sister who had been such a rock for her, was crumbling before her eyes. She barely said anything that afternoon; it was heartbreaking to watch. Wendy had found an incredible inner strength, and despite her own heartbreak, she still managed to share her prayers, and memories, and love with her daughter. Given everything she must have been feeling, she was amazing that day.

I lost count of the long trips I took to the adjacent bathroom. My friends later told me how worried they had been that I might be taking anti-depressants and beta-blockers to numb the pain. I wasn't. I just needed some time away from the intensity of that bedside, time alone with my thoughts; time to gather my strength again and go back in.

In the same way the afternoon became punctuated with those trips to the loo, it also became marked by a number of visits to try to get hold of Gemma's dad, David. But every time I did, it was the same story – voicemail. With each fruitless call, my anger grew. He knew his daughter was ill, why on earth would he turn his phone off just three days after her diagnosis? Inevitably, my anger exploded and reverberated into his voicemail inbox: 'David, I don't know why your phone is turned off, but turn your fucking phone on, your daughter is fucking dying.'

David, our vicar, had witnessed this explosion of anger and suggested we head outside to get some fresh air and cool off. I didn't want to leave Gemma's side any more than I had, but I reluctantly followed him out of the hospital. As the late November sunshine and the cold air hit me, I let out what David described as the loudest, most tortured scream of 'No!' he'd ever heard. All of the pain, the anger and the emotion that I'd kept suppressed for the sake of Gemma, Ethan, and everyone around us came bursting out. (Much later, David told me that he'd had to go and comfort a poor old gentleman who'd been shuffling to the hospital entrance and nearly been blown off his feet by my blast of emotion!)

When I returned to Gemma, a few minutes later, it felt very like the end was near. In my desperation to keep her, I sank to my knees in front of the window, and made one final, desperate entreaty, begging God to do something. The sun was setting behind the trees in the distance as I prayed:

'Lord if you heal my wife, I will travel the world and proclaim your goodness. I will give the rest of my life to telling people about you and what you've done. I'll give up work, money – everything, I'll surrender it all.'

As I prayed, both David and Dan laid their hands on my shoulders and silently prayed that God would give me the strength for what was about to come. They knew that whatever view we have of God, the one thing you can't do with God is bargain with him.

In Gemma's hour of greatest need, my final throw of the dice was all I had left; but it was ultimately a futile act of desperation. As I rose back to my feet, they encouraged me to lie with Gemma for a bit.

By now, the various tubes that had led into Gemma's arms had been removed. The equipment that had been there to try and help her get better was gone. As I lay with her, holding her hand that still gripped that wooden cross, my mind raced through the years we had spent together. All those nights we had slept in the same bed. We could never have imagined that our life together would come to such an abrupt, early end. The agony of knowing it was the last time I would ever lie with her is something I simply cannot find the words for.

As the end neared, I felt as if I needed to make some promises to Gemma. I can't say that she ever really heard them, but I knew our family and friends would hear. And I trusted that God would hear. If nothing else I wanted them to bear witness to the life I was going to try and lead once she was gone. I promised her I would continue the amazing job she had done of bringing Ethan up; I would raise him to be a man she would be proud of. I promised her that I would stand by Wendy and Rebecca; Gemma had always been the person they could turn to, providing a shoulder to cry on and wise words of reassurance. I could never be *that* person; but I promised her I would do everything I could to stand in her place and support them in the months and years to come.

My final two promises were the hardest: I promised her I would not return to the drink, and I wouldn't give up on my faith. But as the story of what happened next unfolds, and the intensity of my grief hit home, those promises would confront me with two of my biggest battles.

I looked up to see the look of profound sadness on the faces of all her friends and family, and the tears that were starting to fall. The clock passed five thirty, and Gemma's laboured breathing became even louder. I knew she was about to go, but I didn't want her to; not like this. Once again, I leant over her, laid my hand on her head and prayed a final prayer of goodbye.

An amazing sunset provided a vivid, beautiful, red backdrop as we gazed beyond where she lay.

As I stood and put my arm around my sister, Becky, the tears flowed. I reflected on our brief life together, and thought of all the times I'd been able to help her, but now in her greatest hour of need, I was utterly helpless.

We enter this world alone, and no matter how many loving family and friends we have around us, we depart it alone. It didn't matter how many times I told her we loved her, or how many prayers I whispered gently into her ear; it didn't matter how much love and support surrounded her that day; this was something Gemma had to face alone.

My eyes never left her face. And as I tried to take in every last moment with her, she suddenly started to look different. The pain of the hours of laboured breathing abated, and a look of pure peace began to shine from her face. Her breathing – for just a moment – became normal, and then with a quiet stillness she fell silent. At aged just 40 years and 180 days, the life of Gemma Rachel Thomas had come to a sudden end.

A CHAMPAGNE SOIRÉE

Our paths had first crossed in late summer of 2001 ...

Before I landed the job on *Blue Peter*, I had spent a couple of years working for the Oasis Trust charity in London as part of their media department. Just a few years later, having graduated from Sheffield University in 2000, Gemma, coincidentally, ended up at Oasis too, doing exactly the same job!

In late September 2001, Gemma's boss (my old boss) Ivor Peters was hosting one of his legendary parties – a late summer champagne soirée. I was single at the time, and as we drove to Ivor's place near Windsor with my friends Kristen and Lucy, I talked about a girl called Sarah who I was hoping would be there. Our paths had crossed a few times at Oasis, and apart from being a very pretty girl, there was something about her that intrigued me. I wanted to find out more ...

It was a beautiful evening with lots of late summer sun, and enough champagne swilling around to fill a swimming pool. As the party got into full swing, I decided it was time to put in a bit of "groundwork" with Sarah, so I left my group of friends and nervously edged towards her. I've always been rubbish at these kinds of things, and never as confident as people might assume. With a glass of bubbly in hand, I edged closer, and rather clumsily forced my way into her little group. I have very little recollection of what I said; but I do remember it not being my finest moment!

Rather than a relaxed chat, it was a quickly curtailed dash to the finish. Rather than a cool, but interested conversationalist, I was little more than a gibbering mess. I decided that the only response to my less than convincing opening gambit was to imbibe some more champagne and try again a little later. But as we stood there enjoying the evening, I was distracted by the sight of a girl I had never seen before. I can remember the moment so well – she was wearing a beautiful cerise top and a stylish skirt. She was tall, with beautiful deep hazelnut-coloured eyes, flowing blonde hair, and a smile that, even though I had never met her before, just radiated warmth. As the guys around me kept chatting, I couldn't take my eyes off her. There was something about her that had completely captured my attention. I got myself introduced to her as soon as I could. Her name was Gemma.

One of the first things she told me was that she had spoken to me on the phone before, about a project Oasis wanted me to be involved with, but I had never got back to her (standard Thomas)! But the way she said it, and the laughs that accompanied the story, immediately made me feel at ease around her.

It's not often you feel that instant connection with someone. You chat to them for what feels like minutes, then look down at your watch to see that two hours have passed. Within no time at all you feel like you've known them forever. I don't remember everything we talked about; but I do remember feeling totally relaxed around her. She had a kindness about her that was so striking. I might only have known her for a few minutes, but I could already see that beyond her physical beauty there was an inner beauty that could do nothing but draw people in. I could have talked to her all night, but eventually I let her go to get another drink, and retreated back to my friends.

I had come to the party hoping to get Sarah's number, but now Gemma had totally captured my attention. I didn't even know if either of them actually liked me; but at that point I was caught in two minds. My friend, Andy, who knew Gemma well from Oasis, was quick to settle it. He painted a picture of someone very special. He told me she was a joy to be around, and everyone who knew her thought the world of her. My mind was made up. Whatever happened over the rest of the evening, I had to get Gemma's number, I had to see her again.

The evening chill descended, and we headed inside. The tunes blared, the champagne continued to flow, and a girl who I had known from my Oasis days was commanding the dance floor with an unforgettable set of moves. A few years ago, we'd had a close encounter at a work Christmas party, but we'd resisted a drunken kiss. As I caught her eye this night, she came over, and it quickly became clear she'd had a bit too much of the fizz. Memories of that Christmas party came flooding back. But before I could make my escape, I was pinned up against the wall, just as Gemma walked into the room, hoping to catch me before she headed off home! What she saw was me in a compromising position with one of her colleagues, and thought the chance had gone.

I saw Gemma and knew it was now or never. With a duck and a swerve, I escaped my colleague's clutches and made my way over to a slightly bemused looking Gemma. A little desperately, I tried to pass it all off as nothing more than a case of our mutual friend having had too much champagne, and asked if I could have her number. To my huge relief she said yes, and for some bizarre reason I scribbled it on the back of a box of matches. We laughed about it all afterwards!

As we headed home later that night, all I could talk about was Gemma. I even broke one of the golden rules – I sent her a text that same night!

I told her how lovely it had been to meet her and how nice it would be to meet up again for a drink. I was roundly castigated by my friend Kristen for breaking lads' protocol, but I didn't care if it made me appear overly keen. I knew then – and I know now

– that when you meet someone that special, you have to grab the opportunity. As my head hit the pillow later that night a lovely text arrived from Gemma saying she'd love to meet up soon and I fell asleep with a smile on my face and a sense of real excitement.

A couple of weeks later, we went on our first date together. First dates are always nervous affairs. You don't want to look like you're trying too hard, but you also don't want to appear like you can't be bothered, and turn up looking a wreck. Do you go for a pre-date haircut or leave it as it is? Smart shirt or T-shirt? Decisions, decisions!

We'd arranged for me to pick her up from her house in Sevenoaks where she lived with her mum and sister, and head into town for a drink and a bite to eat. I remember feeling so nervous as I pootled down the Kent roads in my little Peugeot, I hadn't been on a proper date for ages. And I wasn't quite sure if I should play it cool or just be myself …

Ever since getting the *Blue Peter* job, this was something I'd struggled with. If people have never met you, and only ever seen you on the TV, they can only form their opinion of you based on the persona they see in the corner of their living room at five o'clock on a Monday evening. But when they meet you in person, they might discover that in real life you're somewhat different, perhaps even disappointingly different.

One of the great things about *Blue Peter* is that it's a show that encourages presenters to be themselves. Our editor used to say they were looking for the kind of person your kids could invite over for tea and feel totally at ease with. They didn't want big, screen-hogging personalities, they wanted presenters that the audience could feel like they knew, and that was something I always valued in my six years on the show. There's still a bit of an act, of course. If you've had a bad weekend, or you're not in a particularly happy place, you can't come on air on a Monday afternoon and say 'Hi kids, welcome to *Blue Peter*. Just to let you know I've had a bit of a rubbish weekend, but I'll do my best to crack on through the next 25 minutes!' Whatever mood you're in, you have to suspend whatever else is going on in your life and deliver the show you're paid to present.

Most of the time, this fine balancing act between being yourself and acting the presenter part was okay; but away from the bright lights of the studio, it often left me feeling paranoid. I would go to parties or social functions and have a real fear of what people would expect. While I felt at total ease in front of a camera, socialising – especially with people I didn't know – left me feeling anything but. I started to believe the lie that, because I was on the telly, people would somehow expect me to be this larger-than-life character who could entertain a room with engaging tales of life on the box. But that wasn't me.

I had a great job, and I could deliver the goods when it came to live TV. But in so many other ways, I was the same person I'd always been, full of those insecurities that so many of us have, needing to be accepted for who we are, but fearful that we won't be anything other than a disappointment. In truth, no one expected me to be anything other than myself; but all too often it worried me so much that I tried to appease my anxieties by ploughing into the alcohol and relaxing those social inhibitions.

All this anxiety was running through my mind as I turned into Gemma's road that Saturday evening. But as her house approached, I remembered how relaxed I had felt with her at Ivor's party, and how easy she had been to talk to. I thought: *Just be yourself, don't try and be something you're not.*

I walked nervously up to her front door, and remember thinking: *What if she's not quite what I remember from the other week? What if that spark was a one-off?*

All my concerns evaporated in an instant as the front door opened and that radiant Gemma smile beamed at me once again.

It was such a lovely evening. The conversation never ran dry, it never felt forced, and Gemma felt totally interested in me. I had been on dates before where it felt like they were more interested in Simon the *Blue Peter* presenter than Simon the person. Gemma was the antithesis of that. It might have only been the second time I'd spent time with her, but I loved being in her presence. She radiated a disarming warmth that drew me in and made me feel relaxed.

The evening thankfully passed off without incident, apart from one moment in a Sevenoaks pub ... As we stood there, trying to make each other heard above the sound of a well-oiled local rugby team celebrating a win, a tall burly chap kept looking over, with all the subtlety of a rhino. I kept my eyes locked on Gemma and tried not to catch his; but eventually he came over, and in a rather loud and posh voice asked if I was Simon off *Blue Peter*. Gemma was slightly bemused, particularly by my desperate attempts to try and wriggle out of the conversation. I couldn't say anything other than 'yes' and he told me to wait there; they wanted to give me a little something ... I apologised to Gemma and told her it wasn't always like this. Minutes later, he was back, saying, 'Here's a little something to make your evening even more special,' and handed us a couple of glasses, and a bottle of Veuve Clicquot! It was all a bit embarrassing, but what a lovely thing to do and it gave Gemma a story that she loved regaling people with over the years to come. On a night when I was trying hard to impress, that Sevenoaks rugby team gave me an unexpected head start.

As we drove back to her house later that evening, I felt so happy. She was such an easy person to be around and the whole evening had felt so relaxed. I told her how much I had loved the evening and enjoyed spending time with her. She said she felt the same, and as I looked into her captivating, deep-brown eyes, we kissed.

I hadn't expected to kiss on our first date, I hadn't wanted to go in, all guns blazing, but it just felt like such a natural thing to do. As romantic settings go, a kiss on a driveway in a Peugeot 206 isn't exactly right up there, but in that moment, all of that melted away and I felt like I was somewhere else.

As I headed back to London a few minutes later, I felt so happy. I didn't want to get too carried away too early, but here was a girl who was already beginning to melt my heart. That's one of the amazing things about love, sometimes you find it in the places you least expect.

IN SICKNESS AND IN HEALTH

As the days became weeks, and the weeks became months, that September spark became a bond that would be stretched at times, but would never be broken. One of the many things I loved about Gemma was how she was in social situations. In the same way she made me feel at ease when we first met, she had the same effect on everyone she met. Whether it was just hanging out with our friends or a showbiz-type event, Gemma was a joy to be around, helping me to feel relaxed in the sorts of settings that had so often left me feeling anything but relaxed.

How the person you're with interacts with your family and friends is a really important part of any relationship: we want that person to be accepted without it ever feeling forced. That was never even an issue with Gemma. She was instantly accepted, immediately liked and as the months went on, enormously loved.

I was very much in love with Gemma, and I loved beginning to share my life with her. As with any relationship, it wasn't always easy. However incredible my job with *Blue Peter* was, and however much I might have loved jet-setting around the world on different adventures, it was sometimes hard for her when I was away for long periods.

In summer 2003, we spent a summer holiday camping down in the south of France with friends. At the end of our time away we spent a couple of days meandering up the west coast. Our last port of call was the beautiful coastal town Arromanches-les-Bains – scene of the Normandy D-Day landings. As we sat on the harbour wall on our final afternoon, eating ice cream and looking out to sea, the going-back-to-work blues set in for Gemma. She was passionate about her work in the PR and media department for the Electoral Commission, but she wasn't looking forward to returning to the grind of the daily commute. In contrast, I was rather looking forward to going back to work – and a 10-day filming trip to Belize that was coming up. Understandably this didn't exactly make Gemma's impending return to work feel any easier. As I sat there trying to say encouraging, but ultimately futile things like 'The idea of going back to work is always worse than the reality,' my phone rang – it was Catherine, one of the producers in the *Blue Peter* office. She apologised for interrupting the last day of our holiday and for the short notice, but went on to tell me about a new Disney and Pixar animation called *Finding Nemo* that was coming out later that year. She said the film featured a Clownfish called Nemo who lived on the Great Barrier Reef in Australia, and they wanted to go and film the real Nemo. With me being the only trained scuba-diver on the show, they wanted me to present the film ... and fly to Australia ... on Sunday!

Inside I was bursting with excitement, but sat to my left was my girlfriend, who was already jealous of my trip to Belize. I tried to hide my obvious excitement as Gemma enquired what the call had been about. There was no point trying to dress it up, I just said, 'Darl – I've got to fly to Australia – on Sunday.' It went down like a sack of coal.

Blue Peter is a unique job, which is why it's been so sought after by presenters down the years. In terms of experiences, adventure, and travel there is no job on British television quite like it. One minute you can be making a dolls' gym out of toilet rolls and buttons, on a Monday afternoon in the studio, the next you can be heading off to dive the Great Barrier Reef.

I know how proud of me Gemma was, but it was hard for her, feeling as if everything she did was dull by comparison. My regular

too often, that's when marriages begin to buckle and fall apart. While we wouldn't have chosen to be tested quite so quickly, it helped strengthen the bond between us and laid an unshakable foundation that would be so important in the years to come.

With those early problems behind us, our marriage blossomed. What I loved about being married was just that joy of being able to "do life" together. Whatever life throws at you, whatever experiences you're enjoying, you share them. You support each other.

Gemma became my rock. On those days when I doubted myself, on those occasions when I was finding life in front of the camera hard, she was there beside me, with wise words and loving hugs; always cheering me on. We navigated life together through the good times and the bad. We were a team: Team Thomas. And it wasn't long before our team began to grow.

*

In late September 2009, the greatest of blessings came into our lives with the arrival of Ethan James Thomas. I always knew Gemma would be a great mum – and she was amazing.

I have been so blessed in life in so many ways, and I will be forever grateful that my job afforded us the luxury of allowing Gemma to devote her life to bringing up our boy. Gemma had enjoyed her years working since graduating, but she wasn't a woman driven by the desire for a high-flying career – she was driven by a desire to be the best possible mum.

Over those eight, short years, I saw a relationship grow that was so, so special. They had the most natural of relationships, and so many of the traits that made Gemma the woman she was, I now see in my boy. Her kindness, her sensitivity towards others, her compassion, and her almost limitless patience. He was by no means *a* mummy's boy, but he is *his* mummy's boy, and so much of what she invested in him is now bearing fruit.

In the weeks after she left us, I found a note she had written to Ethan the day before she went away with friends to celebrate her 40th birthday. She hated spending any time away from him; in eight years, that three-day holiday was the longest they were apart. Her simple note encapsulated the depth of love for her boy and the wonderful relationship they shared:

To my darling Ethan. I love you with all my heart! I'll miss you, but I'm sure you'll have a super fun weekend. See you on Sunday! With all my love and kisses, your Mummy xx

As Ethan reached what turned out to be the not-so-terrible-twos, we started to think about trying for another child. We had both grown up with siblings and wanted that for Ethan too. But the weeks turned into months and the months became a year …

Although it had taken us a while to conceive Ethan, we had never really begun to think there might be a problem, and Ethan's arrival bore testament to that. But this time it felt different. The look of disappointment and sadness on Gemma's face as another period arrived became our gut-wrenching monthly norm. We made the decision to go for some tests.

My results came back okay, but one Tuesday afternoon, while preparing for my shift on *Sky Sports News*, Gemma rang, distraught. The tests had revealed a very low egg count, more in keeping with a woman approaching the menopause, not a 34-year-old. The chances of us conceiving naturally were very, very low. It was another absolute hammer blow.

Gemma was crying down the phone, asking, 'Why is it always me who has these problems?' She had overcome the problem of not being able to have intercourse, and then found out she had a fertility problem. It was a painful, lonely burden to carry at a time when so many of our friends seemed to fall pregnant just by looking at each other.

After much soul-searching, we decided to try the IVF route. Although you go into it with your eyes wide open, knowing all the statistics on success rates, there is still nothing that can prepare you for when it doesn't work.

For weeks, poor Gemma had to inject herself and take various drugs every day. Then there was the hospital procedure itself, and after that, the seemingly never-ending two-week wait to carry out the pregnancy test began. As the day arrived, Gemma pulled the test kit out of the draw and nervously made her way to the bathroom. She reappeared a few minutes later, gave me the stick, and said she couldn't bear to look. I turned away from her and stared intensely at the little window, where I hoped and prayed the two magic lines would appear …

One white line appeared. The IVF had failed.

It really is as brutal and as stark as that. IVF is black and white – it either works or it doesn't, and no amount of preparation can ready you for the huge emptiness and pain wound up in that moment. As the tears flowed, it looked like our hopes and dreams of giving our boy a brother or sister were hanging by the slenderest of threads.

We knew we couldn't keep putting ourselves through the ordeal, and so, after several months of relentless trying, we decided to give it one last go. This time, Gemma fell pregnant.

We didn't let our joy overpower us. We couldn't. We still had a long way to travel. But knowing Gemma had been able to carry Ethan to birth, we were hopeful.

Four weeks later, I woke to Gemma in floods of tears. She had discovered some bleeding and feared the worst. Hours later we found ourselves sitting in a waiting room waiting for a scan. The same scan you have during pregnancy. The room was packed with heavily pregnant women waiting their turn. What a stark contrast for Gemma – her hopes in tatters, surrounded by women full of excitement and anticipation. It felt like we were being tortured.

After a painfully long wait, our fears were realised – she'd had a miscarriage. And it was devastating. Having been given the briefest flicker of hope, our dreams of a brother or sister for Ethan were in tatters.

We all deal with the difficulties and challenges in our lives in different ways. Somehow, Gemma had to learn to live with the most fundamental sadness a woman who wants to conceive can have. No matter how much I tried to reassure her, she felt it was all her fault. She said she had let me down. The two big physical disappointments she had experienced made her feel like less of a woman.

Like most men, I wanted to fix it. But I couldn't. I had to accept that only time would heal that scar. As anyone who has been through it knows, it's a tough road to walk. You suddenly find yourself living in a world where it seems like friends can pop out babies like a cash dispenser pops out money. Social media only adds to it, with a constant reel of posts of three-month scans, or announcements about baby number two, three, or four.

I dealt with it all in my own way. I didn't want to talk to anyone. I felt isolated. I was angry, disappointed, and bitter. And eventually it became clear that I was experiencing depression for the first time.

A WOMAN OF COMPASSION

Life with Gemma was everything I hoped it would be. There were challenges, of course, and there was occasional heartbreak. But one thing that never changed or diminished was one of Gemma's most endearing qualities – not just her great love for Ethan and I, but her incredible compassion for others ...

It was Christmas Day 2015. Michael Bublé rang out for about the 20th time that week, the Prosecco was poured, and Gemma began to work her magic in the kitchen, and it wasn't long before the wonderful festive aromas of Christmas dinner were wafting through the house. When we got married, I knew she was a pretty good cook, but it was only after we moved in together after our honeymoon that I realised just how good. She had this amazing ability to rustle up something delicious in no time at all. Our kitchen shelves still lie heavy under the weight of the cookbooks she amassed over the years; sadly, my limited cooking skills will leave most of them forever more untouched.

As she got to work on the finishing touches for Christmas lunch, I suddenly realised that she was crying – and there wasn't an onion in sight! It turned out that her tears were for a lady who had begun coming to our church in Reading, and had struck up an immediate friendship with Gemma. This woman had been dealt some tough blows in life; from an abusive relationship to an ongoing battle with alcohol, borne out of the mental scars she'd suffered.

She wasn't always an easy person to be around, but Gemma showed her a level of love and patience that I wished I had a fraction of. In the weeks after Gemma's death, she told me, 'I didn't know what compassion felt like until I met Gemma.' In Gemma she found a person who didn't judge her, but held out a hand of friendship, compassion, and love.

One night at about eleven thirty, as our heads hit the pillow, Gemma's phone began to ring. It was her friend. She had been to her ex's house for the evening; she'd had too much to drink, there'd been an argument, and she found herself on the street, in the cold, with no money to get a taxi home. Gemma wasn't exactly over the moon to be taking yet another late-night call from her; but rather than tell her it wasn't her problem, she felt we should help and pay for a cab to take her home. At first, I baulked at this suggestion. Why should we be helping her out? But that was a selfish reaction. Alcoholism is an illness, and the bottle had become her way of numbing the relentless pain in her life. Reluctantly I agreed, and a few minutes later a cab arrived at our house, and Gemma walked out in her dressing gown and slippers to give him the money for the fare. An hour or so later she called to say she was home safe and sound, and Gemma and I were able to sleep knowing she wouldn't be walking the freezing streets of Reading trying to get home.

In a service at our church the Sunday after she died, our vicar David paid tribute to Gemma's kindness saying that she had shown an unending love for those people in our church that others found it too difficult to stand alongside.

As Gemma's tears flowed on that Christmas day, she told us what had upset her. As we had left church that morning, Gemma had bumped into her outside and found out that she was going to be spending Christmas day alone in her flat. She couldn't bear the thought of the lovely day and the food we were about to enjoy knowing that her friend was just up the road, all on her own. I looked at her and was struck by her selflessness and her compassion all over again. A few minutes later Gemma's mum and I were bringing her back to enjoy Christmas day with us, and it was wonderful. Not just because she had a day to remember, but because of what it meant to my dear wife. You could see a smile of joy on her face that she had been able to turn a day of loneliness and undoubted pain for her friend into a Christmas she would always remember. Gemma reached out to her and made her feel valued, accepted, and loved. Her friend summed it up best:

'Until I met Gemma, I didn't know there were people in this world like her. She showed me what love is.'

Gemma showed so many of us the way when it came to loving your neighbour; but I wasn't always keen to follow her lead.

A few months after we'd moved to Reading in 2011, we recruited a cleaner – a lovely Polish lady called Ewa. Her English wasn't always the best, but over the years, Gemma became a significant person in her life. I often felt a little offended when I answered the door on a Friday morning and Ewa's face portrayed a slight look of disappointment that it wasn't Gemma!

But one day, after we'd known Ewa several years, I heard the sound of her crying. As I peered down the stairs, I could see Gemma hugging her and Ewa's tear-stained face pressed into Gemma's shoulder. I mouthed a 'What's wrong' to Gemma who shot me back a "leave it with me" look and led Ewa into the kitchen. The best part of an hour later, I heard the front door shutting and headed downstairs to find out what on earth was wrong. It turned out that Ewa and her family had been forced to move out of their rented flat and into another flat with no furniture. Ewa was in distress because she was getting less and less work and they simply couldn't afford to buy any new furniture. As I offered a slightly disingenuous 'Oh that's really sad' response, Gemma had other ideas – 'Darl I think we should give them some money to buy a sofa.' I'm somewhat ashamed to admit that instead of greeting Gemma's amazing thoughtfulness with open arms,

I reacted with a look of incredulity – 'Hun we're not a charity – she's our cleaner for goodness, sake!' Instead of taking Gemma's lead and thinking of others, I reacted in a way that was totally at odds with how Gemma saw things. Instead of seeing Ewa as just our cleaner, she saw her as a friend – a friend with hopes and fears like all of us. In the same way I had been reluctant to pay for a taxi that night, I was reluctant to dip into my pocket to help make Ewa and her family's life a bit easier. A few minutes later I begrudgingly agreed to transfer some money into her account.

It's easy to show people who are struggling or suffering some empathy and understanding; but true compassion is being driven to do something about it. Gemma taught me that. Whereas I just felt a bit sorry for Ewa's predicament, Gemma saw the hurt and need in that woman's eyes and put her Christian faith into action. It wasn't a faith based on hollow words and inaction, it was something that drove her to do whatever she could to help others. When Jesus was asked what the greatest commandment was, he said, 'Love the Lord your God with all your heart and with all your mind and love your neighbour as yourself.' Gemma's tears that Christmas day and her compassion for Ewa were that commandment in action. She could have focused on just making sure her family and friends were well fed and looked after; she could have kept the money for us to spend on ourselves; but instead she put the needs of those two women first, two women who needed to experience that love that Jesus talked about.

I wish more of us (myself included) were able to show that kind of compassion and stand alongside those people who aren't always easy to stand with, to help those who it's easier to ignore. Because they're the people who need to be held by the hand of acceptance, understanding, and love.

But Gemma's compassion and desire to help others didn't stop there. As the Syrian civil war and the refugee crisis began to make the news in 2011, Gemma and I would watch the news unfolding with a sense of horror as the humanitarian crisis played out before us. We were moved by the plight of so many desperate people, packed like sardines into barely sea-worthy boats, making the dangerous break for freedom across the Mediterranean. A journey that, for far too many, ended in tragedy. But the tears that welled in Gemma's eyes sparked a fire in her heart to do something about it.

Over the early months of 2017, Gemma began a pioneering refugee project at our church with the aim of re-settling a Syrian family in Reading. She launched the project in May 2017, and along with a team of volunteers, she spent the final months of her life putting everything in place, including a house for a family to move into later that year. She knew it wasn't going to be easy, but she would often talk to me about how much she was looking forward to the day we would drive to the airport to meet the family and bring them to our hometown. I was looking forward to it too, not just to meet the family, but to see the look of happiness and joy on Gemma's face as those months of hard work came to wonderful fruition.

Gemma wasn't here to see her vision and hard work realised, but a Syrian family *has* now arrived in Reading. Their arrival into our community was a beautiful legacy to Gemma's heart and vision, and so poignant; I'm so sad they never got to meet the woman whose heart had been moved to make it happen. I just know that, if I can get to the end of my days having shown half the love and compassion that she did in those 40 short years, I'll have done well.

So many people had stories to share about Gemma. A few days after she died, our friend, Dan Heyward, who had come to visit Gemma on that Friday, shared this story:

On the Sunday after Gemma's death I preached at church and spoke a bit about the sadness of losing a friend, and being with Simon and his family through the day, and I spoke about the urgency of responding to the love of Jesus because life can be so terribly short.

After the service, over coffee, I was introduced to a woman who had come to our church for the very first time. She said she was a nurse

SIMON THOMAS

in the haematology ward at the Churchill, the same ward Gemma had been on, and said to me that she didn't know exactly who I was referring to in my sermon but thought she could make a pretty good guess. She said, 'If it is who I think it is, then I just want to let you know that she made a huge difference among the staff on the ward. She was genuinely amazing, and she dealt with it in an amazing way. She had a massive impact on the staff.

Even in her darkest and most desperate final hours Gemma was still impacting people's lives and that is the biggest tribute I can ever give her. Despite the physical challenges she had faced and the huge disappointment of not being able to have any more children, she remained a remarkable woman whose flame of compassion and love for others still burnt bright, even when the light of her life was fading.

THE AFTERMATH

How can I put into words the emotions I felt at a quarter to six on that Friday in November?

It felt like a huge bomb had just exploded and we were at the epicentre. The blast was so shocking and so intense that it left us feeling totally numb. The pain and devastation couldn't even begin to register, I was totally and utterly bewildered. After those endless, exhausting hours of hoping and praying that Gemma would somehow pull through, and then the reality of saying goodbye, there was nothing but a sense of profound emptiness. As we stood around her bed everything felt so utterly quiet. In that moment, the rest of the world no longer existed. In the place of her laboured breathing there were tears from those she had left behind.

My mind began to race:

Who do I tell first ... How do I let our friends know – they've been praying so hard ... do I send out a mass text ... do I say something on social media?

... How the hell am I going to tell Ethan ...?!

Before I could pick up the phone, Dr Andy Peniket came over to see me. From the moment I had first met Andy, I'd warmed to him. I didn't just admire him for the fact he had devoted his life to helping people survive blood cancer, he had a genuine compassion about him. Right throughout that week he had had to deliver some hugely difficult news to us as a family; never once did I see a doctor who was just going through the motions.

Andy radiated a warmth and understanding in impossible situations. To sit down with the husband of a woman who four days ago didn't even know she had cancer and deliver the news that she's not going to last the day must be impossibly hard, and I have nothing but a huge respect, gratitude, and admiration for the way he held us as a family during that hardest of weeks.

Dr Andy very gently began to talk through what would happen next. Most of it washed over me, I was barely able to even get my head around what had just happened, but I do remember him talking about the possibility of them carrying out a post-mortem ... I wondered if it would help them understand a little more about this devastating disease and maybe help others. Andy said that was unlikely. So I told him I didn't want one. What was the point? Gemma had gone. And even if they discovered something they hadn't seen before, it wasn't going to change the story. As I rose to my feet to say goodbye, all I could do was hug him. Through tears I thanked him for the grace and understanding he had shown us all week, and for doing everything he could to try and save her. It was a hard goodbye – I could see the sadness in his eyes that despite his best efforts, this was one battle with blood cancer he hadn't won.

*

I picked up my phone and nervously rang my mum and dad. My dad's health hadn't been good for some years and his mobility problems had become so pronounced that they hadn't been able to get from Norfolk to Oxford to be with us. I can't begin to imagine what that day had been like for them. After hearing the distressed voice of their son a few hours before, they must have feared the worst as they waited nervously for more news.

As Mum answered my call, the anxiety and fear in her voice was palpable even though we were a hundred and ninety miles apart. Through my tears, I just blurted out, 'She's gone, Mum, she's gone.' As her voice began to quiver, I could hear the sounds of my dad beginning to sob next to her.

It was a desperate call to make. As a father, I cannot begin to even comprehend what this moment must have felt like for them. Even as our children grow older and take on more responsibility, we never stop wanting to protect them. There was nothing my mum and dad could do that day except weep tears of sorrow for the loss of a daughter-in-law they loved beyond words.

Maybe I should have been focusing on other things rather than worrying about breaking the news to people, but even as everything fell away around me, I knew I had to let people know. I didn't have the emotional energy to call all of our friends, and so at just after six thirty that Friday evening I posted the news on Facebook:

I cannot believe I'm writing this, but my dear Gemma passed away just before 6.00pm tonight after going downhill rapidly today. She was surrounded by her family and friends as we said goodbye and I said a prayer as she breathed her final breath. She was very peaceful as she went.

We are beyond heartbroken. Please pray for all of us but especially precious Ethan who I have to tell tonight. Thank you xx

In those desperate hours, the friends and family who had surrounded us that day were incredible. While we remained in a state of stunned inertia, they attended to all the practical things that you don't want to even think about, but have to get done. Our vicar, David, went back into her room with Becky, and began to collect Gemma's belongings. The others just surrounded us with a shield of love. At times like this, when there are no words; there is huge power and comfort in being present. Whether it's a reassuring hand on the shoulder or a simple hug, it's knowing that despite the pain and confusion you're in, you're not alone. When people say they don't know how to support you, or don't know what to say, just being there, being present, is, in that moment, everything.

However scared we felt, as we prepared to leave that place that night, we knew that we were being held and carried by our friends, and that was something that would mean so much as the storm raged in the days and weeks to come.

As David and Becky emerged from her room with the final few plastic bags filled with her stuff, I caught a glimpse of Gemma still lying there. I felt totally sick at the thought that, in a few minutes, we were going leave this place and head home without her. I asked David what she looked like and he said, very sensitively, that she looked peaceful. I knew I needed to see her one final time ...

The woman who had brought such love, joy, and purpose to my life lay forever still. As I edged towards her bed, I took her right hand for the final time. It was stone cold. Her life had only ended an hour or so earlier, but already the warmth of life had left her body. It was too much to bear, and I wept over her. I thanked her one final time for everything she had been to me and promised her again that I would love and protect her boy in the years to come. As I edged back out of the room my eyes never left her. I would never see her again. From that moment on, my wife would be a memory that would live on in pictures, stories, and most beautifully in the life of my boy, and as I gently closed the door, my mind turned to what lay ahead – telling Ethan that his mum had gone.

A BOY WITHOUT A MUM

We walked out of the Churchill Hospital for the last time, and the chill of that freezing November night hit me hard. The strength in my legs went, and I crumpled onto the cold pavement outside the main doors, screaming, 'Why?' – spitting out all of the anger and injustice I now felt towards God.

I was brought up always being aware of the possibility that there was a God. My dad was a vicar and while faith was always part of home life, my parents never once put pressure on me to conform and believe. But as I grew older and was able to ask those big questions of life and faith that most of us will ask at some point in our lives, my belief in, and relationship with God became a significant part of my life. Without it I'm not sure that Gemma and I would have been able to navigate some of the tough challenges we faced. Our faith gave us a foundation that proved unshakeable in our marriage when everything else around us was shaking; but now those foundations of faith were crumbling.

If the God I believed in was a God of love, how had he stood by and done nothing when I had cried out to him, time and time again? Why had my pleas not to leave my boy without a mum fallen on deaf ears?

I have to believe that the God I believe in heard my pleas; but I have a massive question as to why he let it happen, and my anger with him reverberated into the night – 'Why?' I yelled it out over and over again. 'Why have you let this happen? Why have you left my boy without his mum? Why have you taken her? Why, God? Why?' It must have been heart-breaking for David to see me buckling under the torrent of pain that raw grief visits on you. All he could do was pick me up and hold me.

By the time I had calmed down and we were on our way back to Reading, my mind had already turned to the next nightmare – having to tell my boy that his mum had died.

My mind drifted back two years to a family holiday in Greece. I had always left booking holidays to Gemma. She had a knack of finding beautiful places that didn't cost the earth, and this summer she had found a beautiful hotel in the Messinia region in Greece. All the online reviews were amazing, except one. It was from a lady who had gone there with her family the year before and couldn't fault the place. The only reason she had given it a "terrible" rating was that their little boy's favourite cuddly toy had been inadvertently scooped up in the change of beds, and was last heard of heading to an industrial laundrette in Athens, never to be seen again! That one incident had pretty much ruined their holiday.

One evening, after lapping up another day of Greek sunshine, we returned to our room and I could see that the linen had been changed on Ethan's sofa bed. The bed where he had left his favourite cuddly toy, Ooo Ooo. And there was no sign of his little monkey.

Straightaway, the review came flashing back into my mind. As Gemma and I began looking everywhere, I whispered to her that Ooo Ooo had gone. She told me not to be silly; it must be somewhere. But it wasn't. Just as had happened to that family a year before, the rush to get the room changed had seen Ethan's bedtime companion swept up into a laundry bin, never to be found again, despite the hotel's best efforts to track him down.

As home got ever nearer that night, all I could think about was that day two years before, and the look of inconsolable sadness in Ethan's eyes as we gently told him what had happened. He was heartbroken. It had been with him since birth, and for those first five-and-a-half years of his life, Ooo Ooo and Ethan had become inseparable at bedtime. Despite the well-intentioned efforts of the hotel manager to placate him with a range of cuddly turtles, nothing was going to fill the void left by his little monkey. Such was his sadness that one evening he spent the whole of dinner time drawing and writing a book that ended up being an ode to Ooo Ooo. As I reflected on that moment from the summer of 2015, and how difficult it had been to console him over a toy monkey, the thought of returning home to tell him his mum had gone made me feel physically sick.

He might have been two years older and two years more grown up, but how the hell do you tell an eight-year-old that his mum is never coming home again?

About 10 miles away from Reading we could see the golden arches of McDonald's glowing in the darkness. None of us had eaten that day. Food had been the last thing on our minds, but with the emotional chaos of what was to come at home, we thought it would be a good idea to grab something while we had the chance. It was a surreal experience. When you lose someone you love, it feels like your whole world has ground to a halt and you simply cannot understand how the world around you hasn't stopped as well. One of the many challenges you face is coming to terms with knowing that life must, and does, carry on. When your time comes, it doesn't matter who you are, or how many people will mourn your passing, the world will carry on spinning. The rhythm of life never stops beating, and for anybody experiencing the loss of a loved one this can, at times, feel unbearable.

As we walked into McDonalds, it felt like a smack round the face with something heavy and cold. Here was life carrying on as it always has, and always will. The sound of people ordering their Quarter Pounders, the crackle of fat in the fryer, the excited chatter of kids as they unwrapped their Happy Meals – the incessant soundtrack of normal life felt deafening. As I stood there feeling dazed and staring blankly at the menu, I could feel a sense of anger welling up inside me. *What's wrong with these people?* I thought. *My wife's just died! How can you just carry on as if nothing has happened? How dare you be looking so normal and happy?*

I came close to shouting across the restaurant, 'My wife's just fucking died! How can you look so happy?' – thankfully I didn't. None of these people who were innocently enjoying their Friday night fix of fast food knew Gemma. They didn't know me, and they certainly didn't know what had just happened. But in those raw first few hours after she went, normal life felt like a cruel affront to how I was feeling. It felt like the ultimate expression of insensitivity.

*

The days become weeks, and the weeks become months, but it doesn't get any easier coming to terms with the confusing reality of life carrying on as normal. Often you will hear people who have been bereaved saying it feels like everyone has moved on. In truth, the people who really care about you don't suddenly stop caring. They don't stop thinking about the wife you've lost, and the friend they no longer have. But while the landscape of your world has changed forever, the lives of the people who matter to you most have to continue. Bills still need to be paid. Children still need to be fed. Those dinner parties still need attending. And as time goes on, you either learn to accept this and not take it as a personal affront, or you end up being consumed by a bitterness that makes you feel that the world has forgotten you. Even in the saddest and most desperate of times, life's drum never stops beating its relentless rhythm.

Half an hour later, the glowing windows of our house came into view. I felt totally sick again. My heartbeat quickened, and the food I had just eaten felt like it was about to be deposited all over Dave's upholstery. The moment no child should ever have to face so early in life was upon us.

I nervously opened the front door; I could already hear the sounds of Ethan and his cousins playing merrily in the lounge. The kitchen was a hive of activity. Liz, who had helped bring the kids back a few hours before, was tidying up after tea, and Becky and Gemma's mum, Wendy, were sitting round the table. We hugged and the tears began to flow once again; everybody knew what was coming. There was no need for words. In the next room, an eight-year-old boy was playing innocently with his cousin Thomas, and he was about to have his heart not just broken, but shattered. My heart felt the heaviest I've ever known. As a parent, you want to protect your children, you want to be able to hold them and tell them everything is going to be okay – but life for me, and for Ethan, was about to get as far away from okay as it could ever be. I closed my eyes and prayed that God would somehow give me the right words – this was a moment that couldn't be put off or avoided any longer. Someone had to tell him, and it could only be his dad.

As I approached him, I crouched down to his level and said I needed to tell him something. I could see in his eyes that he already knew something was wrong. All he said was, 'Okay ...' so I picked him up and carried him out of the lounge.

Ethan remained silent as we climbed the stairs to the landing. I sat down in the small blue armchair, placed my hands on his shoulders, and looked into his deep hazel-green-brown eyes. This had been the strangest of days for him. Waking up again without mummy and daddy, being plucked out of school and driven to hospital. Seeing his mum twice, but not being able to hear her speak. His house full of people, but no smiles or laughter ... His eyes betrayed his fear – he knew he was about to hear something he didn't want to, but as he would tell me in the days that followed, he never expected it to be this …

My hands trembled on his shoulders as I began to speak. 'Ethan, you know Mummy hasn't been very well …' He slowly nodded but said nothing. 'Well, today Mummy became really, really poorly, which is why you came into the hospital to see her.' He stayed silent and carried on looking intensely into my eyes, as my heart beat faster and faster. 'My boy, I'm so, so sorry … the doctors tried everything to make Mummy better, but …'

Before the words could even form in my mouth, tears filled his eyes and he cried out, 'Has Mummy died?'

Every part of me wanted to somehow sugar-coat what I had to say, but I knew, for his sake, I couldn't. As his legs began to buckle, I spoke the words I had never imagined saying in my worst nightmares – 'I'm so, so sorry, my boy, but Mummy's died.' His body crumpled to the floor, a gut-wrenching sobbing began to fill the air. It felt like a tsunami was hitting our house and smashing into everything he had ever known. As he rolled on the floor, all I could do was hold him. As the waves of grief began to break, I held him as tightly as I could, his innocent face contorted with pain, Time and time again I told him how much I loved him. I told him how sorry I was, and how much Mummy loved him, over and over again. And when the storm of emotion abated for the briefest of moments, I just kept telling him that we would be okay. That Daddy would somehow get him through this.

My little boy – *our* little boy – had just had his world obliterated.

ALL I WANT FOR CHRISTMAS ...

It was not a night for any of us to be alone. So as the exhaustion of that day finally took us, I laid Ethan onto our bed, lay down next to him, and my sister lay down next to me. We simply held each other as our tired eyes eventually began to close. The enormity of Gemma going had barely begun to register. And that night at least, sleep wasn't the enemy it was about to become. Somehow, we all slept.

My arm never left Ethan. I just wanted him to know that whenever he woke, his dad was right by his side, holding him. And as I woke early that next morning, my arm was still wrapped around my boy, and Becky was still by my side, with her arm wrapped around me.

Have you ever had one of those moments when you wake up and you're not quite sure where you are, or what day it is? Just before reality kicks in and everything comes flooding back?

That Saturday morning I woke wondering: *Why is Ethan in our bed? Why on earth is my sister lying next to me? Where is Gemma?*

For the briefest and cruellest of moments, I had no idea what was going on, let alone what day it was. And that is one of the grimmest parts of grief – every day you wake up to a nightmare. When grief lays its cold oppressive hand on your life, sleep becomes your only escape, and for those short few hours that Friday night, I was mercifully able to escape the horror of that day, but as daylight broke and my eyes opened, I was hurled back into the biggest nightmare of all.

As my confusion began to subside and the grim reality hit home, Ethan began to stir. As his eyes opened, the look of pain from a few hours before had given way to one of deep sadness. And as he snuggled into my chest, and wrapped his arms around me, the tears began to flow again. Like I did so many times over those early months, I wondered what on earth was going through his mind. I wondered what I could say or do to help.

*

I used to live in a rural village in West Norfolk, and I remember one night, my dad had to go out to a meeting. He nearly didn't go. A thick fog had descended on that corner of East Anglia which had made driving down those twisting country lanes even more of a challenge than normal. It was supposed to be a short meeting, but as the clock ticked past half past eight, my mum began to worry. Nine o'clock came and went, and still there was no sign of Dad. All these years later, I can still see that look of panic etched on Mum's face as time and time again she said, 'I knew he shouldn't have gone.' Mum's fears transferred to me. But minutes later, there was the sound of a car on the drive and the hugely reassuring sound of Dad's keys in the door. The fog had been so bad, he'd had to drive back at walking pace. That tangible sense of fear that something awful had happened to my dad never left me. I was eight years old.

As I gazed at my boy's face that first morning, I knew those fears had come true for him. All I could do was tell him, over and over again, that I loved him.

As his tears began to subside, he looked at me and said, 'Daddy, you know it's Christmas soon?' Christmas was the last thing on anybody's mind but reluctantly I said, 'Yes.' 'Well there are three things I want for Christmas ...' As the words began to tumble out of his mouth our new unwelcome reality, began to sink in. 'I want the Playmobil island set I told Mummy about, there's a Lego Minecraft set I really want; but most of all I want Mummy back.' Those words felt like a punch to the gut.

Five days ago, his mum had been lying in this very bed, the clothes she had last worn still lay on the chair by the window, her make-up still sat on her bedside table, everything was as it always had been. Five days! And now, she was a part of his Christmas wish list!

You will often hear about the different stages of grief that people experience. The reality is that grief is not a linear journey. What one person might experience in the first few weeks might be entirely different for another person. But one thing many people talk about in those early days and weeks is denial, a refusal to accept the truth of what has happened. Deep down in my heart, I knew Gemma had gone. But in my head, I simply couldn't accept it. That sense of numbed disbelief was like a shield, protecting me from absorbing all the pain at once. Without it the sheer enormity of what had happened would have been overwhelming. Unbearable. I told Ethan that I would make sure that the Playmobil and Lego were on my Christmas shopping list. And I told him I would do anything to bring Mummy back. But I was unable to muster the words to say I couldn't.

The noise of people waking began to fill the house, but I just lay there looking blankly at the ceiling. My mind was in a complete daze, unable to engage in anything other than empty thoughts. I felt like I had become anaesthetised to the pain of the day before. Eventually I put on my dressing gown and went down to sit in the lounge. In so many ways, everything felt so normal, like any other weekend that my family would come to stay. People were busying themselves in the kitchen making tea and toast, and in the lounge, there was Ethan and Thomas playing on the Wii, as they had countless times before.

As I slumped on the sofa with a cup of tea in hand, and watched my boy playing and laughing, I started to wonder how he was still able to find any happiness on this most unhappy of days. But as the weeks went by, I came to understand that a child's experience of grief is very different to an adult's. It's like a puddle. For a moment they're in that puddle, and they feel sad. They feel fearful about what it is all going to mean for them. They crave some kind of reassurance that everything is going to be okay. But when the pain becomes too much, they can jump out of the puddle and distract themselves with another game or another box of Lego.

As an adult, it feels like there is no escape. You want to jump out of the fear, the worry, and the endless questions about what on earth happens next, but you can't.

As the chequered flag signalled the end of another Mario Kart race, Thomas went upstairs to get dressed and Ethan jumped right back into that puddle. He looked at me sadly, tears welling in his eyes again and said, 'Daddy, can I ask you something? You know you're always at work on a Saturday and Mummy looks after me? Who's going to look after me now?' His worried eyes looked into mine, and, for a second, shook me out of my numbness. I hadn't had the mental capacity to think what life would look like in an hour's time, let alone what was going to happen in the future; but Ethan had. I didn't even want to have that conversation with him. I wanted to shut the door on it, and tell him it was too early to start worrying about things like that; but as I would begin to understand more profoundly in time, you just can't do that. However tough the question, however reluctant you may be to talk about it, you have to. You have to give children the permission and freedom to express their feelings. If every time they ask you an uncomfortable question, your response is: 'I don't want to talk about it,' then gradually, over time, they will stop asking those questions and the door will begin to shut. If it does, where does their grief go then? How do they express what they're feeling? How do they find the answers to their many concerns?

I spoke to a couple of people in the months after Gemma's death, who had lost their mums at a similar age to Ethan, and they both spoke of dads who were unable and unwilling to express their grief. One dad never even mentioned the child's mum after the funeral. Growing up without being able to talk about his mum, or how he was feeling to the person that mattered to him most left him in a very isolated place. As the years passed and he grew into a man, the burden of suppressing all that grief left him emotionally scarred.

The questions children have may not be deep philosophical questions about the meaning of life, but that first question they ask and that first worry they express is nearly always the most significant. And it deserves – and demands – a response. As I scrambled around for an answer to what would happen at weekends when I went back to work, all I could think to say was, 'Ethan, you don't need to worry. Daddy's not going to be going back to work for a while.' Looking back, it seems such a totally inadequate answer because he was worried. It was the weekend, and everything in his world was already looking and feeling unrecognisably different. And for the next four months, it was a worry and a question I would wrestle with endlessly.

What *was* I going to do about work? If I did go back to work, what was I going to do with Ethan? If I didn't, how was I going to earn a living? How would I pay the mortgage? One moment life had felt so straightforward, now it felt that all my certainties were crumbling around me.

FINDING LIGHT IN THE DARKNESS

That first day without Gemma, I was in a constant daze. The friends who had supported us gathered at the house, and, for the most part, we all just sat there. The kettle rarely stopped boiling, the front door was forever opening and shutting, the kids continued to play, but the familiar noises of home life were punctuated by a stunned silence. I can still see my sister Hannah, just sitting on the sofa, staring vacantly into the distance, her mascara smudged with tears, and still wrestling with the guilt of not making it to the hospital in time the night before.

It wasn't the time for words. Nor even for trying to make sense of what had happened – not that we would ever be able to answer that question. This was a time to just be. A time to forget about tomorrow and just survive today.

Every time the doorbell went, or I heard a key turning in the door, I half expected Gemma to walk back in, but of course she never did. Every time I thought of her, every time I remembered her face, or saw her picture on the mantlepiece, my stomach felt like it was being twisted into an ever-tighter knot.

At times I struggled to even remember what her voice sounded like. I would try and imagine her voice echoing through from the kitchen, yet for some reason I just couldn't remember how it sounded. It was horribly disconcerting. How could I forget any detail of a voice that I had heard nearly every day for over 16 years?

As I grew more agitated by this, I would listen over and over again to her voicemail messages. She had sent me the last one just four weeks before she died ... Gemma and some of her friends were making soup for an event at our church, and I had decided to head out and kill some time. Because I was off work and really struggling with my depression and anxiety at the time, she just phoned to make sure I was okay.

Listening to her message again and again that Saturday, just to remember how my wife actually sounded, felt like being transported back in time. Hearing her voice felt, as it always had done, part of the routine of life, so utterly normal. And yet, I was never going to hear that voice in the present, ever again. I was never going to feel the reassurance of knowing she was there, looking out for me – and that new reality hurt. It really hurt, and many months on, it still does.

At other times that day, I'd catch myself staring blankly at my phone, endlessly reading back some of the texts she had sent me only a few days before. It was so painful; an intensity of pain I had never felt before. It felt like my insides were being torn apart.

As morning turned into afternoon, Ethan and Thomas were becoming more and more restless. It had been a long morning cooped up inside and the atmosphere must have felt strange and claustrophobic. As well as being brilliant with kids, one of Becky's many strengths is being incredibly thoughtful and practical, even when she least feels like it. She had seen that Ethan and Thomas were starting to get restless and decided to take them out to get some fresh air and pay a visit to their favourite shop (that does a fine line in cheap, plastic toys that children can't get enough of). They both loved the place, and every time Thomas came to stay, a visit to Terry's was top of his agenda! As Becky got the now excited boys ready for their afternoon excursion to tatsville, I could hear Ethan moaning that he didn't want to wear his coat. The day was crisp, clear, and absolutely Baltic outside! But still Ethan didn't want to wear his coat, and I remembered the almost daily battle Gemma had had on many a school morning as she tried to get him out of the house with his coat on. As I crouched down and put my hands on his shoulders, I said to him, 'Ethan, if Mummy was here right now, what we would she say to you?'

'Put my coat on,' came his resigned reply.

As those words spilled out of my mouth, I could barely believe what I was saying. Gemma had still been with us less than a day ago! But now, without even thinking about it, and without even intending to, I was bringing the memories of Mummy back into the everyday conversations. As Ethan reluctantly put his coat on and walked out into the freezing wind, it felt like an important moment. It was beyond painful knowing that, for the rest of my life, the only way Gemma would live on was through our memories. I knew that however hard it was, I had to keep her part of the conversation.

I headed upstairs to take some time alone. I lay down and stared at the ceiling, thinking of very little. I felt like I was in the aftermath of an explosion. The noise has died down, you're dazed and in pain, but as you try and get back to your feet, you can't make sense of anything because of the devastation all around you. The reality of what had happened the day before had hardly begun to register, but I knew that everything had changed. The winter sunshine poured into the room as I started to think about what Ethan had asked me about work, and what was going to happen to him at weekends. It had just gone three o'clock, and my mind momentarily drifted to the world of football, as I imagined referees' whistles echoing around grounds as the Saturday fixtures got underway. It was a world I loved and had spent the past 13 years of my working life inhabiting. But now it felt an absolute world away. After something as life changing as this, how could I ever care about 22 men running around a pitch chasing a football? How could I ever sit in that studio and pretend to care whether it was a penalty or not? It all felt pointless. Life felt pointless.

I thought about what I'd normally be doing at this time on a Saturday. The live lunchtime game we'd have been covering would be over, and I'd probably be in the back of a cab heading for the train station, ringing Gemma to see how her day had been, and letting her know what time I'd be getting home. The sick feeling in my stomach intensified.

Deep down I knew I wouldn't be going back to work anytime soon. I hadn't been at work for four weeks, and apart from a close circle of work colleagues, no one knew why. Now those weeks were going to turn into months and still no one would know. I needed to let people know. I picked up my phone that had barely stopped bleeping with incoming texts and messages for the past few hours, and posted this message on Twitter:

Today I am crushed with indescribable pain. Just three days after falling ill with acute myeloid leukaemia, my dear wife Gemma passed away yesterday evening, surrounded by her family and friends. If you are a prayer – pray for my boy Ethan. 8yrs, precious and in bits. Thank you.

To this day I don't really know why I wrote what I did. I just wanted to be honest about how I was feeling. I *was* in indescribable pain and I was worried about how on earth Ethan was going to cope with no longer having his mum alongside him. I put my phone down and continued to stare blankly at the ceiling, but then something began to happen that I never expected and certainly never intended.

Just minutes after posting the tweet, my phone began beeping even more as text messages began to flood in. Last night, we had been engulfed by a tsunami; today, a huge wave of support was beginning to break over us. Messages from friends I hadn't heard from in years; texts from the world of sport … By the end of that day, my tweet had been retweeted nearly 18,000 times. By the end of that weekend I had received over 12,000 messages. It was overwhelming. And for a time, it did provide an antidote to the pain. To know that we were being thought about by people we knew and people we didn't, was a huge comfort. Later that evening, I received a text from my old university housemate Andy, who was in Australia, to say that the Aussie rugby legend, David Campese, had retweeted the news. Gemma's tragic story was reverberating far and wide.

*

As I looked back on that afternoon in the months to come, I still don't know why it caused the reaction it did. Yes, my career had given me a platform and a voice that many don't have, but Gemma's story wasn't unique, our grief wasn't any more important than anyone else's. But for some reason the story resonated with people. I think part of it had to do with the speed at which it happened. There was something shocking and brutal about Gemma's story that caught people's attention. If ever you needed a reminder of the fragility of life, this was it. Perhaps it served as a poignant reminder of just how precious life is.

We all crave certainties in life, but Gemma's story underlined the truth that nothing is certain, except the one thing we all fear: death.

Maybe my honesty about how I was feeling struck a chord. Often, when we hear news of someone passing away, we register the wonderful tributes to them, but we don't hear what the immediate aftermath is like for those they leave behind. Death has become so sanitised in our culture. It's not something we want to think about, and all too often it's not something we want to talk about. We still like to employ the good old British stiff upper lip when it comes to those areas of life we find uncomfortable. Maybe, just maybe, laying my emotions bare helped challenge that emotional illiteracy around death.

*

Later that afternoon, as we drank more tea, and tried to talk, a beautifully clear yellow light flooded into the room. The lounge shone with the glorious light of the winter sun. Everything in my head had felt so dark, but as the brilliance of the light striking the walls intensified, I began to feel a sense of hope. An almost overwhelming sense of hope.

So much of the last few hours had felt like an oppressive darkness was closing in. It had felt claustrophobic, inescapable. But as my eyes became transfixed by this light, the words of Jesus came into my mind:

"I am the light of the world. Whoever follows me will never walk in darkness, but will have the light of life."

As I stared ahead and watched the sunlight dancing through the swaying trees in the garden, I remembered the promises I had made to Gemma almost exactly 24 hours earlier as the sun had set over Oxford, and the promise I had made her that I would not give up on my faith. Barely two hours later that same day, I was already discovering that keeping that promise would be the toughest of battles as I railed at God outside the hospital. But as that new sense of hope began to build in me, I had this sense that if I was going to find a purpose in life again, if I was somehow going to find a reason to live again, I had to find the light. I couldn't let the darkness consume me – whatever it took, I had to hold on to my faith and preserve that little speck of hope. Our faith had navigated us through some tough times in our marriage; now I needed it more than ever to guide me through the biggest challenge of all.

Without saying a word, I got to my feet, as my friends and family watched on, and walked over to the French windows where the light was streaming in. I sank to my knees, raised my hands into the air and prayed:

God, I will not forsake you, I will have faith in you.

In so many ways I don't know why I did it. Perhaps I just felt the need to acknowledge – in front of my family, in front of my friends and in front of God – that however dark life felt, and despite the irreconcilable anger I felt towards him, I wasn't going to give up on God.

Talking about his faith, Bear Grylls once said, 'I am no longer too proud to admit that I need my Saviour beside me. Does that make my faith a crutch? Maybe. But what does a crutch do? It helps you stand and makes you stronger. So, yes, when I face overwhelming odds, I need a bit of that.'

And on that Saturday afternoon, that's exactly what I needed too. The odds of me finding happiness and hope again in life were stacked against me. But I'm not afraid to admit that in that moment, when the light broke through the darkness, my faith felt like a crutch, and I was going to lean on it for all it was worth. But raising my hands in the air and praying those words was one thing. Living it out in this strange new world we had been drop-kicked into would be altogether very different, and it wouldn't be long before I discovered, in a new way, just how hard it would be.

STOP ALL THE CLOCKS

As I took Ethan up to bed that second night without Mummy, we were both emotionally spent. He lay down on the mattress at the foot of our bed, so he could sleep next to Thomas, the latest batch of plastic toys bundled up next to him.

There was so much sadness in his eyes. As we hugged, I thought of all those mornings when Gemma and I had woken to the pitter-patter of little feet on the landing, before Ethan had jumped onto the bed and snuggled down between us. At that moment, I would have given anything for one more morning like that, one more "group huggle" as Ethan used to call them. Death doesn't just rob you of a person, it robs you of a way of life, and so many of those little moments that make life so rich.

As I got ready to say good night to him, and say a little prayer, as we had done every night, I asked him if he wanted to share a Mummy memory. It felt like such a weird and uncomfortable thing to do, but I felt I needed to do it. There are an amazing number of brilliant charities and books out there to help families and children cope with the loss of a loved one. But when you're plunged into a situation like this where there is no time to even say goodbye, let alone begin to plan for life after loss, you have to find your own way. When your child's world has been shattered, there's no time for handbooks, no time to talk to child bereavement counsellors – you've just got to get on with it.

That evening, I knew I had to keep Mummy part of the conversation, however difficult and strange it was for both of us. So I told him that every night we should each share a Mummy memory – 'You go first, Daddy,' was his response. 'Okay,' I said, 'my memory of Mummy tonight is her smile.' Ethan smiled back at me, and said, 'My Mummy memory is her roast lunches.' Part of me was kind of hoping for something a little deeper and more profound, but at that moment, this was all I needed to hear. My boy was already being able to talk about his mum amid the sadness and fear, and that meant everything. I grinned back at him and said, 'I promise I'll learn to cook roasts.' Ethan's response was as funny as it was withering. 'Good because you only do BBQs and omelettes!'

In so many ways, that simple and lovely moment became something hugely significant for Ethan's own journey through grief. Right from the very start, he knew he had the freedom to express how he was feeling, he knew it was okay to talk about Mum. The easier option would have been not to do it and avoid the discomfort of asking my boy for a memory of Mummy just a day after she went. But as the weeks became months, keeping her part of our everyday – if only as a memory – would prove so important for him in navigating his life and his grief. It also served as a rather blunt but amusing reminder that, at some point, I would have to expand my somewhat limited cooking repertoire, reverting back to my bachelor days of Super Noodles and outrageously hot chilli con carne wasn't really going to cut the mustard with an eight-year-old!

That was the last night we spent in that room for a long time. It would be nearly five months before I would return to our bedroom and Ethan would return to his. Although we had been able to spend the first couple of nights in there, as the weekend went on, it became more and more painful to even enter our bedroom, let alone sleep in it. There's a famous poem called *Stop the Clocks*, by

W. H. Auden (that was used, so movingly, in *Four Weddings and a Funeral*) that poignantly describes what the immediate aftermath of losing someone is like. In the first verse he wrote:

> *Stop all the clocks, cut off the telephone,*
> *Prevent the dog from barking with a juicy bone,*
> *Silence the pianos and with muffled drum*
> *Bring out the coffin, let the mourners come.*

Our bedroom was that place where time stood still. Gemma's clothes still hung from the door. The last book she was reading just days before, still lay on her bedside table. Her favourite perfume sat on the chest of drawers among the hairspray and bronzers. Everything looked and smelt as it always had done, yet this was a room that now told of a stark and painful absence. And it made me feel sick to be in there.

So on the Sunday night, Ethan and I set up camp in the spare room at the top of the house. He might have only been eight, but I needed him beside me more than ever. While our close family and friends would deal with their grief for Gemma in their own way, we needed to be a team, closer than we'd ever been – we had to be Team Thomas!

I laid a couple of mattresses on the floor for Ethan, surrounded them with a selection of his favourite cuddly toys and tucked him into bed. Like we had the night before, we shared our Mummy memories. Ethan went first and said, 'I'm going to miss her lovely hazelnut eyes.' As I looked on with pride, we agreed that on this night, we would share that memory.

MOUNTAIN BY MOUNTAIN

When CS Lewis wrote about the death of his wife in *A Grief Observed*, he opened the book with this arresting line:

No one ever told me that grief felt so like fear.

Even if he had not written anything else, these words would have been enough. In those first few days after loss, fear becomes your biggest enemy. In its most raw state, grief is what we experience when the door slams shut on love. All the love, affection, and care you had doesn't end, but it now has nowhere to go. It has no space to fill. Love doesn't end with death – if anything, it grows even more – but it can no longer be received. And as the door closes on that earthly love, fear begins to drag you in.

That night, like the previous two, I didn't have a problem getting to sleep, the problem (as I would begin to experience night after night for the next few months) was that I couldn't stay asleep. As the clock passed one o'clock, I was wide awake.

The denial that had cocooned me for the past 48 hours was subsiding and giving way to pure, inescapable fear. As Ethan slept at the end of the bed, my mind was an avalanche of questions and fears as the reality of what had happened, and my anxieties about the future began to hit home. For any of us, the darkness and the stillness of the small hours can turn a minor worry into something altogether bigger. On that night, my fears became like giants.

There are lots of different illustrations you can use to convey what grief feels like, and on that night, it felt like I'd been dumped into a dark, foreboding ocean where a huge storm was raging. All around me, relentless waves were building and then crashing over me. At times it felt like I was drowning, struggling to find the strength to swim back to the surface and gasp for air.

On that night and for those first few weeks it didn't feel like I was living anymore; it felt like I was merely surviving. Some days I was just trying to get through the next hour, others it was about getting to the end of the day. In the early hours of that Sunday morning, the storm was at its worst and two fears kept crashing over me again and again: my career and our home.

When we'd moved to Reading in 2011, we had stretched ourselves as far as we could go with the mortgage. For as long as I kept having my contracts at Sky renewed, we knew we'd be okay. But if the day came when there wasn't another offer on the table, we knew we'd have to downsize.

Most people crave the certainty of home and hearth, and I had worried about our future security before, but now my fears raged with new intensity. What on earth was I going to do about work? Ethan had already asked that question. What *would* I do about weekends? What *would* I do about the holidays when he was off school, and I was travelling the country, covering games for Sky? Suddenly life had become very, very complicated. Everything that had felt so straightforward now felt almost impossible. How would life would work from now on?

When I had left *Blue Peter*, my aim had always been to work in sport. As I left the gates of Television Centre in London for the final time in April 2005, I left with nothing but my *Blue Peter* badge and an uncertain future. After six incredible years on an iconic show, I now had nothing to do. There were no offers on the table, and there seemed little hope of realising my dream sports presenting job. I was 32 years old, four months away from getting married, and jobless.

*

Two months later, thanks to the efforts of my agent, I was sitting in an office in Isleworth with the head of Sky Sports, Vic Wakeling. He wanted to know why I wanted to work in sport, and what my aspirations were. Most importantly, unlike other broadcasters I had spoken to, they were prepared to give me a chance.

Like so many others, my ultimate aim was to present Premier League football. But I knew that while I might have the broadcasting skills and the experience of live TV, this was something completely different to making a dolls' gym out of old bog rolls at ten past five on a Monday afternoon! I was going to have to learn a new trade, and I was prepared to start anywhere to realise that dream.

After many years sat behind the desk on *Sky Sports News* and then five years covering the Football League for Sky, my chance to work on the Premier League finally arrived 11 years later in the summer of 2016. Ultimately, the realisation of that dream was short lived, but for a season and a bit, I absolutely loved it – and it gave us a quality of life that we enjoyed, but never took for granted. Like anything in life, when you have to work for it or have to wait for it longer than you expected, you appreciate it in more ways than if it had just landed in your lap. I knew I was incredibly blessed to be doing that job. I got paid to go and watch the game I loved and then talk about it – it never felt like work. It was an absolute privilege – even during those times when I felt like I lived on the M6!

But even with the best jobs in the world there are downsides, and working in football was no different. I would be away for at least half of most weekends. When Christmas came, the festive period was packed with games, so while the rest of the family carried on enjoying the festivities, I was traversing the country. When the season ended in May, I would get six or seven weeks off, which was always my favourite time of the year; but just as the schools were breaking up, and Ethan was getting excited about the summer holidays, it would be time to get ready for a new season.

Compared to most jobs, these inconveniences were so minor that they barely merit a mention, and they were compensated by the fact that unlike many mums and dads, I got to spend time with my boy during the week.

For those years I worked on the football, life worked. When I wasn't around in the holidays, Gemma would make lots of plans for them both, and I would see them as and when I could. When I was absent at weekends, Ethan had his mum to hang out with, but now everything had changed. The work-life balance that had sustained us for so long was in ruins. As 2.00am came and went, I continued to wrestle with this one question – *What do we do now?*

When it came to parenting Ethan, there was no "we" anymore. I was all he had, and if I did return to work at some stage, what would I do with him? While I was comforted by the countless offers from family and friends to look after him when that time came, did I want him being passed around different people every time I went to work? No one knew him better than me, and I knew he'd hate that being his new "normal". I didn't want him to have to ask towards the end of every week, 'Who am I staying with this weekend, Daddy?' when all he wanted was to be at home. How could I leave him at Christmas, a time of year when he'd probably be feeling his mum's absence more acutely than ever? How could I just leave him like that?

As these fears continued to roll in, I looked to where he was sleeping and knew one thing – there was no way I wanted that life for him. I needed to be with him and more importantly, I wanted to be with him. We had a long journey ahead of us, and it was a journey we would need to walk side by side, for as long as it took. But as that wave of fear crashed over me, another one was already brewing – if I couldn't return to work for the sake of my boy, how would we survive financially?

I felt the panic rising. If I couldn't go back to work, how on earth could I continue to pay the mortgage? I knew roughly how much we had left to pay off, and it was a lot. I knew exactly how much our monthly repayments were, and they were sizeable. Before I knew it, I was on my phone checking all our accounts and working out how much money we had put aside. Despite my tiredness and confusion in those early hours, it didn't take much to work out that if I didn't go back to work, it would only be about six months before we'd be in serious financial trouble. Either I would have to go back to work, or we would have to sell the house.

At any time in life, these sorts of worries would have been big enough on their own, but on the third night without Gemma, they were too much. Everything I was feeling that night – the unbearable pain of losing Gemma, and the questions about life going forward – was overwhelming. My breathing was quickening, faster and faster, until I just started to sob. After that, all I could do was grip the pillow, try to take deeper breaths and hope not to wake up Ethan. The last thing he needed was to wake up to his dad having a panic attack in the middle of the night. As the waves of panic began to subside, I had the briefest of moments where I was able to think rationally, and as I did, two words came into my head – life insurance! We had life insurance; but the only question was, had I put Gemma on the policy?

A few years before, while he was working for Sky Sports, my friend Ed Chamberlin developed stomach cancer. Mercifully, Ed came through, and now fronts ITV's Racing coverage, and has become one of the finest sports broadcasters in the country. The most important thing to come out of that horrible episode for Ed was that he got better and has been able to carry on being a wonderful husband and father. But the other significant thing that emerged from it was the importance of having life insurance and critical illness cover in place, just in case the worst ever happened. Because Sky, like so many other broadcasters employed us on a freelance basis, it meant that, if you were unable to work, for whatever reason, you wouldn't be earning – you can't invoice for work you're not providing. As Ed returned to work, he encouraged us all to make sure we had cover in place, and to ensure it covered us enough. His hadn't, and it proved to be a big wakeup call, as I discovered that although I had a policy, the level of cover it provided was nowhere near enough.

Not long afterwards, I sat down with Gemma and our financial advisor, Roy. We put a new policy in place with much more comprehensive cover, and there were two quotes: one to cover me, and one to cover both of us. Unsurprisingly, there was a significant difference between the two, and as Roy told me in the aftermath of Gemma's death, I was like a typical man that day. You look at the two figures and decide that, because you're the main breadwinner you're only going to cover yourself. I very nearly did exactly that, but I changed my mind after Roy told us the story of a client who was having exactly the same dilemma; in the end, he'd decided to only cover himself. Just 18 months later, just like Gemma, his wife developed acute myeloid leukaemia, and died shortly after. Roy told us that it was the most difficult call he'd ever had to take; the poor husband rang him in tears, desperate to know whether he had covered his wife or not – Roy had to tell him he hadn't. There wouldn't be a payout.

There was now one big question raging above all others – had I covered Gemma?

This wasn't a question that would wait until the morning, there was no way I was going to get back to sleep, so at about 3.30am, I headed downstairs and began to search feverishly through endless folders. I couldn't find my policy documents anywhere. Over the years I had been so organised when it came to filing important documents, but now, when I needed the information most, it was nowhere to be found. The panic of a few minutes before started to grow again. I checked my bank account; I could see the money was coming out every month, but I still didn't know for sure if Gemma was on the policy. I was desperate now. I had to email Roy. I felt callous even asking that question; Gemma had only been gone just over 48 hours and already I was worrying about money. It felt almost disrespectful, but in terms of how I would get through tomorrow, let alone the next few weeks, I had to know now.

I sent Roy this email:

Hi mate – Please don't think I'm mad for asking this so soon, but my mind is in overdrive at the moment. Can't begin to comprehend how we're going to move forward from this and what the future is going to be like.

I am fairly certain the life cover I have was for both Gemma and myself but I can't find anything at the moment except one letter with the policy number on.

Is there any way you can find out what the repercussions are of Gemma's passing if she was covered?

My head is all over the place but I'm desperate to get some peace about Ethan's future and work, where we live – everything.

Thanks mate

Si

As I see those words again, I can hear the panic in my voice, but just a few hours later Roy replied – Gemma *was* covered. Ultimately it was scant consolation; but that moment changed so much.

The journey of grief is like being dropped into a vast mountain range, and unless you choose to give up on life, you're going to have to traverse it. As you scale one mountain, another lies in wait. There is no way around grief; the only way is through it.

On that night, the two biggest mountains lay right in front of me – work and the house. They were so big, so imposing that I couldn't even see what lay beyond them, but when Roy's email dropped into my inbox that morning, those mountains felt like they were pushed to the side. I knew that whatever I decided about work and the future, the mortgage would be paid off. I wouldn't be forced to go back to work; we wouldn't be forced to move.

It also meant that the money we had in reserve would give me that all-important time to try and work out this new, unwanted journey that Ethan and I were now about to travel. In writing this I am acutely aware that this is not the story for countless others who suffer loss. Many, many people aren't afforded the time to work out what happens next. The pressure to return to work and keep food arriving on the table means they barely have time to begin to mourn before they're back to work. At a time when they should be having the space and time to grieve, financial pressures force them back to work. I will be forever grateful for the words of wisdom from Ed and Roy, they saved me from a pressure that I'm not sure I could have coped with, especially given the state of my mental health the last time I had tried to work.

Reflecting on that night, it was the first time I began to understand that grief isn't just about loss. Grief is also about fear. For so long, through those years of being with Gemma, we had journeyed together, life had a direction, we knew roughly where we were heading – life felt like it had a rudder. Even when challenging times came, we had each other to help us navigate our way through the occasionally choppy waters. When one of us fell, the other was there to pick the other one up. At quarter to six that Friday, it felt like the rudder had been torn from the boat. The life we had mapped out together had suddenly been torn to shreds. Without warning, everything now felt disorientating, without a purpose and a direction. So much of my identity was intrinsically linked to her, but without her who was I? On the third night without her, that question was beyond terrifying.

HAPPY CHRISTMAS YOUR ARSE ('FAIRYTALE OF NEW YORK')

As our first week without her began, I couldn't help but feel that my life had suddenly gone into reverse. I was 44 years of age, we were in the 13th year of our marriage, and Ethan had not long turned eight. But without warning, I was a single man once again. One moment I was married, the next I was "a bachelor", "a single parent", "a widower", whatever label people wanted to choose – I hated all of them.

That one marriage vow kept repeating in my head: *Till death do us part*. The reality of life without her was brutal. However much I loved Gemma, and however much I wanted to carry on walking beside her through life, she was gone. Our future together was over.

It's impossible to describe what that feels like. "Life-changing" doesn't begin to cover it. Gemma was irreplaceable. And the pain I felt was excruciating, debilitating. I just couldn't accept she was gone.

"Denial" is a word you often hear when people talk about grief – the refusal to accept what has actually happened, despite knowing the truth, deep down. I didn't want to believe that I no longer had a wife, and I couldn't accept that Ethan was motherless.

I wanted her back so much. And for a time, I couldn't let go of the belief that she would come back, even though everything around me was screaming that she was gone. Sometimes I thought I heard her footsteps in our bedroom and, for a split second, I allowed myself to forget the truth. Or I would stare vacantly out of the kitchen window, half expecting to see her smiling face as she walked in through the gate. Over and over again, I told myself, 'This isn't happening', 'this can't be happening.'

Even many months later I would still call out, 'Darl ...' to her when I got home, and half expected to hear her voice calling down the stairs – and then everything would be alright again. But my call was only ever met with a wall of chilling silence.

I thought denial was something that only affected you in the first few weeks. But that wasn't my reality. I was *still* refusing to accept the truth throughout that first year. I still have days when I walk up to our front door and half expect to see her smiling out through the kitchen window, or catch a glimpse of her busily preparing another tasty meal, but she's never there; the kitchen is always and forever empty.

I think denial helps us to cope with the sheer enormity of loss. When life suddenly becomes so overwhelming and feels so meaningless, the denial helps us to cope with, and survive those early days. If we accept the death of a loved one, and all its implications in one go, it would crush us. Denial helps us to survive the darkest of those early days and begin the long process of trying to adjust to a new way of life, whatever that is going to look like.

As I began to experience that sense of life going into reverse, I stopped wanting to keep up with everybody else. I felt like lashing out at the ultra-filtered social media worldview. It could be hard not to look on with covetous eyes at the images of seemingly happy family life online. I had struggled with the same thing after Gemma's miscarriage following our second round of IVF. It felt to me as if we were surrounded by friends and family who could almost plan their next pregnancy around diary commitments.

Of course we only ever see the parts of people's lives that they choose to share; but rightly or wrongly I felt that same sense of anger with the world now. And I hated it. I didn't want to be that bitter person in the corner who thinks the world is against them; but that's what I was already turning into.

After Gemma's miscarriage in 2013, I didn't want to talk to anyone. As a brother of two sisters, I had always wanted two or three children. I wanted Ethan to have a brother or sister to share life with as he grew up. Our second round of IVF worked, but our joy was short-lived; Gemma miscarried just two weeks later, and it left me feeling angry, disappointed, and above all, bitter. The clinic we had used offered two free counselling sessions to help us deal with what had happened. And within a few minutes of the first session, our counsellor had nailed what was going on with me – she said to Gemma that 'Simon is in his cave and he'll stay there until he's ready to come out. Don't try to drag him out, let him come out in his own time.' I had withdrawn from the world and to a lesser extent, I had withdrawn from Gemma. My frustration that this was a problem I just couldn't fix, no matter how hard I tried, or how much money I threw at it, was intense.

The cave was a dark and lonely place, but in the weeks after the miscarriage, I remained in it and began to spiral downwards into an even darker, more isolated place.

I had never experienced depression. I didn't even really understand what it was. But as the days turned into weeks, I became more and more detached from what was going on around us. I struggled to be around close friends. The church we normally went to on a Sunday morning – once a safe and comforting place – became a painful place to be. Most weeks I would last about 20 minutes before I walked out of the service and found solace in a coffee cup nearby. I was starting to struggle to even get out of bed. Some days I just wanted to stay there and never get out of it again – the darkness was closing in. By the time we got to Christmas that year, I was in the lowest place I had ever been.

Somehow, through all of it, I had managed to keep working. I had been put on anti-depressants and was able to carry on presenting the football for Sky. Even when I turned up for work in a bad place, there was a bizarre sense of security in being on air; live TV gave me some kind of temporary release from how I was really feeling. As soon as we went live, my fight or flight response kicked in – there's nothing quite as exposed as doing your job in front of a camera, and when that red light went on, it gave me the impetus to fight. The black clouds that felt like they were constantly above my head would momentarily clear and for three or so hours, the chains of depression would appear to fall away. But almost as soon as I drove my car out of whichever football ground we had been at, the clouds gathered again.

Apart from a few close friends, I kept it all to myself. I faced my battle alone, unable to admit to how I was really feeling, unable to talk about the depression that had taken a grip on my life. I felt totally cut off from the world around me. It was like being in some kind of parallel universe – life carried on as normal around me, and I was still a part of it, but I felt totally divorced from real life. It's deeply disconcerting to feel like you are no longer living, you're just existing.

A couple of days before Christmas that year, I went out for a drink with a few friends. I couldn't think of anything I wanted to do less, but Gemma practically pushed me out of the door telling me it would do me some good. I remember that evening so vividly. We went to a pub in Caversham called The Griffin and the pub was swaying to the sounds of the festive season and the anticipation of the holidays to come. As The Pogues' glorious 'Fairytale of New York' rang out, I found comfort in a glass of something strong. But instead of finding some temporary respite, the clouds above me grew bigger and darker. The sounds of my friends talking around me felt like echoes in my head. The music blaring out of the speakers sounded like someone playing a record at the wrong speed.

As we walked home, the pit I was in felt larger and even darker, and a new and threatening thought entered my head:

In that moment, I wanted to end my life.

We walked down the causeway that leads to the farm estate we live on; the others were far enough ahead not to notice me as I peeled away from them, jumped the fence, and disappeared into the field. I stood there, all alone in the night, and the thought returned: *I don't want to be here anymore.*

I had had enough. As the tears of hopelessness flowed, my thoughts turned to how I would do it – an empty field doesn't exactly offer many options! But before I knew it, my friends had realised I was no longer with them, and were walking back down the causeway shouting out my name. Almost without thinking, I shouted back that I was having a wee and re-joined them, trying to act like nothing had happened.

We ended up back at my friend Dave's house, drinking some of his single malt whisky, and the festivities continued. But I couldn't keep the act up for long, and in front of four blokes, I began to sob, uncontrollably. They looked at me, bewildered, not knowing what to do or how to react.

Dave knew I needed to get away. He walked me round to our house where Gemma was waiting, The three of us sat on the sofa in the lounge, and through the tears, I kept on saying again and again, 'I don't know what's wrong with me.' They held me, listened to me, and prayed for me. I told them that I just wanted to give up on life; that something had got hold of me that had taken me to the lowest point I'd ever been to.

Maybe that night gave me the catharsis I needed, and over the following weeks, with medication, counselling, and talking to Gemma and our friends, the clouds began to thin and clear, and I finally felt able to re-join life. As the sun began to burn brighter, I was once again able to love and appreciate the huge blessings I already had – an amazing, loving wife and a son who loved me unconditionally. They accepted me for everything I was, weaknesses and all. And for the next few years, that was the life I was able to lead. As a family, we had reached a point where we were at peace with what we had. Yes, there would always be that residual heartbreak that Ethan was going to grow up without a brother or sister, but we knew that we had been hugely blessed just to have him in our lives.

The spectre of depression hid itself away, but then, out of nowhere, the clouds began to gather again ...

OUT OF TIME

I have no idea what triggered my second episode of depression. It was easy to see what impact our infertility problems had had on my mental wellbeing the first time, but four years later, life was as good as it had been for a long time. I was loving my second season of presenting the Premier League for Sky and our family life was the strongest it had ever been. I wasn't worried about anything, but that didn't stop the clouds gathering again. One minute I was happy and at peace with life, the next, those feelings of disconnection from the world began to crowd in again. Only this time, it came with a sense of anxiety like nothing I had ever experienced before.

The first time I started to feel real anxiety was a Thursday in late September. Sky Sports had started a new show that season called *The Debate*. It's a good show, but without wanting to sound arrogant, it should have been a walk in the park for someone who'd been in sports broadcasting for over 12 years: two guests, and one hour to discuss the main football talking points of the day, job done.

Yet as I awoke the morning I was due to present *The Debate*, I had a strange, sick feeling in my stomach. I lay there wondering what on earth was happening. It felt like waking up before a really important exam having done absolutely no revision. I felt a horrible, nauseous sense of discomfort.

I spent the morning at home going through my statistics for a game I'd be presenting on the Saturday, when Gemma rang, suggesting we meet up for lunch before I caught the train to work. As I walked in to Reading to meet her, I couldn't shake off my unease or escape the endless questions flooding my mind: *What if the guests aren't very talkative? What if I can't think of another question? What if I'm just shown up to be really rubbish at my job?* It seemed totally irrational, yet at that moment, this new, unwelcome anxiety was very real.

As we sat down to lunch, I tried to pretend everything was okay, but after pushing my pasta around the bowl for the 25th time, Gemma looked at me and said, 'What's wrong, Darl? You're not yourself.' I looked into her eyes and told her I just didn't know. All I could tell her was that I had woken up really nervous about work and didn't know why. In the 16 years I had known her, I had never been that nervous about work. Yes, there had been occasions when the significance of the game demanded a healthy dose of nervous adrenaline, but I had never experienced such a tangible fear that it could all go very wrong. That day I did.

I hoped it was a one-off. Maybe I'd just slept badly, and I was overtired. I got through it that time, but as the days passed, the feeling didn't go away; it only intensified. Every time I was due to work, the anxiety returned, and as it increased in intensity, my mood darkened. Suddenly everything was starting to feel too much, especially work. Games I would normally relish started to become games I feared. None more so than the match between Liverpool and Manchester United that I was due to front on October 14th. Such is the rivalry between these two giants of English football that it is always one of, if not *the* biggest game of the season. The chance to present it live from Anfield should have been an opportunity to savour. But I was dreading it. Even though the game was a couple of weeks away, it had started to play on my mind – a lot. Every time I thought about it, pangs of anxiety undermined any enthusiasm I would once have had.

It began to affect our home life too. A week before the big game, I had a rare, work-free weekend. I'd been so looking forward to the chance to spend some quality time with Gemma and Ethan. On the Saturday we were due to go to two birthday parties. It should have been a nice day with family and friends, but as my darkening mood took over, it turned into a day I'd rather forget.

I have never kept a diary; but that weekend, for some reason, I wrote down what I was feeling:

Saturday 7th October, 2017:

Everything feels like it's crashing down around me again. Work and anxiety becoming really bad – Liverpool against Manchester United next weekend is dominating my thoughts. Wanted to make the most of this free weekend and enjoy time with Gemma and Ethan – it's been a disaster. Completely let my mood ruin Saturday and the trips to Rocyn and Charlotte's parties. Let my family down – again! Why am I like this? Feel hopelessly down.

Sunday 8th October, 2017:

Genuinely feel sick. I have never felt this way about work before. I just want to crawl back into bed the whole time and pull the duvet over my head and forget the world. I feel depressed, it's back. I don't know who to talk to.

That weekend was the last we would ever spend together without work, and with Gemma well. It should have been a weekend for me to look back on fondly, but it ended up being a weekend to forget. All the joy of our life together was being sapped by my depression and anxiety. I can only look back on it with a deep sense of regret.

The game that had turned into my worst enemy arrived. I wouldn't describe it as my finest moment in broadcasting, but I somehow got through it. (After a monumental amount of hype, it predictably ended up nil-nil!) But that was only the beginning ...

With Ethan's autumn half term approaching, Gemma and Ethan were going to see her dad in the south of France with Gem's sister, Rebecca. It was always a busy time for me with Premier League games at the weekend, and League Cup fixtures midweek. In previous years it hadn't been a problem, but this time I was dreading them going.

As the day of their flight drew ever closer, I felt more and more anxious about being apart from Gemma. I always missed them both when we were apart, but accepted that, with my working life, I couldn't be an ever-present at home. She was only going for five days; it was ridiculous to feel so uncomfortable at the idea of spending five days apart. But with everything that was beginning to unravel in my mind, those five days began to feel more like five months.

On Thursday night, Ethan went off to bed excitedly, looking forward to his 4.00am alarm call and the flight from Stansted (he loves those early-morning flights). But I was little more than a bag of nerves. I was restless; I couldn't even focus on watching the television. Every time Gemma asked if I was okay, I gave her the most unconvincing reply of 'I'm fine.' She knew I wasn't, and unbeknown to me had already begun to discuss the possibility of her staying at home and Rebecca taking Ethan to France.

That night, I couldn't sleep. The knotted feeling of anxiety in my stomach had become a familiar bedfellow, and it just wouldn't shift. I spent the night staring at the clock and counting down the minutes until the 4.00am alarm. My restlessness was keeping Gemma awake too, so at just after 1.00am, I reluctantly headed up to the spare room so she could at least get a few hours of rest. It was the last thing I wanted to do, I didn't want to leave her side.

For the next three hours I watched the clock counting down to 4.00am, and then heard the sounds of people on the move. As Rebecca and Ethan got ready to leave, Gemma came to find me. When she gently asked how I was doing, I couldn't contain my pain and fears anymore and started to sob into her arms, pleading with her to stay. 'Please, Darl, don't go, don't go.'

I could sense in Gemma that while she desperately wanted to help me and understand what was going on, she was struggling to comprehend how going away for just five days was causing me to feel like this. But the clock was ticking, and they needed to leave if they were going to be on time for their flight. Gemma told me she needed to go downstairs and finish getting ready, but promised she'd come back up to say goodbye. But really, she went back to speak to Rebecca, just as she had the night before, and they agreed that she shouldn't leave me.

Gemma came back in, crouched down beside me, and wrapped her arms around me, saying, 'Darl, I can't leave you like this. I've had a chat with Rebecca and she's going to take Ethan to see Dad and I'm going to stay behind.' They should have been just the words I wanted to hear. But amid the haze of confusion I was feeling, I had a fleeting moment of clarity, and, just for a moment, the haze lifted. For the past eight years, Gemma's dad had been living with myeloma, a type of blood cancer that develops from the bone marrow. In the early days he had come very close to losing his life; but over the years that followed, his treatment brought the cancer under some kind of control. It wasn't an illness he was ever going to recover from; but it was a cancer he was able to live with, and still enjoy a full and happy life.

As her kindness sank in, all I could think about was Gemma, her dad, and Ethan – who had such a special relationship with the man he lovingly referred to as Pompa. Although David's health at this time was good and the myeloma was under control, we all knew that we needed to make the most of those times we got to spend with him, especially given he was living one hundred miles south of Lyon. Gemma needed to see her dad, and in that moment, I stopped being consumed by my troubles and told her she needed to go; she needed to be with her dad. I knew how much Ethan had looked forward to this trip, and it wouldn't have been fair for Ethan to have to go without his mum. I put my hands on Gemma's shoulders, looked into her worried eyes and said, 'Darl, you have to go. We don't know how many more years your dad is going to be around for, you need to see him. I'm going to be so busy with work that I'm not going to see much of you anyway. Please go, Darl, you have to go.' In truth, I struggled to say those words; I needed her more than ever. But deep down, I knew how important it was that they went.

Gemma hugged me tightly, and gave me a tender kiss goodbye. Then reluctantly, she got up and left. And as she went, the haze descended again. I curled up on the bed, contorted and broken. It took everything I had to stop myself shouting out, begging her to stay.

Moments later, the little figure of Ethan appeared at the door and rushed over to give me one of his Daddy huggles. I had to muster everything in me not to burst into tears again, and wished him a lovely trip with Mummy and Auntie Becs. Then he leant over and whispered in my ear, 'Daddy, you're going to be okay, I love you.'

Of all the many things I love about our boy, his sensitivity is one of them. He had sensed things weren't right with Daddy; he had picked up on the fact I was going to struggle with them going away, and in that moment, my eight-year-old boy was reassuring his dad. Moments later, he was gone, and I heard the sound I had dreaded throughout that sleepless night – the gentle thud of the front door shutting. My heart quickened, I leapt to my feet and ran down the stairs to the first-floor landing, and looked out into the darkness.

I could just about pick out the three figures as they made their way to Auntie Bec's car and saw the little figure of Ethan scampering onto the back seat. I couldn't hold back my emotion anymore as Gemma climbed into her seat. I shouted, *'Don't go!'* Weeks later, Becs told me that Gemma had heard my shout, and she'd had to reassure her sister once again.

My gaze never left the car lights as they pulled slowly away, and then finally disappeared through the gate. They had gone. For all of five days! But as I collapsed onto the landing in tears, something more significant was happening, something I would wrestle with for weeks after Gemma's death. For whatever reason, and it's something that still troubles me to this day, the feeling of separation from Gemma, at that moment, on that Friday morning, was more intense, and even more painful than the permanent separation I was going to experience just a month later. How on earth could that be so? How could five days away from her feel more agonising than the knowledge I was going to be spending the rest of my life without her? How could a half-term trip to France feel more overwhelming than death?

To this day, I don't fully understand it. But when you experience mental illness, logic disappears out of the window. The everyday bumps on the road of life, suddenly seem like mountains, the challenges of work become seemingly insurmountable, and everything that usually feels normal becomes totally abnormal. Under normal circumstances, my reaction to Gemma going away *was* totally abnormal; but given the way the last few weeks had gone, perhaps it *was* my new normal.

Through the toughest period of my working life, Gemma had been like a rock for me. She was the one person I knew I could lean on. I could confide in her, and she always seemed to understand me. Because very little in my life was making any sense, the briefest separation from her seemed impossible to deal with.

Whether it was Gemma's influence, or his own nature, Ethan was starting to show a strength, understanding, and emotional maturity that would prove so significant in the months to come. On the Sunday evening in France, he asked Gemma for her phone and sent me a text before he went to bed, without any prompting, or any help. Accompanied by his trademark mass use of emojis, he said:

I'm going to bed now Daddy. Love you lots 😄😄😄😄😄😄😄😄😄 😄😄😄😄😄😄😄😄😄 *I'm praying for you* 🙏🙏🙏🙏🙏🙏🙏 *Love Ethan xxxxxx*

Those five days without them were incredibly hard. Somehow, I got through the games I had to present, but every one was accompanied by a growing anxiety and ever more confusion.

I still didn't know why I was feeling the way I was. The pattern was exactly the same. Every time I went on air, the anxiety dissipated, and every time I came off-air, I would wonder what all the fuss was about. But by the next game, all those feelings of worthlessness, insecurity, and inadequacy would come flooding back.

On the Wednesday, while Gemma was returning home, I was making the journey from Swansea to London. On the Tuesday night, I had fronted the League Cup fourth round tie between Swansea City and Manchester United, and after another mostly sleepless night, I got on the train to London for the cup tie between Tottenham and West Ham. As I reflected on the last two games I'd presented, I could see that, objectively, everything had gone okay. I hadn't made any mistakes, I hadn't had a meltdown on air, I had done my job. But none of that helped; I still couldn't shake off the knotted, sick feeling of worry building in my stomach.

I tried to write my script for the half-hour build-up to the game, but couldn't write a thing. Over and over again, I persisted in telling myself – sometimes out loud (to the bemusement of nearby passengers) – 'I can do this.' It made no difference. If anything, I just felt worse. As the train pulled into Paddington Station London, I texted Gemma:

My work anxiety this morning has been terrible. Went to the loo about ten times on the train. Stomach knotted. It's a nightmare. I feel so helpless to end it at the moment. Just got to hold on. x

A few hours later I emerged into the early winter sunshine bathing Wembley Way. The imposing figure of Wembley Stadium was ahead, the arch glinting in the sunlight. It's the sort of sight that would usually have filled me with excitement, but as I walked, ponderously slowly towards the stadium, I felt dread.

As I entered the TV compound in the bowels of the national stadium, my phone rang. It was Gemma; their flight back from France had just landed. As soon as I heard her voice, I felt a massive sense of relief – she was back. I was honest with her; I told her how much I had been struggling. That's when she decided to do something that she had never done in my nearly 20-years of broadcasting – she said she was coming in to see me – and she wouldn't take "no" for an answer. 'We're coming to see you, even if it's just for five minutes.'

In all the years I'd known her, I had rarely heard Gemma sound so insistent. And so, at just after four o'clock, I headed out from the stadium, staring intently at the app on my phone showing me where they were. Then, suddenly, I saw a familiar yellow hoodie and the smiling face of my boy as he pulled his little red flight case behind him. It was such a joy to see that face again.

And then, there she was ... Gemma rounded the corner a few seconds after Ethan, and I can only describe the joy of seeing her again, as feeling akin to the joy I felt as she walked down the aisle on our wedding day 12 years before.

It was a bewildering reaction. This was a Wednesday afternoon, at Wembley in late October, not the packed, sunbathed church of St Nicholas in Sevenoaks on that unforgettable day in August 2005. But emotionally, I felt exactly the same. I felt joyful. I felt relieved. I felt connected.

We only had half an hour together, but it was such a special moment, and I savoured every single minute I had with them. As we said goodbye, knowing I would see them again a few hours later, Gemma's parting words of 'You know you can do this, Darl,' gave me the reassurance to get through the next few hours. And, like all the games before, even in the midst of everything that was going on in my head, I held it together and delivered what I was paid to do.

Thinking back on those five days troubled me in the weeks and months that followed Gemma's sudden death. The deep uncertainty that my depression and anxiety had caused me in those autumn weeks served to heighten the sense of security in life that Gemma gave me. Without her, I felt helpless, alone, and scared. With her, I had someone to cling on to, someone to guide me through life – I had my rock to lean on. But I also wonder if something else was happening.

Looking back, it almost felt like I was being prepared for the much more brutal and final separation from Gemma. Like it was part of the process of readying me for what was, at that stage, only four weeks away. In his book *Mere Christianity*, the author and lay theologian CS Lewis made this observation about God and time:

If you picture time as a straight line along which we have to travel, then you must picture the whole page on which the line is drawn. We come to parts of the line one by one: we have to leave A behind before we get to B, and cannot reach C until we leave B behind. God from above or outside or all around, contains the whole line, and sees it all.

Maybe, just maybe, the intensity of feelings I had towards Gemma during those five days in the final weeks of her life left was all part of God's preparation. If God is outside our understanding of time, did he know what was coming? Painful though it was, this deeply unsettling period forced me to rinse out every moment I had with her – even a cappuccino at Wembley's Pret a Manger!

MELTDOWN AT OLD TRAFFORD

Gemma was home. And yet, by the end of the week my anxiety was debilitating. On Saturday 28th October, I fronted what turned out to be my last ever game for Sky, as Manchester United met Tottenham Hotspur at Old Trafford.

I knew I needed to get some sleep in the bank for the weekend, so I decided to take an over-the-counter sleeping remedy. Big mistake. When I woke on the Friday morning, the day before the game, I was worse than ever. I felt like I'd sunk a bottle of gin. I tried to write my script for the game, but I could only focus for about 20 minutes at a time before having to retreat back to bed. I couldn't work out what was going on. For years, I had prepped a game in exactly the same way without any problems, but now, it was proving almost impossible.

Later, Gemma gave me a lift to the station. When she asked me how I was feeling, I could barely muster a word. I kissed her goodbye and trudged off with a feeling of total dread. What was happening to me? It felt like the job I had worked so hard to get; the job I loved so much was starting to strangle me with anxiety.

As the train ploughed northwards, I tried to focus on the game to come. I couldn't. As Manchester Piccadilly came into view, all I could think about was checking in to the hotel, and getting to my room as quickly as I could, without bumping into anyone from work. Normally I would have dropped off my bag and headed down to the bar to enjoy the evening with my colleagues. But on that evening, it was the last place I wanted to be – I didn't want to see or talk to anybody.

After the bad experience the night before, I didn't take anything to help me sleep. But the result was the same – I didn't sleep a wink. The pointless alarm rang out at 7.00am and I reluctantly got dressed for work. I wasn't in the mood for breezy morning chats, so as I passed through reception, I kept my head down, grabbed the first available cab and headed for Old Trafford. The sky was grey, the rain was falling hard, and the buildings passing by, looked drab and lifeless. Everything about that morning reflected my state of mind.

Old Trafford loomed into view. I told the cab driver to drop me off "anywhere." I ended up at the wrong end of the ground, but I didn't care. I walked through the driving rain until I found the outside broadcast trucks and sat down, with soaked trousers, in a complete daze. A daze that didn't lift that entire day.

At 8.30am we had our usual production meeting, but it felt like an out-of-body experience. I tried to focus while our producer, Jack, went through the first hour of the show, but I felt completely disengaged. As he pointed out the graphics I would be talking about in the build-up to the game, I felt like a drunk being asked to walk in a straight line.

Gemma knew I was struggling, and just before we headed up to the studio, she sent me another, in a long line of encouraging texts:

Darl, I know it's horrible and hard but you will get through this and you're not alone. Loads of people are surrounding you with their thoughts and prayers. Love you darl. Xxx

I sat down in my usual chair on set and realised that I hadn't registered anything we'd discussed in the production meeting. At half past eleven, we would be on air for our hour-long build-up to the game, and with less than two hours to go, I barely had a clue what we were doing. It was horribly unnerving.

Throughout my working life I had always prided myself on turning up for work prepared if not over-prepared! But not that day – and not through want of trying. I felt as unprepared as I had ever been. I managed to stumble through the rehearsal, but as our on-air time of 11.30am rapidly approached, and Graham Souness and Jamie Redknapp were getting themselves comfortable in the chairs next to me, I felt a sense of panic beginning to overcome me – I had to escape.

In nearly 20 years of live TV, I had never experienced a moment like it. I made my excuses – last minute trip to the loo and all that – and headed to the disabled toilet. At least there I wouldn't be disturbed. I shut the door behind me and sank to the floor, crying, uncontrollably.

In a small part of my mind the cry was *What the hell is wrong with me?*, but the bigger part was gripped by fear. All I could do at that moment was grab my phone and ring the only person who would truly understand. My wife. My rock. My Gemma.

As ever, she was the reassuring voice of calm. While my body was shaking, and my breaths had become shallower and more rapid, Gemma spoke truth and reassurance without dismissing my pain. 'Darl, I know you can do it. God has given you this gift and he won't let you down. He knows you have the strength to do it, you know you can do it, and I know you can do it. Now please darl, tell Jack your producer how you're feeling.' I did exactly as she said. I got back to my feet, I rang Jack and told him what was going on, I returned to my chair and minutes later at 11.30am, the voice in my ear-piece said 'We're on air' and the title music began to ring out. There was nowhere to run now, I had to deliver. Somehow, I did. As we got to the end of the hour-long build up and the game finally began, Gemma sent another text. Although she was nearly two hundred miles away, it felt like she was right beside me:

Watching now Darl – looking good. You'd never know ... well done xxx

In the minutes after we came off-air, Gemma sent through another message:

Just watching back some of the build-up again and it's brilliant – you are so good. I know you feel awful but honestly it all looks great ... just so you know.

Weeks later, I told my boss, Gary, about that day in Manchester and he told me that if anything, my performance levels were higher than normal. But that turned out to be the last time I would ever present a game for Sky. Five days later, everything came crashing down. It was another Thursday, and my turn to present *The Debate* again later that evening.

Once more my morning's prep time had been punctuated by frequent trips back to bed and the sick feelings of anxiety were worse than ever. I joined Gemma in the kitchen for lunch before heading off to catch my train, but just sat there gazing blankly at my tomato soup, not saying a word. Gemma was getting more and more distressed, but I simply couldn't muster the words to explain. Like five days before at Old Trafford, my breaths started to get increasingly rapid and without saying a word, I left the table and headed for the stairs. As I glanced at Gemma, I could see tears in her eyes and a look of fear etched on her face. I will never get the chance to ask her what that moment felt like for her, but I can only imagine it must have been horribly disconcerting to see the man she loved falling apart in front of her.

I didn't make it to our bedroom, but slumped into a heap on the stairs and started to cry uncontrollably as I had done at Old Trafford just a few days before. In that moment it felt like my entire world had come crashing done. All the peace and happiness of our lives was collapsing around me.

Gemma hobbled up the stairs with her broken foot, and sat beside me. She held me, kissed me, and spoke gently reassuring words. And then she prayed, a beautiful, powerful prayer asking God to help me. In that horrid, scary moment, to be in my wife's compassionate arms felt so secure. She was a refuge from the fears now raging in my mind.

I went to lie on our bed, and a few minutes later I could hear Gemma on the phone to my boss, Gary, explaining what was going on. I worried how he'd react, would he just recommend taking a couple of days off to get ready for the game at Stoke on Saturday? Would he understand what I was going through, or would he just think I was being weak? Would I even be allowed to return to work when I was in such a mess?

All of these ultimately irrational fears were never realised – Gary couldn't have been more understanding. As Gemma passed the phone over for him to speak to me, instead of being met with the response I feared, he was nothing but supportive. He wanted to understand what I was feeling and, more, and more importantly, how they could help. He told me to take as much time as I needed to get myself better. Later that afternoon, the head of Sky Sports, Barney Francis, rang to offer me his support too. My fears about how Sky would react were totally unfounded. The message that resounded again and again was that they wanted to do everything they could to support me.

(The narrative that mental health is met with a wall of ignorance is, thankfully, starting to change and if more companies treated this area with the sensitivity and care that Sky treated me, it will change even faster.)

If those horrible few weeks of anxiety had been the biggest challenge I had ever faced, the events of November 2017 made them feel terribly minor in comparison. If I had struggled to deal with all of that, with Gemma by my side, how on earth was I going to deal with anything without her?

The one person who had held me, and protected me was gone, leaving me to face whatever life threw at me, alone. I knew that if I ever returned to work, and had a repeat of what happened at Old Trafford, and just needed to hear her voice of reassurance and comfort, her phone would forever more remain silent. That voice of compassion, those messages of encouragement had disappeared forever.

That realisation filled me with fear. It had been such a reassuring part of our life. I had taken it for granted. When that is taken away from you, then you realise in a whole new way, just how important all the seemingly insignificant bits of your day-to-day life really are. You never really know what you have until it's gone.

It left me feeling even more scared and alone. How could I carry on without her? How could I "do life" without my co-pilot?

LIFE IN A PARALLEL UNIVERSE

A new week was beginning for Ethan and I, facing life without Gemma, and I was starting to feel like I had been drop-kicked out of the life I had known and into another, unfamiliar universe. Over the course of the next few weeks, a phrase I would often hear when it came to grief was the "parallel universe". And as the enormity of what had happened began to hit home, I began to understand some of what it meant.

My surroundings still looked and sounded the same, the cat still meowed on that Monday morning as she always did, impatiently waiting for her food; the news stories of the day echoed out of the radio as they did every day, and the cars heading out on the school run still rumbled past outside. It was all exactly the same. But everything felt totally different.

I was still in among all those sights and sounds I recognised as daily life, yet I was in a completely different place. My family and friends surrounded us, supporting us, caring for Ethan, but their universe now seemed totally at odds with mine. I no longer felt truly *with* them.

I felt like I had been ejected from "normal" life and launched into a place where nothing made sense anymore, a place that looked familiar, yet felt so utterly different.

I remember staring blankly out of the kitchen window that first Monday morning, and seeing one of the mums from our estate driving past with her kids in the back. As her car disappeared from view and she headed off on the school run, my eyes glanced at the clock, it was ten past eight. Nine times out of ten, Gemma would be running late, but this was the time that she would be getting into the car to take Ethan to school. As I looked out of the window again, I could see our car, redundant now, on the drive, I could hear my boy playing with Thomas in the lounge, and the starkness of this new reality hit me again. The school run – something so routine, so ordinary – was now going to be forever different. Unlike the little child who had just passed with Mum at the wheel, Ethan was never going to have his mum alongside him again, as he navigated the many years of school life that still lay ahead. It was another simple, yet horribly painful reminder of a part of life that would never ever be the same again.

But it was also a reminder that my grief was going to be multi layered. Not only were we starting the walk down the road of grieving the loss of a dear wife and mum, we were beginning to grieve something else – the lost years. In 2018, the average life expectancy for a woman in the UK stood at 82.9 years. Gemma had turned 40 just six months before, and if she had lived a full life, she would only have been approaching "half time" in her life. The myeloid leukaemia that had exploded into her bloodstream in late October didn't only take her life, it stole from her the rest of her life.

When you think of grief like this, it's all too easy to give in to the self-pity. You can start to feel like you're the one who has been hard done by. But so much of my sorrow was for her. She had so much more to live for, so much more to do; so much more love, life, and wisdom to pour into Ethan and others. The vibrancy and zest for life that she had exuded at her 40th birthday party just four months before spoke of a woman embracing life. With the refugee project at church beginning to gather momentum under her leadership and passion, it felt like she was entering an exciting new chapter in her life; not the final chapter. The book of her life would forever remain unfinished.

The last ever wedding anniversary card she wrote to me breathed her sense of excitement for the future:

Oh, Happy Day! Twelve years ago today. I love you more than ever Darl, and am very proud of you and excited for the next part of our journey together.

As she wrote those beautiful words of optimism, her life had but four months left to run.

In the same way cancer stole those years from Gemma, it also wrenched them away from Ethan. She only got to cherish eight-and-a-bit years of her precious boy's life. One of the many things we discovered when the time came to finally clear out her belongings was a diary she kept about Ethan's first few years. The first few pages tell in detail the trials and tribulations of breastfeeding and the daily routine of Ethan's daytime sleeps, and of course, the battle to get any sleep herself. But as the pages go on, and the early years of his life pass, there is a very moving record of a conversation between them when Ethan had reached four years and ten months on 8th August 2014:

Just had to write this down. I started a conversation at bedtime (as I have a few times recently, as I mourn the passing of the pre-school years) about how I wish Ethan could be four forever and not have any more birthdays – so that he'd always love me.

He got a bit upset and said, 'But then I'd never get any more presents!' I said I was joking, and he tried to reassure me (as he often does) that he will still love me and give me huggles when he's five.

Then I said when he grows up, he'll probably find someone that he loves even more than Mummy who he'll want to marry and have children with. He seemed unsure and said he wanted to stay with me ... I tried to reassure him (and actually got on to the subject of getting old and dying but I said it would be fine because we'd be together with Jesus in heaven!) I then said our usual sort of bedtime prayer; but when I finished, he burst into tears.

Gemma recorded their conversation:

E: *I really don't want to grow up any more.*

Me: *Why not?*

E: *Because I want to live here with you forever and don't want to live on my own.*

Me: *But you'll have your own family who you will love even more.*

E (crying even more): *But I want to stay here with you. When I'm a policeman and I have babies can I stay here with you? Please??? PLEASE, MUMMY?*

I then had to spend a good five minutes reassuring him that he could – that it would be fine if he wanted to. He was still a bit sad when I said good night. We had the biggest cuddle.

He's so sweet. I love him with all of my heart.

I am so glad she wrote these moments down. In the years to come, Ethan will be able to read them back and hear his mum's love for him calling out of every page. And for me, reading those words for the first time stirred up a whole host of emotions. For a start, I never knew Ethan wanted to be a policeman – his career aspirations have changed somewhat since! But here was Gemma expressing what so many parents feel: that joy and pride in watching their children grow up, underpinned by the sadness of knowing that time passes all too quickly. We know the day will inevitably come when they need to spread their wings and begin to explore life for themselves.

It was only a year on from Gemma's miscarriage; we both knew we were only going to have these magical moments once. And Gemma's words told of a woman who was pouring every ounce of love and attention she could muster into the life of her boy.

Only three and a bit years later, that amazing bond between mother and son was cut tragically short. It was my biggest heartbreak. Somehow, I could just about deal with my own grief; but I couldn't cope with the pain and sorrow I felt for Ethan and

Gemma, knowing they would never get to enjoy another magical moment together. Never again would he see her smiling face in the playground at the end of the school day. There would never be another trip to France together to visit Pompa, no more family holidays for the three of us. No more goodnight kisses.

All of the potential life milestones that lay ahead for Ethan – going to senior school, passing exams, maybe one day graduating from university, getting his first job, finding someone to share his life with and perhaps having children of his own ... they will all happen without his mother.

It's almost impossible to know what to say to someone who has experienced this. What *do* you say to someone who has lost the mother to their child?

It is almost too difficult to entertain the idea, let alone find the words to offer some kind of comfort. If you're a parent, you know the thought of not seeing your child grow up is almost unbearable. Knowing that your son or daughter will mature into a man or woman without you being there to cherish every moment is too frightening to even contemplate.

I think about it now, more than ever. The Christian response to loss can sometimes be as unhelpful as it is helpful. Occasionally people would tell me, 'At least Ethan will one day see his mum again in heaven!'

They meant well. They were trying to offer comfort, but all too often, it felt like empty platitudes. As a man of faith, the hope that death isn't the end did help keep me going. It gave me a shard of light in a dark and hopeless place. But not straightaway. At first, in the cold light of the days after Gemma's death, it gave me little comfort.

How was the hope of a heavenly reunion one day going to help either of us in the here-and-now? As Ethan said to his teacher one day, 'I have a very long wait till I see Mummy again.' A child's concept of time is so very different to how we experience it as adults – a week feels like a month, and a month can feel more like a year. But as an adult, time seems to pass so fast, that we want to pull up the handbrake and slow it all down.

Ethan's hope that he will, one day, see his mum again is massive. He believes this isn't the end; but in earthly terms he *does* have an inordinately long wait (hopefully) until that day finally comes.

The hymn 'Thine Be the Glory' tells us, *'Death hath lost its sting.'* The reality, even for someone who believes in eternal life is somewhat different. Death hasn't lost its sting. It isn't a fatal sting anymore, but the pain of losing the people we love still hurts like hell.

When someone loses their life at a young age, the mourning of the lost years is one of the most excruciating parts of grief. It sits alongside the immeasurable sorrow you feel for the person who has gone, and hits you with a sadder, bleaker vision of the future for your children.

Knowing that Gemma wouldn't get to see the life she brought into the world grow, mature, and flourish was my single biggest struggle. The years of life they looked forward to would never be realised. As I look at Ethan asleep in bed, watch him playing, see him running out of the classroom door to greet me, or hear his thundering feet running to jump on our bed in the morning, it's a daily battle not to let that pain for the life he has lost consume me.

As a dad, all I wanted to do was fix it. I wanted more than anything to be able to tell him that everything was going to be okay. That we just needed to get through the next few months and then Mum would be back, with a smile on her face, telling him how proud she was at how he'd dealt with life without her.

This is the harsh, stark reality of grief – there is no end point to work towards. You're dealt the biggest challenge or your life, but the challenge doesn't have a goal to reach. All you can really do is try your best to find some kind of life again in the knowledge that the happy ending you want most for the child or children left behind is impossible. The day Gemma reappears is never going to happen.

Every time I saw Ethan looking sad or breaking down in tears, it felt like a knife being driven through my heart. I want to take all of his pain away, but I can't, it's something that will walk side by side with him for the rest of his life. In time, the pain will feel less intense – but it will never leave him. He will still experience joy and laughter, as he showed, even in those early weeks, but it will forevermore be coupled with a sadness that his mum isn't there to experience that joy with him.

When you feel that depth of sorrow, anger is never far behind ...

Less than two weeks before Gemma fell seriously ill, we had watched Channel 4's brilliant *Stand Up to Cancer* night with a *Gogglebox* special. Gemma had always been an avid *Gogglebox* watcher – and I can still hear her now, laughing away at Steph and Dom and their humongous glasses of vino!

But on that night, *Gogglebox* had a very different flavour with a cast of celebrities including Ed Sheeran, Sharon and Ozzy Osbourne, and Liam Gallagher, and their families. As well as featuring some of the usual shows for the cast to comment on, the programme was interwoven with incredibly powerful stories of men, women, and children who had battled cancer. Their stories had the celebrity cast in bits, and left Gemma and I in floods of tears on the sofa.

One story in particular struck us in a deeper way than any other. It was the story of Annalesha, a young wife and a mum of two beautiful kids, who had been diagnosed with breast cancer. As the powerful film played out, we were hoping and praying for a happy ending to such a desperately sad story. It was agonising to watch the images of her playing in a sun-filled park with her two children, and to hear her talking so bravely about the possibility of not seeing them grow up. As her story continued, a black screen suddenly appeared stating simply:

In July 2017 Annalesha lost her battle with cancer.

We sat in stunned silence. Annalesha was so young, and had been so brave. She had spoken with such hope, and yet this cruel disease had won the day. Her happy, beautiful marriage was cut horribly short, and she would never get to enjoy the enormous privilege of seeing her children grow up. As we wept for that poor family, I turned to Gemma and said, 'I cannot believe just how much this bloody disease devastates lives.' Little did we know that night that in exactly three weeks' time, that bloody disease was going to tear our lives apart.

For all the incredible advances in medicine, for all the countless millions spent on trying to find cures and better treatment, for all the doctors and scientists who devote their lives to defeating cancer, it continues to destroy the lives of thousands of men, women, and children every single year. It robs children of their childhood. It cuts down the hopes of young men and women who have so much life to live. It rips families in two, ends marriages, and leaves countless children without a mum or a dad. Cancer is still wreaking a trail of destruction through countless lives.

Like many, we watched *Gogglebox* that night hoping and praying that those stories wouldn't be our story. But cancer has never been a respecter of who you are and what you have, it doesn't care whether you're young or old; it is indiscriminate. Cancer is a cruel thief that steals our hopes, dreams, and lives.

As my anger towards the cancer that had taken Gemma's life grew, so too did my resentment towards our doctor. In those early weeks of 2018, I couldn't get the question out of my head – how on earth had he not picked up on how ill Gemma was?

When Gemma had sat down with him that Monday morning, she was only four days away from dying – how had he not seen the change in her from the week before? Why didn't he send her for a blood test just to be on the safe side? There were times when I partly blamed him for Gemma's death, even though I knew by now that even if he had sent her for a blood test that Monday, it would probably still have been too late to save her.

If I was going to find any hope and joy in my life again, I knew I had to deal with this. I couldn't allow resentment and bitterness to take over my life. No amount of anger was going to bring Gemma back.

I regret some of the things I said publicly about him in the weeks that followed, but after several long conversations with my new doctor, it eventually led to me sitting down with him in mid-February. I wanted to find out exactly what had been said in that room when Gemma saw him alone.

Thirteen weeks on from Gemma's final appointment, I sat down in the surgery and awaited his arrival. As he walked nervously in, the emotions began to flow. I shook his hand and he expressed how sorry he was. I could see tears welling in his eyes. He told me the story of that morning, and I could only trust that what he was telling me was the truth. For some inexplicable reason Gemma had never told him just how ill she was. She had told him of the headaches and fatigue but hadn't told him how bad it actually was. She never mentioned that she had been struggling to make the three-step trip to the en-suite bathroom. She hadn't revealed that lifting her head off the pillow to speak to me was almost too much. She failed to mention the fact she had barely eaten for days. To this day, I can't even begin to understand why she never told him the full story. Surely she would have wanted to do anything to make sure she got better, so why wouldn't she have told him everything? Maybe she was simply too ill, too shattered to make any sense.

In the end, I had no choice but to trust his words. Doctors don't need condemnation, they need more help to spot the signs of blood cancer better amid the unrelenting pressures of NHS targets.

While I believe he could have acted better, he's a good man. As I left, all I could do was give him a big hug. We're all human, and we're all muddling our way through this thing called life.

THE BACON BOYS

Throughout that first weekend without Gemma, we were embraced and comforted by our family and friends. And as we nervously entered that first full week, their support showed no signs of letting up. The doorbell had been ringing all that weekend as more and more people came to pay their respects, and it showed no sign of falling silent on that first Monday without her.

Becky went to answer the next ring at the door, and I heard the familiar County Durham accent of someone I had known for many years. I looked up to see my old *Blue Peter* mate, Matt Baker, standing in the hallway. Matt had joined *Blue Peter* just six months after I started on the show, and over the next six years we became inseparable as we shared so many adventures together. In the years after *Blue Peter*, our careers had taken us in different directions, and there had been times when it felt like our friendship had drifted, but seeing him there that morning, showed just how deep our friendship ran.

Matt had been in two minds about making the trip to see me and had even rung our old *Blue Peter* editor, Richard Marson, for advice. He knew Richard, of all people, would truly understand loss. Tragically, Richard had lost his 14-year-old son, Rupert, nearly 10 years before. When Matt spoke to Richard, he told him how much he wanted to come and see me and support me, but he was genuinely concerned about whether it was the right thing to do. He didn't know if I would even want to see him so soon after it had happened. Richard's response was simple: 'What's the worst thing that can happen? He isn't up for seeing anyone and doesn't want to see you?'

Matt came in and gave me a massive hug. It was all I needed. The fact that he had come over, not knowing what kind of state I might be in, meant everything. So often when someone we know is bereaved, we struggle to know how to support them. We desperately want to help, but we don't know how. We want to say something, but we don't know what, and often, we're so worried about getting it wrong, that we say nothing or do nothing. The easier option for Matt would have been to stay away, drop me a text, or pop the standard "With Deepest Sympathy" card in the post – he chose the harder, braver option and came to see me. Something that is normally so straightforward, like popping in to say 'Hello' takes on a very different complexion when grief comes to call.

Matt listened as I spoke about the events of Friday. He reassured me when I voiced my fears for the future, and he offered to help me in any way he could. It was all I needed. When grief is so raw, it isn't the time for answering the big questions. It isn't the time for finding solutions to the myriad problems you're suddenly faced with. And Matt didn't try to do any of that. But by being physically present, it underlined what I was beginning to appreciate more and more – however hard this unwanted new journey was going to be, we were not alone. In *Matters of Life and Death*, Professor John Wyatt wrote:

"Suffering is not a question which demands an answer, it is not a problem which requires a solution, it is a mystery which demands a presence."

That was our experience. Ethan and I were suffering; we were just trying to make it to the end of each day. It wasn't a time for trying to work out why it had happened. And there weren't any solutions waiting to be found. The one problem that we all wanted to solve more than any other was Gemma's. But there was no solution to that problem – she was never going to be coming back.

All too often, we think we need to support the bereaved by coming up with smart answers or quick solutions to the many questions they're facing. But there simply aren't any answers. In the early days, it's all about just being there and helping people know they're not alone. It's about letting the bereaved know that whatever the challenges that lie ahead might be, they won't have to face them alone. A gentle hand on the shoulder, a hug or a sympathetic ear is often far more reassuring – and more powerful – than words can ever be.

I needed my friends and family close – and they were there for me. Their presence and love moved me and exceeded all my expectations. And then there were "The Bacon Boys".

As my depression and anger with the world kept on getting worse after Gemma's miscarriage, I found it got harder and harder to be at church. Slowly, Sunday by Sunday, I was withdrawing from church life. On the weeks I went with Gemma and Ethan, I struggled to engage with it, and would often escape to a nearby coffee shop, where I'd nurse a coffee and stare vacantly out of the window. It wasn't a protest at our church or the people in it; I just wanted to be alone. But as the weeks went on, I ended up becoming more and more isolated from the people who wanted to help me the most. Ultimately my steady withdrawal from church life ended up being counter-productive. Instead of helping me, it had the opposite effect, leading me into a darker and lonelier place.

After that first wave of depression had passed, I was determined to make sure guys at our church were better supported. I could see that, all too often, when men at our church were facing tough times, their response would be just like mine. As the Sundays came and went, I would see them looking increasingly disengaged with everything going on around them. Some of them would step out part way through; some would stop coming altogether. Instead of leaning into the support that already surrounded them, they withdrew, just like I had done. And sometimes, they would never come back. I wanted to do something to stop guys slipping through the net, so I set up a men's group with the aim of encouraging and supporting us all through the good times and the more challenging times. Every other week, we met up in Pret a Manger in Reading at 7.00am to drink coffee (often with a bacon roll thrown in). We'd chat and sometimes even pray together.

Whether we profess to have a faith or not, the one thing that unites so many men is this: we're not very good at talking to each other when we're faced with difficulties. We're good at talking about the surface stuff. We're in our comfort zone when we're chatting about the fortunes of our football team, we feel at home talking about work, family life, or the kids when things are going well – but when a spanner is thrown into the engine of life, we tend to shut down. We find it almost impossible to be vulnerable. The Bacon Boys was our way of getting those conversations going, and reaching out to support one another.

If you were to ask any of my friends what I was like before I met Gemma, most of them would say the same thing – I was a closed book. I was useless when it came to talking about how I was feeling, or opening up about my problems. Vulnerability wasn't part of my make-up. If anyone ever asked me how I was *really* doing, they'd get a monosyllabic response; I was emotionally illiterate. But the challenges we faced in our marriage changed all of that. We had only been able to navigate through those difficulties by talking and by allowing ourselves to be vulnerable, whether it was to each other or in front of a counsellor. Slowly that "closed book" had started to open, until I was in a place where I felt more at ease expressing my true feelings. After many years, I felt more at ease being vulnerable. But being vulnerable is something that so many people, especially men, find so hard to do. Instead of being an expression of courage and strength, it's seen by too many as an admission of weakness.

The Christian leader and author, Pete Greig, wrote this about the power of vulnerability:

"When life is tough they tell you to be strong. Don't be strong. Be weak. Unclench your fists. Dare to be vulnerable. Honest weakness takes courage. It affirms our common humanity, deepens friendship and elicits grace."

That's not the bloke's way though, is it? Daring to be vulnerable and having the courage to admit we're not as strong as we appear isn't something we do very well. I wanted The Bacon Boys to allow us to dare to be vulnerable, to unclench the firsts, and deepen our friendships. But getting to a place where men feel comfortable opening their hearts to each other takes time. You have to allow yourselves to journey to a place of trust so you can loosen the cultural chains of manning-up. My vision for The Bacon Boys was that we would become that group, that band of brothers who would stand side by side in good times and bad. Little did I know that the first person to really benefit from this was going to be me!

In the days that followed Gemma's death, The Bacon Boys were an almost constant presence in our house. Whether they came on their own, or in little groups, their visits never let up. They didn't come armed with "wise words" or Christian platitudes – they were just there for me. Sometimes I was barely able to say a word; sometimes I just wept. And sometimes, I managed to talk – and share memories of Gemma.

As this stream of visits from the boys flowed over the next few days, my family and friends said they were like a band of brothers who had created a cocoon of love and support around us – it really moved them. Surely, this is what church should be all about? This is what love looks like. It's easy to love and support each other when life is good; the real test of faith, friendship, and love comes when the chips are down.

That November, The Bacon Boys became everything I had hoped and prayed we would be. And a whole lot more. Their part in keeping me afloat as the early storm of grief raged, helped keep me from drowning. They were a bright ray of light in the darkness.

DEAY DADDY

3 # GREY DAY

Daddy It's getting HARDER AND HARDER AND HARDER!

But I STILL LOVE You LIKE THIS MUCH

Hate Now MORE THAN THIS!!! REALLY LOVE
AMAZING RIGHT!

In the Title It says # GREY DAY
Because Mummy Died She was a great mum But I still have you

Love Ethan

DEAR DADDY

CHRISTMAS
EDITION # 8

HI Daddy JUST six 6 more days till CHRISTMAS!!!

MY version of 12 days of CHristmas # 5 days of love

1. My daddy in the campervan
2. two aunties Dancing
3. three Friends playing
4. four gand parents sleeping
5. Five dishes from mummy

LOVE Ethan XX

As well as The Bacon Boys, I had the support of so many of my oldest and closest friends; none more so than Dave (or Giggsy as he's known to his friends). I have known Giggsy for over 25 years. He and his wife Debs were a big part of the reason why we ended up moving from London to Reading, and Debs became one of Gemma's closest friends. Despite their own personal pain at what was unfolding in Gemma's final week, they barely left our side. From Debs taking Gemma to A&E on that Monday night, to collecting Ethan from school on that saddest of Fridays, to standing alongside us as Gemma went – their support was immense. Giggsy wasn't a rock; he was a mountain.

Even while he was juggling his family and work commitments, he was almost an ever-present at our house, working with military precision to ensure a stream of visitors for me. There was even a planner! I caught a glance of it one day, showing who was coming to visit, on what day and at what time, if there was a gap in an afternoon or evening, he would be back on the phone to fill it. If people were getting in touch to ask what they could do or how they could help, Giggsy was quick to get a visit booked in. Such was the intensity of those first few days that I don't think I really appreciated all he was doing; not just for me, but for Ethan and Gemma's family as well. He really did think of everything when it came to how best to help and support us.

None of us (thankfully) had ever been through anything like this before. None of my close friends had lost a partner, none of them had a blueprint for how you support someone who has suddenly lost their wife. But Dave, with the support of an army of our friends, just got on with it. We never had to worry about where the next meal was coming from (not that I was that hungry), and I didn't even have to worry about whether Ethan was being entertained – none of the practical challenges that each day brought fell at my feet. They were all embraced by the immense wave of support that was protecting us.

For anyone who gets launched into the unsettling world of grief, practical help is so, so important. The mind becomes so overloaded with fears, anxieties, and overwhelming questions about the future that even the simplest tasks become too much. There were numerous times during those early weeks when something as straightforward as making a cup of tea became a major challenge.

There were other indicators of the stress too. Gemma's death threw up so many unanswered questions about what life was going to look like going forward that my brain became overloaded, and my short-term memory began to suffer. I could barely remember what I was supposed to be doing in a few minutes' time, let alone the next day. And I would regularly start a conversation with someone and then completely forget what I was saying. My mind was behaving like an old computer; the tasks it once carried out in seconds were now taking forever.

It wasn't until some of the questions about our future began to get answered that the space in my brain started to free up, and my memory began to return.

This part of the process is another reason why the whole experience of grief is so horribly disconcerting. There were times when I really did feel like I was beginning to go mad! With my brain resembling the consistency of a suet pudding, the practical help we had in those first weeks became such an enormous blessing. While no one can take away the biggest burden of all – the pain of losing a loved one – they can lighten some of the burden that accompanies it. At times, while I sat silent and lost in my world of grief in the lounge, the kitchen was a hive of activity. In one corner my sister Becky would be preparing the next meal, while round the table sat friends who were helping to lessen the administrative headache that comes with a death. There are bank accounts to be closed, mail lists to be ended, phone contracts to be cancelled, questions about pensions to be answered, and death certificates to be posted. I never had to worry about any of those things.

A close friend of ours, Lucy, who had lost her mum very suddenly, just eight months before, spent hours attending to all the grim, but necessary administrative tasks. The most I ever had to do was remember where a document was, or provide some missing information.

People often struggle to know how to support the bereaved, but simply having practical help, whether it's on the menial tasks or the major ones, is a huge blessing. When people are on the floor, just offering to get the shopping, or cooking a meal can help to pick them up again. It's not a time for clever answers or pearls of great wisdom; it's a time to roll up your sleeves and get stuck in.

I'm not sure how we would have got through those first few weeks without Giggsy and that army of others who just pitched in whenever they could. If everyone had a Giggsy and a team of friends alongside them, the path back to the light would be easier to tread.

SIMON JAMES THOMAS: WIDOWER

On that first Monday, our vicar and friend, David Walker, sent us this message:

Dear Simon and Becky – sadly today is the day to take on some practical steps. You will need to get a death certificate and contact an undertaker. I will try and get to you later today, but you will need to start the rather grim process of paperwork and organising. Call me if needed. With lots of love David.

There was something grim and also something surreal about reading David's message. Just the words "death certificate" were enough to stop me in my tracks. I couldn't get past knowing that just a week ago, Gemma lay in our bed upstairs. But now, seven days later, I was about to go back to the city where she had lost her life and collect her death certificate.

Giggsy offered to drive, and another of my oldest friends, Graham, accompanied us. I reluctantly got in the car and we headed back to Oxford. As we drove through the Chilterns, the memories of the week before came flooding back. If I closed my eyes, I could hear the sound of the ambulance sirens again, and I could see the image of Gemma lying beside me, with the oxygen mask held to her mouth. The look of fear etched on her pale face.

I could barely compute how much had happened, how much had irrevocably changed in such a short time.

Another friend, Dan, was waiting for us in Oxford. Dan used to be part of our church in Reading but was vicar of a church in Oxford, and had been with us in the room the day Gemma went. He wanted to be there that day to support us. It wasn't something he was duty bound to do, we weren't even close to his parish; it was just another incredible example of a friend being there when it mattered.

I was about to carry out one of the grimmest tasks anyone has to perform. My heart should have been thumping, and the sick feeling that had been my constant companion for the past three days should have been worse than ever, but I felt a bizarre sense of peace and calm as we followed the signs to the death registry office. It was less than four days since Gemma's death and the enormity of it hadn't even begun to sink in. I was still in denial; still half-expecting her to walk in through the door at home. There was no way I could truly engage with the gravity of what I was about to do. But I also believe that I was experiencing the same divine peace that I had felt in the immediate aftermath of Dr Andy Peniket's conversation with me on that Friday morning.

We sat in a room that was more warm and welcoming than I had feared, and the registrar took all the necessary details. As she worked, she said, 'Can I ask who are these lovely chaps who are with you?' Without thinking, I immediately replied, 'This is part of Team Thomas, these are my friends who are here to support me.'

In the following months I started to use #TeamThomas on social media posts, but this was the first time I had used that phrase since Gemma had gone. It did feel like we were part of a team. A team of family and friends that was going to carry us through the storm-ridden waters of those first few faltering weeks of grief. The registrar said, 'You're lucky to have such amazing support. Not many who come here are supported in the way you are.' Her words really struck me and I asked whether most of the people who came here, came alone. She responded with one, sad word: 'Yes.'

Hearing that made me realise how incredibly blessed I was to have this team around me – friends who were taking time off work or using holiday days to be there for us. But it also made me feel incredibly sad that so many people have to do something as grim as registering a death alone. The registrar told us that some people came alone out of choice, but for the majority, it was because they didn't have anyone to support them. Grief is a heavy enough burden for anyone to carry, and in its early stages, the weight feels too heavy; too all-encompassing to bear. Having to bear that burden alone sounded impossible.

I began to imagine what it must be like entering a room like this with no one to support you, accompanied only by feelings of bewilderment and sorrow. I looked again at my friends, and felt a huge sense of relief and gratitude knowing they had my back.

The registrar's black fountain pen signed the last certificate and she handed them over so I could check all the details were correct. And there it was, in cold, formal black writing, on the same kind of green paper that our wedding certificate had been written on all those years ago, the words that even now, I still find so hard to read:

Date and Place of Death – Twenty-fourth November 2017, The Churchill Hospital, Old Road, Headington, Oxford.

Name and Surname – Gemma Rachel THOMAS

Name and surname of informant – Simon James THOMAS

Qualification – Widower of deceased. Present at death.

Cause of death –

(a) Intracerebral Haemorrhage

(b) Acute Myeloid Leukaemia

Never before have I had to read words that were so overwhelmingly sobering. If I was struggling to believe that she had truly gone, here was the proof. Black writing on green paper, with the registrar's signature drying at the bottom.

The words that hit me the hardest were about me ... Four days ago, I had been Simon James Thomas, husband of Gemma Thomas. Now. I was a "widower". It's a word that feels as cold as it sounds.

LIKE MOTHER, LIKE SON

In those first few weeks, grief felt like an oppressor without any mercy. I felt as if I was being tormented. Barely a moment would pass when the pain of her loss didn't make me feel like I was being suffocated. The only escape was the three or four hours I was managing to sleep at night. With my mind overloaded with questions and fears about the future, I thought getting to sleep would be almost impossible, and that my mind would never be able to switch off for long enough to fall asleep. I *was* able to get to sleep; I just couldn't *stay* asleep.

When the bereaved talk of having to adjust to a "new normal" in the aftermath of loss, short nights become the new normal. Waking up at two thirty was a bad night, half past three became okay, and anything close to five o'clock began to feel like a lie-in. For a time, I fought it. When I woke, I would lie there for hours tossing and turning, and trying to think of anything other than what had happened. But it was futile. I could never switch off. My friends and family became increasingly worried about my lack of sleep, and tried everything to help. My bedside table turned into a mini pharmacy. Friends making calls to my doctor or making trips to the chemist became a part of the new daily routine as we tried almost every kind of drug available. I had pills with the power to knock out a small rhino. They didn't even make the slightest difference.

Eventually I came to accept that sleep deprivation is one of the many unpleasant facets of grief. At a time when you need all the energy that you can muster just to get through each day, sleep becomes your enemy, and instead of fighting it, I came to reluctantly accept it. Rather than lying on the bed for hours, staring into the darkness and listening to the sound of Ethan sleeping close by, I would get up, put on my tracksuit trousers and hoodie, and head downstairs to make myself a tea or coffee. And then I went and sat in silence in the lounge.

I tried watching the television, but whatever I watched – whether it was re-runs of *The Jeremy Kyle Show* (why on earth did I watch that?) or a box set – I just couldn't engage with it. I tried catching up on the latest episode of *Designated Survivor*, which Gemma and I had watched avidly, but I found myself rewinding every two minutes, as I could barely focus on the screen, let alone keep abreast of the plot. I tried everything to pass the time, but nothing worked. Whatever the hour, the tormentor that is grief never leaves you alone.

Most mornings as it got towards six o'clock, I would head back upstairs to our room, and lie next to Ethan on the floor until he began to stir at about seven. Often, I would lie next to him for an hour and just stare at his peaceful face, grateful that, for a few hours, he had been able to escape the nightmare of his new life.

I wanted to be there for him, so that however he felt when he woke, he knew his dad was right there beside him. Most mornings, we would just hug; but one morning, only days after she went, he woke at six. As his tired eyes began to open, I whispered to him, 'Why are you awake so early?' 'I'm feeling sad about Mummy,' came the quiet, softly spoken reply. The day had barely started and already the pain of it was hitting him once again. But then he asked, 'Daddy – what are we going to do with all Mummy's clothes?' It was not a question I was expecting, and after less than a week, it wasn't something I had even begun to think about. All I could think of saying was that it wasn't something we needed to worry about for a while, but that one day, when we were ready, we could sort them all out and give them to a charity shop that helps people with cancer. 'Daddy, can I choose some of Mummy's clothes to put in a memory box?' 'Of course,' I replied. My emotions felt so conflicted. On the one hand, I felt an enormous sense of pride that despite everything he was going through, he had the emotional maturity to talk about the kind of things I wasn't ready to even think about. But on the other, I felt a desperate weight of sadness that we were even having this conversation. He should have been asking what we were all going to do at the weekend; instead he was worrying about what was going to happening to his late mum's wardrobe!

That conversation was only the beginning of what would come to define Ethan's response to loss – his openness, and ability to express how he was feeling. Later that day, he asked if we could watch *Paddington* again. At the start of the film, Paddington is living with his Aunt Lucy and Uncle Pastuzo in the jungle of darkest Peru. When an earthquake strikes their home, they're forced to seek shelter underground. But they don't all make it. Uncle Pastuzo can't reach the shelter in time and doesn't survive. The next morning, we see Paddington discovering his uncle's hat, and as he begins to realise what has happened, you can see the sadness of loss etched onto Paddington's loveable face. Ethan turned to me and quietly said, 'That's what happened to me, Daddy, except for me there wasn't an earthquake.'

All kids develop an awareness of death from an early age, and for parents it can be hugely disconcerting when your children start mentioning it for the very first time. In the preschool years, children will often see death as something temporary and something that can be reversed. They know that people can die, but, to begin with, their understanding of what that means is limited. That state of blissful ignorance doesn't last long; soon enough kids begin to appreciate that all living things will eventually die – and that death is final. In January 2015, Ethan experienced that for the first time when Gemma's grandma or "Great Big Grandma" as he liked to call her, passed away at the age of 93. Ethan was five, and in his first year at school. As he came to terms with his first taste of loss, Gemma wrote:

Great Big Grandma passed away in January. Ethan was amazing as we talked lots about dying and how Great Big Grandma's batteries were running out. He knows she's gone to be in heaven.

And then at Easter:

Ethan: *'Why are people buried on a cross when they die?'*

As we've just had Easter, I thought he was asking why Jesus died on the cross, so I started on that track, but he kept saying, 'No – why are people buried under a cross?' I realised he meant gravestones (we had walked through Sonning church yard today). So I said that when you die, your soul, heart etc. goes to heaven to be with Jesus and your body is buried as it's not needed anymore.

E: *'Why? What happens to it?'*

Me: *'Well it rots basically.' (I was keen to get downstairs for dinner!)*

E: *'Mmm ... I think I'd like the whole of me to go to heaven!'*

Me: *'Think of Great Big Grandma's old, worn-out body that didn't work anymore ... why would you want to take that with you when you get a new body in heaven so you can jump and even maybe FLY?'*

Ethan's eyes lit up at that.

As parents, we want to protect our children from the harsher realties of life for as long as we can. We don't want the waters of childhood innocence to be muddied by our mortality. Those conversations can't have been easy for Gemma. But she always listened to Ethan's questions, she allowed him to express his fears and responded with the kind of imagination and wisdom that I wish I had.

And then I began to realise that her emotional maturity lived on in him. So much of the wisdom that poured out of such a young boy spoke of his mum. She gave him permission to voice his fears and responded with love and patience. The love and wisdom she poured into his life in those eight short years started to bear fruit in the year after her death, but more than that; they will be the cornerstone of the man he eventually becomes. And for that, I will forever be grateful for the mum she was.

In the same way Gemma had been a rock of love and wisdom for Ethan, he was fast becoming a rock for me – a pillar of love and strength that I had never expected from an eight-year-old.

NEVER GIVE UP!

We'd spent the first few days cooped up inside the house, tentatively starting to plan Gemma's celebration (I couldn't face calling it a funeral) and I knew Ethan needed a change of scene, so I warily suggested heading out for lunch. It was the first time I'd been behind the wheel since it all happened – up to then my friends had taken it upon themselves to take the wheel, and not allow an increasingly unhinged Thomas loose on local roads!

Wendy, Rebecca, and our friends Lucy and Becca came with us, and as he clambered into the car, Ethan asked, 'Daddy, where shall I sit?' For the first eight years of his life it had always been the same – Daddy drove (mostly), Mummy sat next to me, and Ethan sat in the back behind Mummy. As I got into my seat, I immediately caught sight of her little make-up bag, still in its usual place in between the front seats: the make-up she would use while stuck in school-run traffic, the blushers and lipstick she had still been using only a few days before. Ethan asked again, and I looked over to the grey, leather seat next to me, and knew she would never sit alongside me ever again. As that knotted feeling of pain twisted in my stomach once again, I said, 'Ethan, do you want Mummy's old seat to be yours now?' I could hardly believe what I was saying, but I couldn't bear the thought of that seat lying forever empty. Ethan and I were a team and I wanted my boy right beside me. With a throw of his plastic child's seat into the front and a scramble over the gear stick, he plonked himself down in Mummy's old seat and said, 'Now it's my seat, Daddy.' All I could do was smile. It was a poignant moment, but ultimately a happy one too, as Ethan began taking his first steps into our "new normal".

Thankfully there were no accidents on the epic one-mile drive to Caversham! But as I pulled into the Waitrose car park, the usual hunt for somewhere to park began. Round and round we went, trying to find an elusive space. Usually this wouldn't have been anything more than a mild irritation, but the more I drove around, the more agitated I became. I started muttering words an eight-year-old does not need to hear. Every time I thought we'd got a space, we found one of those irritating tiny cars hidden away in there, and I thumped the steering wheel in frustration. What would normally have been a small annoyance was turning into a panic attack. My heart beat was quickening. My breaths started coming fast and shallow. And worst of all, everything was starting to feel impossible. Before anyone else could intervene, Ethan piped up, 'Daddy, what's wrong?' I can't remember what I said to him; I just remember the panic, and thinking I didn't want him to see me like that.

Right from the start, I had wanted to be open and honest with Ethan about how I was feeling. I wanted to be able to cry in front of him. I wanted to be able to express how much I was missing his mum, and how painful it was – but I didn't want him to see me lose the plot. So whenever I'd felt the anger building, or panic setting in, I had quickly learnt to take myself away from him, so that I never subjected him to the rage inside of me.

For any child who loses one parent, their single biggest fear turns to losing the other parent as well. Ethan had seen his mum at the start of one school week, but she had gone by the end of it. Why wouldn't he fear that the same thing could happen to his dad as well? Seeing his dad having a meltdown in a Waitrose car park was not going to help ease his fear; but in that moment, he didn't need my help. I needed his ...

Before anyone else could say anything, Ethan leant over, grabbed my arm, and said six simple words that will stay with me for the rest of my life: 'Daddy? Team Thomas never gives up.' As those incredible and touching words came out of his mouth, I turned to him, smiled, gave him a huge hug and said, not for the last time, 'Ethan you are amazing, you really, really are.'

And as we hugged, the panic that had begun to grip me subsided, the fog cleared, and we found a space – eventually. In the same way that Ethan needed his daddy more than ever, he was revealing to me, in his own, amazing way, that he was going to be the single biggest influence on how I would navigate this most unwanted of journeys.

Ethan only missed one week of school after Gemma went. If I had got my way, he wouldn't have gone back that term. But in the end, I had to bow to the wisdom of people who actually knew what they were talking about regarding child bereavement. Not long after we lost Gemma, we were put in touch with a local charity called Daisy's Dream that supports and cares for families in our area who are going through the same nightmare. Like a lot of these brilliant charities they are small and struggle to get the funding they need; but the work they do in supporting young lives scarred by the experience of loss, is immeasurable. Much as I wanted to keep Ethan at home with me for as long as possible, Gill from Daisy's Dream looked at it from a different point of view. For any child who experiences the loss of a parent – and by the age of just 16, around one-in-twenty children in the UK *has* lost a parent – they have to face up to a world that has changed beyond all recognition. All of the things they believe are certain in life now feel anything but; the foundations upon which they are growing up feel like they're falling down around them. The landscape of their whole life changes. We teach children to embrace life with optimism, but loss makes them afraid.

Gill's advice might not have been what I wanted to hear, but she was right. When a child suffers loss, they need normal structures and routines to stay in place as far as possible, and that means going back to school. If I had kept Ethan at home until after Christmas it would have left him wondering and worried about what on earth was happening in his life. His life – as he had known it – would have felt like it was all disappearing. Reluctantly I agreed to take him back on the Friday, just a week after Mum had gone.

Ethan's school was nothing short of incredible in making him feel as comfortable as possible. His headmaster and teacher came to visit us the day before he returned, to spend some time with him, and reassure him that everything would be okay. His entire class had written letters to him, and he sat with his teacher on the sofa and read each and every one of them; his face a picture of concentration as he pored over them. Later that day, I sat there and read what his friends had written and could only weep tears of joy at just how much my boy was loved and how much his friends missed him. One letter from Fir Class simply said this:

Dear Ethan

We are so sorry about your Mum, but we will always think about you and support you. You still have your friends and your Fir team.

Another wrote:

Dear Ethan

I know the sad news, but this is also sad. Every time I hear your name, I'm full of sorrow; but when you get the letter I made you'll be happier. Fir Class and all your friends are missing you. We hope you'll be back soon. We love you.

I was dreading his return to school. In the same way I had never wanted to be apart from Gemma in the weeks before she fell ill, I didn't want to spend a moment away from my boy. It felt like the gradual process of adjusting to this new life was happening too fast. I couldn't face the thought of walking into the playground and hearing the hubbub of normal life echoing around me. I couldn't bear to see all of Ethan's friends being dropped off by their mums, knowing that was something he would never experience again.

I also feared seeing people again. How would they react? What were they going to say? What *could* they say? What if everyone was feeling too uncomfortable to say anything? As I sat there on the Thursday night, I wanted to ignore all the advice and keep my boy at home for another week at the very least. He didn't want to go back either; but I reminded him it was only one day, and then we'd have another weekend with his cousin Thomas and his Auntie Becky. That news alone was enough to briefly lift his mood and convince him that tomorrow would be okay.

Later that evening as I sat in the lounge, staring at the soothing, dancing flames of the fire, Auntie Rebecca came down from saying good night to Ethan and told me that having said a goodnight prayer with him, he had asked her how much his mummy had loved him? Rebecca told him that mummy loved him more than anything in the world, and as she said it, his face lit up. Through a huge smile, he said, 'I'm so glad that Mummy and Daddy married each other because otherwise I wouldn't be here.'

ARE YOU FEELING BETTER YET?

The next morning was like so many others (apart from my grief alarm clock waking me at 3.00am!). At seven o'clock, Ethan and I headed down to the kitchen in our dressing gowns, just as we had, every other school morning. I could even hear the usual sounds of movement upstairs, but it wasn't his mummy getting ready to take her boy to school. Everything felt the same, and yet everything felt so very different.

We settled into our well-drilled morning routine. First, Ethan ate his Weetabix, with his usual dusting of chocolate, and protested again about not wanting to go to school. Then he took an age to get his pyjamas off and pants on. As usual he wanted me to do up the top button on his shirt (at what age do kids finally master this?) and protested at having to do his own tie knot. As he tucked his white shirt into his trousers, I glanced at our bedroom door. Normally there would have been some encouraging words from Mum: 'Do what Daddy says, darling,' or 'Come on, Ethan, you know how to do a tie knot.' But that room lay eerily silent now.

Ethan headed down to watch telly, and I could feel the sense of dread growing. I couldn't face not seeing him for six and a half hours; I needed to be with him. I couldn't face the return to the school playground.

As our usual leaving time of 8.05am moved closer, I filled his water bottle and grabbed an apple from the fridge for his break time snack. As I popped them in his rucksack, I remembered the snack notes I had sometimes written for him and placed in his lunch box. Gemma had usually sorted out his lunch; but when I did it, I'd started to put in little notes for him to find at lunchtime. Sometimes they were just silly dad jokes, but other times they were words of encouragement. As I zipped up his rucksack, I wondered how he was feeling about the day ahead. How on earth would it feel going back to school a week on from the day when everything in his life had changed? How was he going to feel seeing his friends kissing their mums goodbye? How would he feel saying goodbye to me, and walking back through those school gates? If ever there was a time for an encouraging snack note this was it.

I pulled out some paper and wrote:

Ethan — You're Daddy's SUPER HERO.

Love you, Daddy xxx

For the rest of that school year, I wrote him a note every day. Whether he was having a good day, or a not-so-good day, I wanted him to know that daddy was always thinking about him, and I was proud of him. I put in lots of notes about his mum too; I wanted to make sure she was still a huge part of the conversation, and part of his life, even if only through our memories.

Snacknote – 24th January, 2018

Ethan I see so much of Mummy in you.
Her love, compassion and kindness. She lives on in you!

I love you, Daddy xxx

The sands of certainty in Ethan's life were shifting, but the snack notes were something he could depend on. And on those rare days when I forgot to write a note, I would drive to the school and drop one off.

Thankfully we didn't have to make that first trip to school alone. Auntie Rebecca had offered to come with us. As we climbed into the car and headed out of the farm, it felt like some kind of bizarre re-entry into life. For the past few days, we had been mostly shut off from "normal" life. But now as we headed off on the school run it felt like we were the space shuttle re-entering the earth's atmosphere. All around us, the normality of life going on as normal hit us like the friction of earth's atmosphere on re-entry.

The usual crowds of children gathered, shivering in bus stops. There were the same endless queues of traffic waiting to get over the bridge, and the predictable blasts of horns from frustrated drivers. All these normal sights and sounds of a Friday morning in late November felt like another cruel assault on my grief. I felt apart from it all. The short drive to school felt like an out-of-body experience.

I took the right turn into the school car park and caught the gaze of one of the mums walking by. She clocked the car, realised who it was, and offered a weak, uncomfortable smile, then turned her gaze to the pavement. As I reversed into a space, I could sense pairs of eyes everywhere, looking on from the nearby parked cars – some people offered a sympathetic smile or wave; but it was all too obvious that others wanted to do anything but catch my eye.

As the clock neared half past eight, Esther, who was Gemma's closest friend at school, came over and linked arms with me for the walk to the gates; it felt like some kind of funeral procession. Most of the mums and dads were lovely. Some just said how sorry they were, some simply laid a hand on my shoulder as we passed. Others came up with tears in their eyes and hugged me, saying sorry, over and over again. I didn't want to look like some kind of victim, I didn't want everyone feeling pity for us, so I kept my head up, and, rather than avoiding eye contact with people, I looked at them, expecting to say 'Good morning' to anyone I knew. It was too much for some. As they caught my gaze, they looked away, and others looked like they were trying to do everything they could to avoid walking past us.

I don't blame them.

For the bereaved, it's easy to become upset and offended by the ways some people react, especially when you're seeing them again for the first time. We want people to reach out to us, we want to know we're not alone. The problem is that so many of us are ill equipped to know how to deal with grief. If a parent dies at a ripe old age, we have a more comprehensible frame of reference – that is just life. That is what's supposed to happen. We get old, and like Gemma said about Great Big Grandma, our batteries run out. It's sad. It's painful. Of course it is. But it's an expected part of life's journey.

So what do we say to someone who has just lost a loved one at the wrong time in life? Sentiments like, 'I'm so sorry but what an amazing life they had' or 'They had a great innings' don't really cut the mustard. How do we express words of comfort in the face of tragedy? How do you convey sympathy to someone who, a week ago, had a wife, and is now a widow?

I want to believe I could have found words that wouldn't have sounded crass or trite; but I'm not sure I could have. Maybe that would have been me, avoiding eye contact or tripping over my tongue, trying to say something meaningful.

In truth, the vast majority of the people we met that morning were nothing but lovely. It's such a small school that there is a real sense of community and togetherness. I had worried that I might have felt like an outcast, but I felt loved and supported. Some of the most meaningful moments came from those who couldn't find the words, and just laid a hand on my shoulder instead. Those moments were more powerful than a hundred, *I'm so sorry's!* Sometimes we can feel so helpless to know what to do when grief confronts us, and sometimes the simplicity of human touch is all that we need.

People's reaction to Gemma's death in the weeks and months to come moved me and amazed me in equal measure. There were times when I was profoundly affected as I heard and saw what Gemma had meant to so many people. But there were other times when I felt like screaming, 'I've not lost my dog! I've lost my bloody wife!' In one of my rare ventures out in the early days, I was at our butchers for a batch of sausages to keep Ethan and his cousins going for a few days. As I waited, a lady came and stood behind me in the queue. Out of the corner of my eye, I could see that it was a lady I knew from the estate we lived on. We'd passed the time of day countless times. But as I turned around, about to say 'Hello', she looked straight at the floor. It was so quick and so unsubtle that it was impossible to misread what was happening – she simply couldn't bring herself to even look at me let alone say anything. She could only look down at the white tiles of the butcher's floor.

On another occasion, only a month after Gemma died, I bumped into a friend, and after exchanging strained pleasantries she asked, 'Are you feeling better yet?' I looked at her somewhat confused – 'I've not had the flu,' came my immediate reply. She responded, 'No, I meant about Gemma.' My face twisted into a look of total bemusement and incredulity. Had she really just said that? Did she honestly believe that only a month after losing my wife I'd be fine? All I could muster as a response was, 'It's not as easy as that.' Later, she had apologised; she'd only wanted to ask if I was okay. It had just come out all wrong. And this is why knowing what to say to the bereaved *is* so hard. Either we can't say anything because we can't find the words, or we're so scared of saying the wrong thing that we end up doing exactly that. She was just trying to articulate her concern for me in the face of an impossibly horrible situation. As the months went on, I had to try to learn that people weren't being deliberately insensitive or crass, they were just trying to reach out to me.

The reactions I found hardest to cope with were from people who seemed unable to even acknowledge what had happened. I lost count of the times I would bump into someone I hadn't seen since we'd lost Gemma, and they would talk to me like everything was totally normal. After exchanging the standard opening greetings, they would fill any uncomfortable pauses with questions like, 'How's Ethan doing?' or 'What are you doing over the summer?'

We had lost almost everything, we were still struggling to find some kind of life again, and yet some people were talking to me as if nothing had happened.

Some people asked what we were going to be doing at Christmas, as if it was going to be a Christmas just like any other. Just by asking those sorts of questions, they were, in their own way, acknowledging that something *had* happened, they just seemed unable to say what. Even many weeks on, I would bump into people when I was out and about, or see friends at events, friends I hadn't seen since I had lost Gemma, and they would talk to me like they always had; but Gemma was never mentioned. It hurt. It hurt a lot. Sometimes, I wanted to grab them and shake them, and shout, 'Do you know what it's like to lose your wife?' But I would just walk away in disbelief, shaking my head.

At the time, these encounters didn't just leave me feeling hurt, they left me feeling angry. I couldn't understand how people could talk to me like literally nothing had happened; I couldn't begin to understand how anyone could talk about how cold the weather had been when I'd just lost my wife.

It was all too easy to see them as people who didn't care; people who were so wrapped up in their own lives that they didn't have the time or the inclination to engage with what was happening in mine. But as time passed, I came to see this part of grief in a different way. These people *did* care; they *did* want to know how I was doing; but like so many of us in this country, when we're confronted with grief, we struggle to talk about it.

Why should it surprise anybody when people find it hard to talk to the bereaved? For many in our circle of friends, this was the first time that their lives had been touched by death. There was no script to work from, no experience of how they should react to fall back on; people were just trying to do their best in an almost impossible situation. More often than not they got it right; but sometimes it felt so horribly wrong.

And what were people supposed to say to me when they didn't see me until weeks, or even months after Gemma died?

Maybe they were scared that it was too late to talk about it? Or they thought it would be insensitive to say, 'I'm so sorry to hear about Gemma.' Perhaps it felt uncomfortably like an admission that they should have said something a long time before. But ultimately it comes back to the same problem. When death is visited on us unexpectedly – and so horribly early in life – we struggle to know how to deal with it. It causes us to confront our own mortality and the disturbing possibility that if it can happen to them, it could happen to us. That's a tough concept to deal with.

So if people cross to the other side of the street to avoid you, knowing it's impossibly insensitive, the chances are that they want to say something, but they can't even begin to find the words to express what they actually want to say. Or else, in their scramble to find the right words to say, it all comes out in awkwardness, with forced smiles and questions about the mundane things of life.

But there was one response that, in many ways, said it all better than any other. I was in a coffee shop a few weeks after Gemma had gone. As I stood in the never-ending queue listening to the hum of chatter and the hissing of the coffee machines, a woman in front of me kept glancing around at me. She looked familiar; but I couldn't think where I'd seen her before. Eventually she came out with it: 'Are you Simon?' I told her I was. She went on, 'I used to be a mum at Newbridge (Ethan's old nursery) and knew Gemma. I'm so, so, sorry for what's happened … it's just fucking shit!' She looked a little embarrassed at the words that had tumbled out of her mouth, but I could only smile and give her a big hug. In that one sentence, she had summed it all up. Instead of struggling to find the words or searching for well-meaning platitudes, she had nailed it.

What had happened to Gemma was unjust, it was cruel, and it was shit. Sometimes there is no need to search endlessly for the right words. All we really need to do is call it what it is.

DECEMBER MOURNING

By the end of that first week without Gemma, my mood was darker than ever. And on that Saturday morning, it led me to a very bad place.

As ever, the grief alarm clock forced my eyes open at just after four. (Nice to have a weekend lie-in!) That morning, I didn't have the energy to get dressed, I just put on my dressing gown and went downstairs. I sat in the lounge, looking blankly into the distance, and as the tears began to flow again, a huge sense of hopelessness began to descend.

A week earlier, I had tried so hard to commit to finding a new sense of purpose in life, but now I was starting to believe that there wasn't any point. I tried to tell myself that life was still worth living; that there would, one day, be moments to enjoy again. But in that moment, I lost sight of it all – even the enormous privilege and responsibility of bringing up my son. As I stared into the future it felt like there was nothing to look forward to any more. Our new world felt so lifeless and grey.

The slow night hours passed, and morning light seeped into the lounge. I could hear my sister in the kitchen, but I didn't want to talk. I hadn't the energy or the words to express how I was feeling, so I walked into the hallway, put on my Wellington boots and walked out of the front door, shouting to Becky that I needed to get some fresh air. I didn't really know what I was doing or where I was going – I just had to get out.

The early December air was damp, but mild, and the skies were a leaden grey – the world looked like I was feeling. I walked out of our garden gate, still in my dressing gown, and the pent-up anger just erupted out of me. The tears fell, as the anger I had felt towards the world, and God, and every bloody thing spilled out.

I was shouting, over and over again, screaming out "No!' louder and louder, in huge, wrenching bursts of rage. The sense of injustice that Gemma's life had been stolen from her, and the anger that my boy had been left without his mother was flooding out. I looked like a lunatic – twisted up and railing at the world, in my dressing gown and boots! I barely noticed the joggers on the opposite banks of the River Thames as they stopped and stared.

As my anger dissipated, I stumbled over and sat by a tree on the banks of the river. I was left feeling hollow and broken. I had never experienced such a sense of hopelessness. I had a family that loved me, an army of friends who were rooting for me, and a son who needed me more than ever, but in those moments, none of it mattered.

I stared at the swans floating past, full of beauty and grace, and I envied them their simple existence. I was done. I couldn't take any more pain. I just wanted to end it. I stared into the cold, murky water of the Thames, closed my eyes, and imagined letting go, giving up.

But as I imagined it, as I let the thoughts consume me, Ethan's face filled my mind. It was so clear. The expression on his face was the same as I'd seen the night he looked into my eyes when I told him Mum had gone. My fists clenched, my body tensed, and I drew on what little strength I had to stop me from throwing myself headlong into the water.

A few yards away in the house, my little boy was probably down in the lounge playing with his cousin, not knowing where his dad was. His face never left me in those next few minutes and as I began to sob, more quietly now, I knew I could not give up. It was not an option. My boy was going to need me more than ever. The very last thing he needed was to lose his dad as well. It sounds the most selfish of thoughts to have, but when hope feels like it has died, perspective evaporates.

There was something else in that moment of realisation. I sensed a presence alongside me on that riverbank – I felt the presence of Jesus. I could feel him, just sitting beside me, crying with me. I know, if you don't have a faith, this will sound ridiculous; but on that morning it felt so very real.

The Jesus I have read about in the Bible and know from my faith understood, more than anyone, what true darkness felt like. When he died on the cross, the darkness he experienced was so profound that the light died with him. As he breathed his last, he came to know what it was like to feel the agony of separation, of being cut off from his father. The Jesus I have followed throughout my life is a man who understands the pain, sorrow, and suffering that death brings. In that most desperate of mornings I could feel him, right beside me, his presence was tangible. In that one, powerful moment, when my darkness had closed in, the image of Ethan and the presence of Jesus shone two rays of light into the pervasive gloom of that morning.

I slowly rose to my feet and headed back to the house. As I walked up through our garden, I could picture the scenes from just four months before – Gemma's 40th birthday garden party. I could see the queue of people waiting for their wood-fired pizza and smell the delicious aromas wafting from the brick oven. I saw our guests eating, drinking, and chatting on the grass bank as the music played. And I could see Gemma, dressed in a beautiful, but vaguely ridiculous pink feathered headdress laughing and loving her special night. That evening, the garden had exuded light, life, and love.

I opened the front door and Becky asked if I was okay. I simply said, 'I just needed a good shout.'

After bereavement, life feels so utterly bereft of joy and purpose that you start to believe there's nothing left to live for anymore.

The pain and bleakness of your "new" life stares you down at every turn, blinding you to the blessings you already have. For the briefest of moments that day I lost sight of the enormous blessing of my boy. I lost sight of this incredible group of family and friends who were surrounding us. I lost sight of all hope, and for a few minutes felt nothing but hope-less.

There would be other gut-wrenching lows – when the weight of loss felt too much to bear – but that was the moment when I came closest to giving up. Thankfully, the darkness that day didn't win.

JUMPING PUDDLES

The love and support of family and friends was keeping me afloat, but it was my boy who gave me the biggest drive to live again. I knew that giving up was not an option, I had an eight-year-old boy, and now I had the unwanted, but enormous privilege and responsibility of bringing him up on my own. In what felt like the darkest moment of my life, he was the ray of light that increasingly penetrated the gloom.

But I knew the day was coming when the two of us would have to go it alone. This incredible group of people gathered around us would have to leave, and we would have to find a new life and a new way of living it.

The weekend before the week of Gemma's "celebration" we returned home to Norfolk to stay with my parents in Cromer. I had been wrestling with how I was going to talk about the funeral to Ethan. As I lay in bed with him – still asleep next to me – listening to the sound of the waves crashing on the nearby promenade, I knew I couldn't wait any longer. As Ethan began to stir, I knew it was the time. I took a deep breath and said, 'Ethan, I need to talk to you about next Thursday ...' Daisy's Dream had told me a good analogy to help children to understand why we have funerals, so I started describing to him how Mummy's life was like a letter.

'All the things Mummy did are written in a special letter which is her life – the day she was born, the day she started school and the day she left school, the day we got married, the day you were born, and the day Mummy went to heaven. We've all got special letters – and all the names of the people we loved and loved us are in them, and all the many experiences we have had, like our holidays together. The letter is our life. When we die that letter goes to heaven to be with Jesus; but the envelope that contained the letter is left behind and we have to do something with the envelope.' Ethan immediately asked, 'So is the envelope Mummy's body?' I took another big intake of breath and said a reluctant, 'Yes.'

Gill from Daisy's Dream had warned me that kids at this age are by nature curious, they will want to ask questions about everything, and hard though it is, you're going to have to go there with them. 'What's going to happen to Mummy's body?' came Ethan's next question. There was no dressing it up anymore, I was going to have to tell him everything. In all my wildest fears, this was a conversation I had never expected to have to have with my boy. Like so much of my new life, it felt like an out-of-body experience. I could barely engage with the gravity of it as I explained what was going to happen.

I told him that all of Mummy's family and friends would gather with us at our church in Reading, and we were going to celebrate Mummy's life.

'Is Mummy's body going to be there too?'

I would have done anything to have stopped the conversation there, or handed it over to someone else to explain; but it fell squarely on my shoulders. I had to answer. I couldn't dress it up or save it for another time. 'Yes,' I replied. His curiosity and questions never let up, and didn't stop until we'd reached the cremation itself. No child should ever have to ask about the funeral of a parent; but tragically so many do.

At the end of it all, he looked at me and said, 'But what about football and Beavers?' Ethan had already moved on from the unpalatable details of next Thursday, and was back in the here-and-now. I couldn't help but just smile and say, 'My boy. You don't need to worry about that, you've got a whole day off school and everything else.' 'Good,' came his reply, 'that means I get to play with Thomas!'

If ever I needed a greater understanding about how a child processes grief, this was it. This was the puddle analogy in all its simplicity. For a few minutes, Ethan was almost submerged in the sadness of having to talk about his own mother's funeral, but the next moment, he had jumped out of that puddle and was focusing on the prospect of a day off and playing with his cousins! Not for the first time, I wished I could be him, just for a day, just to be able to escape the deluge of adult questions about the future. I too wanted to be able to jump out of that puddle and think about simpler things. But that is one of the hardest parts of grief, especially in those first few weeks – there is no escape. Every waking hour is filled with a relentless barrage of troubling thoughts.

Later that morning, after our traditional trip to the amusement arcade where Ethan emerged with his usual armful of plastic prizes, or "expensive tat" as I like to call it, we headed down to the beach. The day before, a storm had swept across most of the country, the North Sea had been stirred, and massive waves were crashing onto the stony shore. Everywhere you looked, the white foam that had been whipped up by the tide was quivering in the wind and glistening in the sunlight. You could see and feel the relentless rhythm of life.

Ethan threw pebbles while I gazed far out to sea. I felt a rare moment of peace. I was back in my hometown, a place that had been such an important part of my life, and a place that Gemma had grown to love. But our peace was quickly shattered as the wash from a huge wave rushed up the beach and filled our shoes. It was a cold winter's day in December, and the water was absolutely freezing. As the shock of the cold water hit Ethan's little feet, he let out a yelp and then began crying in pain. As swiftly as I could, I gathered him up in my arms and ran to the nearby promenade. Pain was etched all over his face. I sat him down on the wall, pulled off his sodden shoes and socks, took off my coat and wrapped it around his now red feet. I tried to warm them up as quickly as I could, and through his sobs, he cried out the words that felt like a dagger to my heart. 'I want Mummy. I want Mummy back.'

I had never felt more alone. To see my boy in pain and distress, and to hear him calling out for his mummy as any child does when they're in pain, was impossible to bear. Ethan wanted the one thing that I could never give him. His mother's love was now just a memory, and as I held him tighter and tighter, all I could do was again say, 'I love you,' over and over again. A winter's walk that had, for the briefest of moments, brought a glimmer of peace had turned, in an instant, into heartbreak and pain. Not for the first time, and certainly not for the last, grief felt like a tormentor that never let go.

A few minutes later, hot chocolate and marshmallows worked their comforting magic on Ethan in The Rocket House café that Gemma used to love. I couldn't take my eyes off the huge waves that continued to pound the beach. There is something mesmeric about the sea, its restless movement and sheer power draws you in and transports you away from the stresses of life. Willingly, I let it take me.

Moments later, a family sat down on the sofa opposite us – mum, dad, and a little boy – and once again, my brief moment of peace and reflection was shattered. Right there, sitting in front of us was a very physical reminder of what we once had. I tried not to stare, and struggled to hold back the tears as I remembered all the times we too had sat there as a family of three, enjoying the holidays; enjoying life. I was about to descend back into the pit when Ethan saved me, once again.

Seeing the sadness in my face, Ethan turned to me and said, 'Daddy, turn that frown upside down,' and gave me a kiss on the cheek.

With a simple act of affection and a phrase he had remembered from *Paddington 2*, Ethan turned a moment of huge sadness into one of happiness and pride. We hugged, and I whispered to him that he was a very, very special boy. Later that night as I wrote down some of my memories of that day, I wrote this about him:

Another moment where amidst the darkness, God's light is shining. I know I have to be a rock for my boy, but already he's being an even bigger rock for me.

PRESSURE WAVES

As Gemma's celebration moved ever closer, Ethan's questions became more frequent. I was getting used to the different tones in his voice and I could tell when he was about to ask something that might prove difficult to answer. So when I put him to bed one night and he asked, 'Daddy …?' in that certain way, I steeled myself and replied with a nervous, 'Yes?' 'Daddy, you know Mummy died really quickly?' My 'yes' in reply sounded even more nervous, but Ethan went on in a very gentle, matter-of-fact way. 'Daddy – you could die really quickly too. I mean you could die tonight, but you could also live to a billion.' I couldn't help but laugh at the last bit, but the rest made my blood run cold. His counsellors had warned me about how real this worry becomes for children who lose a parent – but to hear him vocalise it for the first time was hard to take. I wanted to alleviate his fears by telling him not to worry and that I'd always be there for him … but you can't do that. You cannot promise a child something that isn't true.

I tried to reassure him that although Mummy did die very quickly, she had been feeling unwell for a while, and that Daddy was feeling well. But once again he said, 'But you could die tonight, Daddy.' It was so tempting to tell him not to be silly, but I couldn't. In his mind, he had seen his mum go very quickly, so why couldn't the same thing happen to Daddy? It was a stark reminder of the place we now found ourselves in – I was his closest family; there was no one else now. I held his little hand tightly as he drifted off to sleep.

I stared at the ceiling, feeling a huge weight of pressure beginning to rest on my shoulders. If I was all he had left, I had better make sure I was going to hang around for as long as I possibly could. His fears about losing me too echoed around my mind and I prayed, 'Please Lord, don't let me die like Gemma, don't leave my boy on his own.' I left Ethan to sleep, hardly believing that I had just prayed those words.

All of that week, it felt like an unwelcome tide of momentum was sweeping us towards that dreaded Thursday. With two days to go, I once again awoke at stupid o'clock and found myself downstairs, sipping tea with the fire roaring into life. In the quietness of those early hours, I wrote:

The growing feeling of sickness is disquieting. The finality of Thursday is filling me with dread and the intense fear of what lies beyond is almost crippling. Just walking around the house as the business of the last two weeks has begun to tail off is horrid. Our home, the place Gemma poured so much of her love into making so beautiful now feels like it is becoming my enemy – I don't want to be here. How can we carry on living here without her? My stomach is a constant knot of sickening nerves. How am I going to get through this? How can I survive when the reality of this new life really begins to hit after Thursday? How can I ever go back to work after this? I want to curl up into a ball, hide from the world and pretend this isn't happening – but there is nowhere to hide.

The house had grown quieter. The knocks on the door had become less frequent, the kitchen was no longer a hive of activity. Little by little, the gradual shift into what would eventually become our new reality was underway. Thankfully, our two ever-presents – Auntie Rebecca and Dan – were still with us.

Despite having to deal with the acute pain of losing her sister, the sister she called her best friend, Rebecca stood side by side with me during some of my lowest points. Even when the waves of grief were pulling her under too, she still found a remarkable strength to lift me back up when I fell. Whenever I spoke about my biggest fear, the fear of the day coming when it would just be Ethan and myself in the house, she always responded with the same reassuring words – 'Simon, no one is going to leave you here alone for a long time.'

Whenever grief hits, people will often be surrounded by an initial wave of sympathy and support, but as time goes on, and the routine of life continues, people can't be present as much as they were. If you're blessed, as we were, you will find that some will stand by your side for longer and support you in ways you never expected. In the same way my close friend Dave had been such a tower of strength, an old friend from our days at Sky Sports became a pillar of support. I had first got to know Dan Lobb when I joined Sky in the summer of 2005 and over a number of years, we enjoyed many a shift together behind the *Sky Sports News* desk. As time went on Dan became a good friend of mine and Gemma's; he had a glint-in-his-eye sense of humour that would regularly reduce her to fits of laughter.

We hadn't seen Dan for a few months when she fell ill, and as news reached him of her death, he was absolutely distraught. As I spoke to him on the phone the day after she went, I could hear the emotion in his voice, as he apologised time and time again for not having seen more of us in the last year. To me, that didn't matter, what did matter most in that moment was the fact he had picked up the phone. The easier option for any of us is to avoid the potentially uncomfortable call, and express our sympathy through a text, a social media post, or worst of all, a praying hands emoji! Picking up the phone to a friend who has only been bereaved for a matter of hours takes courage, it takes us right outside of our comfort zone.

Dan really stepped up to the plate that day, and in so many other amazing ways in the weeks to come. He became a regular visitor in those first few weeks, with his beautiful dog, Lottie (much to our cat's disgust).

Often, Dan would accompany Ethan and I on the school run, knowing how hard I was still finding that part of daily life. He would walk with me to the playground and then we'd go and find the nearest coffee shop, where he introduced me to the delights of a flat white (I had always been a cappuccino man). Best of all, he listened as I poured out every emotion possible. He listened as I expressed fear after fear about what the future might hold. And he listened as I wrestled with questions about my faith. Dan never tried to leap in with quick solutions. And despite not having a faith himself, he was never judgemental. He just exuded a love and understanding that became a huge help to me in somehow navigating the stormy waters of early grief.

Thanks to Dan, Auntie Rebecca, and Dave – and his daily planner – my big fear of spending that first night in the house with just Ethan wasn't realised for the first 16 weeks! Dave made sure that we were never alone, and if no one else was free, he would turn up with his little rucksack and sleep over. When I look back on that period, I realise how blessed we were. This kind of long-term support isn't a part of everybody's experience of bereavement. Sadly, most people have to get used to a new, lonely life almost from the start. But for me, having all those weeks of knowing that every night, we would have someone there with us, allowed me to gather the strength and courage to finally do it alone. To face the moment that I had feared more than any other.

On the Monday before Gemma's celebration, we had the briefest foretaste of what that new life might be like. Rebecca was off for 24 hours to have a spa day – it was her opportunity to take some very necessary time to prepare for the week to come – and it was the least she deserved after everything she had done for us. Dan nipped out with her, just to move his car, leaving Ethan and I alone in the kitchen. I thought nothing of it, but almost immediately Ethan turned to me and said, 'Daddy – it feels so lonely here without Mummy.'

Without realising it, for the first time since she had gone, it was only the two of us in the house – and Ethan had picked up on it in an instant. Dan was only gone for a couple of minutes; but it felt more like 10. One day, in the not too distant future, this was going to be our everyday life. Just the two of us, trying to carry on, forever trying to deal with the gaping absence in our home.

I remembered the dreams we'd had when we'd first moved to Reading six years before ... dreams of a house filled with the chitter-chatter of children as we added to our family. Dreams that were too painful to think back on now. Our only hope was that somehow, one day, it would feel like home again. But at that moment, with the memories of Gemma ringing out from the corners of every room; this was not a place I wanted to be in anymore.

DO NOT WEEP AT MY GRAVE ...

There is the denial, and the out-of-body feeling of living through bereavement, and the sense of being lost in a parallel universe ... so much of grief is so utterly surreal. The day before Gemma's celebration was one of those days.

As I walked towards the school gate to pick Ethan up, I got a call from the funeral directors. I dutifully stood outside the gates (obeying the no phones in school policy), and he ran me through the final details for the next day. It was such a bizarre moment. As mums and dads huddled in the cold and waited for their children, there I was, talking on the phone about my wife's funeral! In one ear I could hear the daily banter of the playground, in another I was being asked if I wanted Gemma's coffin to be brought in at the start of the service or to have it in-situ as everybody arrived. If ever there was a moment that encapsulated the parallel universe of grief, this was it. Physically I was present in that playground; but mentally, I was an absolute world away.

*

The winter sun streamed through the windows; the church was packed. People I knew and people I didn't crammed themselves in, leaving many more standing at the back. The atmosphere breathed a huge sadness, but I felt a tangible sense of love.

The night before, I had barely got through the first paragraph of my tribute to Gemma before I collapsed in floods of tears. That day, somehow, I found the strength to stumble my way through it. Catching Ethan's eye and seeing him gazing back at me kept me together.

I have listened back to the recording, and there were times, as I stood by her coffin, when my anger at the injustice of her life ending so soon was palpable; but I'm glad it was. I was angry. I did have massive questions about what this God I was following was actually about, and instead of dressing it up to make it more palatable, I could only express what I was actually feeling, and underline once again (as if I needed to) what a huge hole Gemma had left behind.

In the same way that this experience was challenging every aspect of *my* life, I wanted to challenge everyone else that day. I didn't want them leaving that place just saying things like, 'What a lovely service,' or 'What a wonderful way to remember Gemma.' I wanted to make them think. In the same way this was changing my perspective on life, I wanted it to change theirs, and as I neared the end, I said this:

'So often in life we hear these words – seize the day, *carpe diem*, live each day as if it was your last, and yet we know that in the business and pressures of life how difficult this is to do. As I've looked through the many, many photos of Gemma these past few days I've seen her in a new and more beautiful way. She looks more radiant than I ever remember her. I will never get the chance to tell her how beautiful she is again, but I would do anything – I would give up our house, I would give up my job, I wouldn't give up you, my boy; but I would sell all that I have, to just have one more hour with my Gemma. In the space of just three, fear-filled days Ethan lost a mum and I lost my wife. Life is precious. Life is so, so precious.'

Funerals are one of the strangest of life's rituals. For the people who gather to remember the "dearly departed" it is a chance to pay their respects and say their goodbyes. But for family and close friends, it's an altogether different experience. I mentioned my friend and former *Blue Peter* Editor, Richard Marson, who tragically lost his 14-year-old son, Rupert, to suicide in the summer of 2008. To mark the 10th anniversary of his death, Richard wrote a remarkable blog that described in raw, but incredible words what his loss felt like, and he said this about Rupert's funeral:

'There were compliments about the music and the words, and how well it was stage managed. And funerals are a piece of theatre, a ritual which helps most of those attending to process the death and move on. Not so much the family left behind.'

I felt so much like Richard. Despite being surrounded by this large throng of family and friends, I felt so desperately separate from it all. The music played, people said beautiful and sometimes funny things about Gemma, but I was marooned in a place of total disbelief. Even as I gazed at her white coffin with the flowers below spelling out the simple word *"Darl"* I was barely processing what I was actually looking at.

In the weeks to come when I would listen back to my tribute on yet another sleepless night, I could barely remember even standing there, or the emotions I was feeling. As we gathered afterwards for the wake (I hate that word – can someone come up with something better please!) I spent most of the afternoon in the corner by the table, where people had left cards and gifts, barely speaking to anyone. Every time Ethan came over to see if I was okay, I hung onto him for all he was worth. Here I was in a room full of people who loved Gemma and loved us, and yet I couldn't have felt more alone.

When I looked on at friends catching up with each other, and heard the occasional sounds of laughter, it conjured up a plethora of mixed emotions. Part of me was happy to see so many people there for Gemma, and us; another part of me wondered what was the point of it all. Why was I spending all that money on giving people a pleasant time on this most desperate of days? I resented knowing that in a few hours, they would be able to go back to their lives with everything as it had always been, while the rest of us had an "appointment" at the crematorium! I looked at the couples standing side by side, and as I watched them chatting away, I felt a huge wave of jealousy that they still had each other. After only a few minutes I just wanted to get out and go home. It was like some kind of perverse wedding reception; but instead of it being the happiest day of my life, it was the worst.

*

Later that day, as the December light faded fast, a small group of family and friends gathered at the nearby crematorium. It was everything I expected and worse. Gloomy, lifeless, and utterly devoid of hope. For most of that day, I had somehow kept my surging emotions at bay, but as we stood in the cold, waiting for the hearse to arrive, the gravity of the day and the finality of the moment to come became too much to bear. Wracked by unbearable pain, I sobbed and shouted and railed at the sky.

My legs could no longer support me, and I slumped onto the cold gravel. People gathered around me, and friends hauled me back to my feet. Many of them laid hands on my shoulders and people began to pray that in this most desperate of places, in this most painful of moments, God's peace would come and rest on me.

It was a moving moment; but before I could even let the words sink in, I saw car lights piercing the gloom in the distance – Gemma's final journey was about to reach its end.

We had spent six years living less than a mile from this place, and we'd driven past it at least four times a day, back and forth on the school run. There had even been times when after getting stuck behind yet another funeral cortège, I'd joked that, one day it would be us. Just a bit of black humour in response to the uncomfortable reminder of our mortality. But now, inexplicably, it was one of us.

I was screaming out again and again as the polished Jaguar moved ever closer. Even now, when we were about to say our final farewell, when everything around me said she was gone, I couldn't accept what was about to happen.

The chapel was a small, claustrophobic room; the sense of despair was palpable. But as our vicar, David, said the traditional words of the ceremony, the room suddenly began to feel different. As the song I had chosen played, these words sang out from the tin pot speakers:

You give life, You are love
You bring light to the darkness
You give hope, You restore
Every heart that is broken
Great are You, Lord.

('Great is the Lord' – David Leonard, Jason Ingram & Leslie Jordan)

As I stood there, with my eyes fixed on her final resting place, the pain of emotion from only minutes before strangely started to dissipate. Instead of tears, I began to feel an indescribable sense of peace. If there was ever a place, ever a moment that I least expected to feel like that, this was it. And as the song carried on playing, I started to smile. For the first time that day I was able to feel a genuine thankfulness for all that Gemma was, and all she had been to me. Instead of staring endlessly at her coffin, I shut my eyes and began to picture her smiling face. Rather than feeling a sense of hopelessness about the future, I started to believe that somehow, one day, life could be good again.

As David closed the short service with the words of committal, I went and stood by her coffin, touched it briefly and began to walk out; but as I did, I could sense everyone behind me beginning to gather around it. Some laid hands on the coffin, others made the sign of the cross, others just watched on in silence. I don't know why but something about this made me feel uncomfortable and without thinking I suddenly said, 'Sorry to be a bit uncouth and break crematorium etiquette but she's not here, I'm off ... bye Darl.'

With that, I turned around and without looking back, walked out. The ceremony, the ritual, and the day were over, but these last three weeks had only been the start of life's new story; the reality of life without Gemma was about to bite.

EPISODES

In many ways, the period of time that precedes a funeral postpones, for a time, the unpalatable reality of what lies ahead.

We had been surrounded by an incredible group of people supporting us, and pushed along by the momentum of formalities. I had been at the heart of planning the celebration – that was the only way I could be sure that it would be, in some small way, worthy of her.

Plenty of people warned me that, it's only after the funeral that your grieving really begins, and the reality properly strikes. They were right. As I lay in bed that Thursday night, I was emotionally and physically spent. The next day, December 15th 2017, I wrote:

Today, as I feared it might, the pain has gripped me in a new way, it feels suffocating, it feels like there is no way out.

I had to go into our bedroom today. The winter sunshine was streaming through the windows and it felt like everything was glowing, it all looks like it always has done. Gemma's toiletries still sit on the top of the chest of drawers, her beautiful bracelets and necklaces still hang from their silver stand, her array of beautiful scarves remain draped over the blue chair by the window – this is a "stop the clocks" room. Everything screams: she's still here; but she's not. I slump to the floor. I can't do this; I can't get through this, but I have to for the sake of my boy.

I went into his room this afternoon – he's still sleeping with me upstairs. For the first time in weeks his room is actually tidy! As I looked at his bed with his vast array of cuddly toys covering the pillow, I started to think of all those nights I'd gone into that room to kiss him good night. Every time, before my lips had even left his cheek he would say, 'Can you get Mummy now?' How can it be that he will never get to say those words again? I'm in so much pain for my boy, this is so unfair, we couldn't give him a brother or sister, was it too much to ask that he could grow up with a mum and a dad?

Today is three weeks since she went. The longest I've ever been apart from her is five weeks on a Blue Peter *summer expedition. Soon it will be five weeks, and then six and then seven – on and on it will go until the day will come when it won't have been weeks, it will have been years. Barring me making 90 years of age I'm probably already past the half time point in my life, but if God grants me a decent life, I've got so many years ahead without her.*

I cannot stop crying today – it feels like my grief has started all over again.

But as my pain increased, so too did my boy's remarkable strength. Despite his own sorrow, his strength helped carry me. A strength that belied his years. Something I don't fully understand, but will be forever grateful for is that unlike mine, Ethan's sleep was never affected. Never once did he have trouble getting to sleep, and never once did he wake up in the middle of the night having had a nightmare. In many ways, given everything he was going through, it's something I can't fully comprehend, but at a time of few blessings in life, this was a massive one.

The Saturday after the celebration, I was in a bad way. I'd been down in the lounge since about half past three. I felt beyond tired, my body felt weak, yet my mind wasn't allowing me to sleep for longer than two or three hours. As I lay on the sofa and muttered to myself, 'I can't do this,' I hadn't noticed Ethan in the doorway behind me. He'd heard every word, but instead of being scared, he came over and gave me the biggest of hugs. His skinny body felt so fragile as I gripped him for all I was worth, yet I could feel this extraordinary strength radiating out of him.

I told him again how much I loved him, and how proud Mummy would be of him. I whispered in his ear, 'Will you pray for me, my boy?' I felt so desperate, that I couldn't think of anything else to say. But without hesitating, he did exactly that:

'Dear Lord. Please will you help Daddy to have a good time even without Mummy and we pray that he will be able to be really brave. Amen.'

Ethan's strength galvanised me once again. Without him, I don't know how I would ever have been able to find light in the darkest of places. Even when the darkness closed in around me, Ethan's light continued to shine. He was always waiting for me on the other side.

Later that day, we went for a walk into Reading. As we walked, he turned to me and – with that tell-tale change in his tone that signalled a difficult topic of conversation – said, 'Daddy, can I ask you something?' Nervous, as ever, I said he could. Ethan went on, 'You know the day when Mummy died? Why didn't Mummy come home that day? When you took me up to the landing to speak to me, I thought you were going to tell me she was going to be okay. I thought doctors and nurses are there to make people better?'

As a child, Ethan's understanding of hospitals was straightforward: they are where people go to get better. But Mummy didn't get better, and it had left him asking why. I scrambled around for an answer, I wondered if I should have given him some warning and prepared him better, but I couldn't change what had happened; the leukaemia hadn't given us any time to work out what was best. I told him that doctors and nurses *are* there to try to make people better; but sometimes, like with Mummy, people are so ill, that not even the best doctors in the world can make them better. I hoped that would be as far as he wanted to take it.

He bent down to pick up yet another stick, and simply said, 'Okay ... so was Mummy a bit like a car that had broken down and they couldn't fix?' 'My boy,' I said, 'I couldn't have put it better myself.' And we carried on walking.

*

I was still ignoring the grief adage: be kind to yourself.

The next day, we'd planned a walk with friends. But the rain fell so heavily that the walk was over before we had even had time to put our boots on. As we sat around trying to think of something positive to do with the day, I offered to go and get some lunch. Up until that point, I just hadn't had to worry about cooking. We had been spoilt by friends cooking for us at home, and delicious meals being delivered by the kind people at our church, like a Christian version of Deliveroo! But on that day, we hadn't got anything to eat. So I took it upon myself to go and get something. I gathered the shopping bags and headed for the front door as our friend, Lucy, offered to come with me. At that point, I should have said, 'Yes.' Instead, I just looked at her, and angrily said, 'I need to get used to this, I need to do this alone.'

Big mistake. As I headed out into the damp morning, I knew it was a bad idea; but the stubborn part of me wanted to prove to everyone that I *could* do this. I *could* do life without Gemma, however hard it was going to be. I slammed the car door shut, thinking ridiculous thoughts like, *I'm going to show them*. But of course, there was nothing to prove. I didn't need to show them anything. Gemma had been gone barely a month; the time for going it alone could wait for another day. My friends were there to help me, and protect me from doing too much too soon. I should have accepted Lucy's offer. As I pulled up in the rainswept Tesco's car park, I knew it was the last place I should be. I knew I wasn't being kind to myself, but I wouldn't listen to the inner voice of reason. Inside the supermarket, it all felt completely overwhelming. I looked at my untidy shopping list and glanced up at the endless aisle numbers, but I couldn't make sense of it. The simple act of gathering a few groceries felt too much.

I pointed the trolley down various aisles, but couldn't find anything. Even finding a simple head of broccoli felt ridiculously challenging. The sounds of irritable kids, frustrated parents, and the endless store announcements were beginning to grate. As I tried to hunt down a chicken to roast, I could feel my heartbeat quickening. My breaths were coming faster, and a familiar sense of panic was beginning to overwhelm me once again.

I wasn't shopping anymore; I was shambling around in a quivering daze, and the tears were falling. I remembered the many times I had shopped there with Gemma. She had always been so clued up on what she wanted and where it was – all I had to do was push the trolley like a faithful dog and load the bags at the end. But now she was gone, and I had been plunged into some kind of retail hell where nothing made sense. All around me were the sights and sounds of a normal Sunday morning in Reading. But I felt like a lonely, messed-up freak. At one point, I nearly picked up a corn-fed chicken and hurled it down aisle 16 in a fit of rage. Life felt cruel, and I couldn't have felt more cut off from the world.

I arrived back home and the emotions of the past hour came bursting forth. I dropped the bags to the floor in the kitchen, and hurled my keys across the room, smashing the pot they lived in. I couldn't face talking to anyone, and headed straight upstairs. My office chair got in my way as I walked through to Ethan's bedroom, and as my anger overflowed, I kicked it across the room, narrowly missing the computer and Lucy who was coming out of the room! I slumped to the floor, and Lucy and Dave (who would later refer to these moments as "episodes") sat with me and held me. Words weren't needed; I just needed to be held.

I wasn't being kind to myself that day. Instead of taking Lucy's offer of help, I had stubbornly put myself through something I didn't need to do. The time for solo shopping trips should have waited for another day.

Thankfully Ethan didn't get to witness this episode. Of all the emotions I was comfortable sharing with him, anger wasn't one of them. The last few weeks had been disconcerting enough for him; he didn't need to start fearing for his dad's mental wellbeing.

A few Sundays later, I had to protect Ethan from another angry episode. As I sat in the lounge after lunch with Gemma's mum and sister, Ethan was trying to download a Playstation update, but with no success. Inevitably the call of 'Dad – can you help me' arrived on cue. I sat down with him to try and sort out the problem, but what should have been a straightforward task fast became almost impossible. As my frustrations at not being able to help him grew, I could feel my breathing becoming shallower once again, and more rapid. I started to panic. As I was getting ever more agitated, Ethan was getting visibly more worried. A simple request for help had sent his dad into a full-blown panic attack.

With anger welling up inside me, I stormed out into the cold. I just wanted to scream, but I was too near the house, and didn't want Ethan to hear me. I went to open the garden gate, but couldn't open it; it was stuck. The anger overcame me, and with one almighty kick, I smashed the gate off its hinges. Thankfully, the gate came off worse.

I paced around the garden, breathing more deeply, and the anger and panic began to subside. A few minutes later I walked back into the lounge and thankfully, Ethan was none the wiser.

When I think back on moments like these, I don't recognise myself. It feels like I'm describing the actions of someone else; but this is what traumatic grief does. The shock waves were still reverberating, and they had the power to make the most mundane of tasks feel like trying to scale a mountain.

The grief took Auntie Rebecca in a different way. Later that day, I found her, lying motionless on the floor of her bedroom with Wendy by her side. The only signs of life were the tears running down her cheeks. We sat with her in silence, holding her hands, struggling to know what to do, when a diminutive figure appeared at the door. Without a moment's hesitation, Ethan walked over, knelt down and gave his auntie the biggest of hugs. Wendy and I looked at each other with a huge sense of pride. Moments later, he was off again. I thought he was probably heading back downstairs to complete another Lego creation, but instead, he came back and placed a small wooden cross in Auntie Rebecca's hand. It was a similar cross to the one that Gemma had been holding when she died. I was in awe of Ethan's love and compassion for others. All the years of love that Gemma had poured into his life, were now being poured into the lives of others.

Before going to sleep that night I wrote this about our bedtime conversation:

We both agreed that our Mummy memory tonight was when she told us that she loved us. As I finished saying our nightly prayer, he asked me if I would sleep next to him tonight on the floor – I told him of course I would. As I kissed him good night and got to my feet to turn out the light, he said something that he hadn't said for days: 'Daddy, I'm feeling very sad.' As I lay back down next to him, he starts telling me about an episode of The One Show *he had seen a few weeks before (I'm guessing during Children In Need week). He tells me that he remembers seeing the story of a boy whose daddy had died, and how he'd watched it and felt so sad and had hoped that it would never happen to him. Then he said he couldn't believe it when I came home that night and told him that Mummy had died. This is so heartbreaking to hear.*

As incredible and inspiring as Ethan was, watching him navigating himself through his own sadness was absolutely heart-breaking. In so many ways, it provided an incredible insight into the way a child's mind works and how they process grief as he jumped from his puddle of sadness into thinking about how life was going to work going forward. What was the rest of his life going to look like? What was "family" life going to be like with just him and his old man? The next day, that window opened even further. As we drove home from school, with Granny in the back and Ethan in the front, a conversation began that I was never expecting to have, especially less than a month after she had gone, and it started, as usual with a question:

'Daddy – you know when people lose their mummy or daddy, do they sometimes get married again?'

I tried my best not to swerve off the road and into the nearby ditch. I could see Granny's eyes of surprise looking back at me in the rear-view mirror thinking, *Good luck with this one!* I thought the question might surface one day, but I hadn't expected it quite this soon. I wanted to tell him it wasn't something he needed to worry about yet, but I knew I couldn't. If this was something that he was thinking about, if this was a part of life going forward that he was worried about, I couldn't just shut him down. If I did that, what other big questions would he feel he couldn't ask? Where would he be able to turn to express his fears? Not for the first or the last time, I had to go there with him.

I told him that sometimes people do get married again after losing a husband or a wife. That most of us like to have someone to share our lives with, and maybe, one day, Daddy would get remarried; but it wouldn't be for a long time. I also tried to make light of it, saying, 'I doubt anyone will be interested, Ethan. I'm getting on a bit now!'

The cogs were still turning though, and eventually, he asked, 'If you did get married again, Daddy, they wouldn't be my real mum would they?'

His questions felt like a fast bowler aiming an in-swinging ball at my middle stump. There was nowhere to hide. I tentatively pushed at his latest delivery with my bat of limited wisdom, and told him that whatever happened, if Daddy was to ever get married again, no one could replace Mummy. And we wouldn't want them to, because we are all unique, we are all irreplaceable, and we would want to love the woman for who she was. With that he returned to playing with his latest tub of car-seat-wrecking green slime, and no more was said.

Later that evening he shared one of his more surprising Mummy memories. As he sat with Granny on the sofa, listening to his bedtime story, he suddenly said, 'I miss Mummy's squishy boobs. Nothing can replace Mummy's squishy boobies.' For the first time in what seemed like a very long time, we all collapsed in laughter. My boy – a beacon of light and laughter in the darkness.

BOTTOM OF THE GLASS

In her final hours, I promised Gemma that I would not return to the drink, and for the first three and a half weeks after she died, a drop never passed my lips. But then Christmas came ...

I have always had a love–hate relationship with alcohol. Before university, it had played very little part in my life save the occasional teenage house party where someone would always end up cracking the lock to their parents' booze cupboard and the Cinzano or Martini would start to flow (Why was it always something ghastly?!) and we'd all feel horrendous the next morning! It wasn't until I headed for Birmingham University in the early 90s that my eyes were opened to a culture I had never been a part of.

Fresher's week was like an alcoholic bomb going off. It felt like the vast majority of activities and events put on to ease your integration into university life largely revolved around consuming vast quantities of drink. Get stuck in and you instantly felt accepted; abstain and you ended up feeling like some prudish outsider. At a time when you're adjusting to life away from home and trying to make as many new friends as possible, immersing yourself in this new culture provided an easy way in. The problem for me was in my character.

I have always been an all-or-nothing personality type. In many ways this was a positive attribute – whatever the challenge I was presented with, I threw myself into it, not least the challenge of trying to land my dream job on *Blue Peter*. While it may have taken me a lot longer to get the gig than I had ever planned, I gave it absolutely everything. I never took "no" for an answer, and even when I was turned down for the job for a second time, it still didn't put me off giving it one last go and succeeding on my third attempt. But for all its positives, this part of my personality became my Achilles heel when it came to alcohol.

In the same way alcohol gave you a sense of acceptance at university, it became a source of refuge in my years on *Blue Peter*. In those three and a half years I spent trying to get my dream job, the prospect of being famous intrigued me, but I didn't crave it. For the first few months on the show, being recognised was a bit of a novelty. As time went on, the question changed from 'Isn't it that bloke from the telly?' to 'Isn't that Simon from *Blue Peter*?' As a taste of fame goes, this was very minor stuff, but whether you're a rock star or a children's TV presenter, nothing quite prepares you for losing your anonymity.

As the years on the show passed, the pressure of potentially being recognised made me increasingly paranoid about the simplest things – even a trip to the shops was fraught with worries about what I was wearing and how I was looking. What if I was approached by kids who watched the show and discovered I was nothing more than a huge disappointment? I started to over-think everything.

My paranoia was often at its most acute in social settings. In my years on the show before Gemma entered the scene, I'd avoided showbiz functions like the plague. And if I did reluctantly go, I felt like a fish out of water. I had got it into my head that because of what I did, people would have certain expectations of me – that I would be the life and soul of the party, regaling everyone with endless tales of adventures.

In truth no one expected me to be like that, least of all the people who knew me best; but I had allowed myself to believe that they did, and all too often, I found my confidence in a glass of something. It gave me comfort and courage, and allowed me to be the person I stupidly thought people wanted me to be. It's a familiar story. The dependence creeps up on you without you even realising it. And as time went on, it became my social crutch.

There were times in my marriage when it was a source of real tension. Gemma liked a drink, but unlike me, she knew where the off button was. She might not have understood my dependence, but I never felt judged by her, and her devotion to me never wavered.

There were a number of times during our marriage when I gave the drink up – for a whole year on one occasion – but eventually, almost inevitably, I always went back to it. No matter how many years I had spent in front of the camera, whether at the BBC or Sky, I couldn't stop worrying.

What if people discover who I really am? What if they realise that I'm just a fraud who's half decent talking to a camera?

The pressures of doing my job in a very public and exposed place triggered a paranoia that I would ultimately never shake off. and I coped by finding solace in the bottom of a glass. The relief it gave me was only ever hollow and fleeting.

Four months before Gemma fell ill, I decided enough was enough, and I did it – I went teetotal. There was no big moment of crisis or enlightenment; I'd just got tired of it being a tension in our marriage, and in my life. In the same way my all-or-nothing personality had sparked a love–hate relationship with the bottle, I knew that half measures were never going to work.

Giving up is such a grey area; it comes with an unspoken expectation that at some point you will go back to it. People's reactions to you saying 'I've given up' are often very different to how they react if you say 'I don't drink.'

In the countless times when I'd given up before, they'd say, 'Come on, if you've only given up for a few weeks, one won't hurt!' It's a bizarre reaction. If someone came to a dinner party and told you they had given up meat, you'd never dream of forcing a rump steak into their mouth; but people seem to find it harder to accept when it comes to drinking.

In the weeks that followed my decision to *stop* drinking, people's reactions were entirely different. When I said, 'I don't drink anymore,' there was nothing but respect for my decision. Instead of looks of incredulity at me opting for a Diet Coke, people seemed to respond with understanding, rather than judgement. For five months, I felt nothing but peace with the decision. Instead of feeling like I was missing out, I found a strength that I had never felt before. Instead of drink being something I craved, it became something I rarely thought about. I remember the pride Gemma felt that this was, at last, firmly behind us. And as a result, our relationship and my faith had never felt stronger.

Four months on from that life-changing decision, as Gemma entered the final hours of her life, I promised her that I wouldn't return to the booze.

In front of her, and in front of my family and friends, I publicly pledged that I wouldn't drink again. That was one fight I didn't need, not now, and certainly not in the months ahead.

But I think that if Gemma had known what was coming, she would have worried about it. She would have known that, as I was about to face the biggest test of my life, there was every chance I would turn back to the drink to help get me through it. And I knew it too.

THE GREAT DECEIVER

For the first three and a half weeks after we lost her, I kept my promise. Despite the flood of emotions overwhelming me, the thought of having a drink barely entered my head. Even when people drank a comforting glass of wine around me at home (they always asked if I was okay with it first), I still didn't crave the pain-numbing antidote of alcohol. However hard things were, alcohol was not the answer. If I was in a bad place now, I didn't need to take myself somewhere even worse. But then Christmas arrived, and the wheels began to fall off.

If ever there was a year when I wanted to cancel Christmas, this was it. Never before had I felt so totally disengaged with the yearly festivities. The tired Christmas songs rang out on their endless loop, and the television adverts taunted us with their parade of happy families and perfect Christmas dinners! It all felt like a deliberate reminder of all that we had lost. The season of peace and goodwill felt like the season of turmoil and cruelty. If I could have fast-forwarded time to January, I would have done it in a heartbeat. But as they say, Christmas is for kids, and however much pain he was in, Ethan was just as excited about it as he had ever been. So I had to go through the motions of wrapping presents, pulling crackers, and putting on the bravest of faces.

Becky and her husband, Neil, knew just how tough Christmas was going to be, and invited us – and Gemma's family – to spend it with them. They were amazing, despite the huge pain they were experiencing themselves. All of the stresses that accompanied Christmas were taken away. All I had to worry about was wrapping a few presents and getting through it. Even the stress of buying gifts for Ethan's stocking (something Gemma had always done) was looked after by a wonderful group of women from our church, who produced an amazing array of gifts that left the stocking redundant and needed a pillow case to hold them! In the same way we had been carried through the first month by the love of our family and friends, we were now being carried through the toughest of Christmases.

But, in spite of it all, the pain of losing Gemma never relented for a moment.

The day we arrived at my sister's, I sat down in their lounge and adopted my now standard position of staring vacantly at a flickering fire. In the conservatory next door, I could hear the sounds of laughter from Ethan and Thomas, and as I listened, the strangest thing happened – I started to feel jealous of my boy! I started to wish I could *be* him. I wanted to be able to grieve like a child could. To have those moments of inevitable sadness, while being able to escape them in the trappings of childhood, free from the endless questions and fears about the future. I wanted to jump out of that puddle of pain, if only for a few minutes.

I knew I was being utterly ridiculous. I wasn't jealous of my wonderful boy; I just wanted my torment to end.

As darkness fell that day, I told my sister I needed to get some fresh air and went for a walk. When I pulled my coat on, I knew exactly what I was doing. A few minutes later, I arrived at the nearby Co-op store and headed straight for the bottles of spirits.

Everything inside me was saying, 'no, don't do it,' but I couldn't take my eyes off the bottles of spirits that sat behind the counter. The last month had taken its toll. I'd had enough. I wanted –

needed – to escape the pain, if only for an evening. Like a relapsed drunk, I waited nervously in the checkout queue, constantly looking around to make sure no one I knew was nearby. And then, I did it. I bought a bottle of vodka. My heart was pounding as I paid for it, hurriedly put it in the plastic bag, and walked out of the shop feeling more like a shoplifter than a Christmas shopper. As I made the short walk back, it became an increasingly agitated conversation between two voices in my head:

Remember the promise you made to Gemma? You don't need to do this. You don't need to put your family through the worry. Ethan doesn't need his daddy hitting the drink.

The bottle swayed back and forth in the bag as I walked, and the other voice answered back, strong and clear.

You need this – you need to numb the pain, you need an escape, you deserve it, everyone will understand.

I already knew exactly what I was doing, and I felt powerless to stop it.

My thoughts began to turn to how I could sneak the bottle back into the house without anyone knowing. With a loosening of my belt buckle I pushed the bottle down the front of my trousers and hoped for the best. I must have looked ridiculous! To my relief no one was nearby as I entered the hallway and headed upstairs to my room. I hid the bottle in my suitcase and hoped no one had suspected anything.

It started slowly ...

I re-joined the family and grabbed a can of Diet Coke. Then, as innocently as possible, I got up and popped back to my room with a half-drunk can. Making sure no one was around to hear me, I topped it up with Smirnoff. With each sip that I took, the pain began to subside. For the first time in weeks, I felt a sense of release from the worries and fears that had filled every minute of every day. And for a time it felt good.

The trips back to my room became increasingly frequent. I didn't think it would look at all odd that I kept going up to my room with a can in my hand, but really, it must have looked vaguely ridiculous to everyone else. And while the temporary relief felt good, the change in my demeanour didn't go unnoticed. I might have kidded myself that after four months without so much as a sip, I could handle one of alcohol's strongest blends. But everyone could see what was going on.

I went to the garage to pluck another can of Coke from the fridge, and Becky came to find me. I was already halfway to being properly drunk, but I can still remember seeing the tears in her eyes. She knew exactly what was going on.

One of the many lies alcohol tries to sow is that no one will notice; no one will even smell it on your breath. The more you drink the more convincing it sounds. But I wasn't fooling anyone, least of all my sister.

I tried to tell her through my own tears that I had just had enough of the pain. But the guilt was crushing. I knew I was letting everyone down, not least Gemma. My sister had every right to make me feel like a naughty schoolboy who'd just been caught with a pack of Silk Cut in his bag, but she was never judgemental; she was nothing but loving. She knew more than most how much I was struggling, but she also knew how destructive heading down this path could be.

I agreed to let her pour the final third of the bottle down the sink, and tried to convince her it was a one-off. I promised I wasn't going to go back to it again …

I spent the rest of Christmas trying to fulfil my promise. But there were times when it consumed my thoughts. Some days I would win, others I would be seeking opportunities to sneak out and buy another bottle. The allure of being temporarily free from the pain was hard to resist.

I was crafty though; I found ways to hide it, even going as far as buying a bottle of water, emptying it, and then refilling it with vodka. But every time my lying and deception was short lived; while I was "enjoying" the temporary reprieve from pain, everybody else was becoming, understandably, ever more concerned. And at times, that concern manifested itself as anger. I was angry too – I hated lying to my family, I hated the fact that only weeks ago I had been in such a strong and happy place. Now this battle with the bottle was raging in a way it had never done before.

As conversations took place behind my back between concerned family and friends, I felt like people were getting at me; that they couldn't possibly understand. But it wasn't that at all. They just couldn't bear to see someone they loved making his plight even worse.

*

I had a quiet New Year's Eve. I took to my bed at nine thirty to avoid the optimistic sounds of Big Ben. But everything came to a head on New Year's Day.

We spent the day at my parents' place in Cromer and enjoyed the head-clearing effects of a winter's walk by the North Sea. But as the relentless sounds of waves crashing onto the pebbles filled the air, I knew that the time to head home was fast approaching. And I knew that in 24 hours, we would finally have to confront the new daily reality of life without Gemma.

I have never feared a new year in the way I was dreading the start of 2018. At home, it was soon going to be just the two of us, and there wouldn't be anyone to keep an eye on me. I knew the drinking couldn't continue, but I had one last night in Norfolk …

I feel a huge sense of selfishness, guilt, and shame as I write this, but I had already given myself permission for one more night on the drink. I wanted one more shot of relief from pain; but it ended up taking me somewhere much darker and more sinister.

Again, I drank in secret, and again, people were quick to spot what was going on. Another bottle of vodka was poured down the sink. I made it through the rest of the night, but as I lay in bed later, the fears about returning home began to crowd my mind. I felt sick at the thought of life at home without Gemma. And with each hour that passed, my sense of hopelessness grew. I couldn't face this; I didn't have the strength to take on this new life we had been catapulted into.

For a time, the alcohol flowing through my veins had numbed the pain and softened the fears, but now it was taking my mind to a much darker place. As the rest of the house slept, I got out of bed, walked quietly down the stairs and out into the garden. It was a freezing night, and I could feel the brittle, frostbitten grass beneath my bare feet. As I looked up into the night sky and the beautiful constellations of stars above me, I wanted to end it. Like that morning on the river bank at home, I no longer had the strength or the will to carry on.

I sank to my knees and prayed that God and my family would forgive me as I lay down on the grass. I was only wearing a pair of boxer shorts, and the frozen lawn felt like glass was being broken on my chest. I closed my eyes, not wanting to ever wake up again. I was waiting to die, waiting for hypothermia to take me; but then, what had happened on that morning by the river, happened again ... I could see the unmistakeable image of Ethan's face, his innocent eyes looking back at me. They were the eyes of a boy who needed his dad more than ever; a boy who had just been dealt the hardest blow any child can receive; a boy who didn't deserve to lose his dad as well. I couldn't do it. However hard it was going to be to carry on, I couldn't give up.

As I rose to my feet and started walking back to the house, I couldn't stop crying. How had I ended up here? How could I even contemplate ending it all? I crept back up the stairs, grabbed my duvet from my room and headed to the room where Gemma's sister, Rebecca, was sleeping. No one had any idea what had just happened; but I knew I was in a very bad place and needed someone to keep an eye on me.

Rebecca stirred and woke, and I told her I was struggling, and asked her to keep an eye on me. That's one of the last things I remember from that night. As the early hours of the next morning passed by, I became more agitated and confused, and that's when I started headbutting the wall. I just wanted to inflict as much physical pain on myself as I could. Later, Becky told me that three of them had had to sit on me to stop me self-harming myself any further.

The next thing I remember was coming out of the loo and finding a paramedic waiting for me on the landing. My family had become so concerned about my mental state that they had called for an ambulance. Very gently, Becky and Rebecca tried to explain what had happened and why I needed to go to hospital, but I was too confused to know what was going on. Time and again, I asked them to ring Gemma and tell her what was going on; I was so disorientated that I had become convinced that she was still alive.

As the ambulance sped towards the Norfolk and Norwich hospital, the memories of that ambulance trip with Gemma just a few weeks before started to come back, and I became gripped by fear that I had got acute myeloid leukaemia as well. Again, I asked them to ring Gemma and tell her I was okay.

I was an absolute mess. What had meant to be one last night on the drink had turned into a nightmare for my whole family. If ever I'd needed a lesson on why drink and grief don't mix, this was it. Slowly, the alcohol in my bloodstream reduced and my mind started to clear. I knew then that, whatever it took, I couldn't lose this battle, I had to beat the booze.

Over a year on from that forgettable night, I still feel a huge sense of shame that I put myself in a place where life didn't feel worth living anymore. Shame that my own pain seemed more important than anyone else's, even my own son's. And shame that the promise I'd made Gemma had been so spectacularly broken. I felt a huge sense of guilt too. My sister and her family had been nothing but loving and supportive. They had looked after us during the most difficult of Christmases and I felt as if I had let them down. And they were *still* looking after us – unbeknown to me, conversations were taking place between concerned family and friends as they tried to work out how they could help me through this. Later that day, my friend and rock, Dan Lobb, arrived on the train from London to drive us home the next day.

I sat at the table with them all later that evening and they told me, as lovingly as they could, just how concerned they were. It was a sobering listen. At times, it felt like everyone was getting at me, or they were all against me. At times, I felt no one trusted me anymore; that they didn't think I could be the father Ethan needed me to be.

I shouldn't have felt any of those things. This was a group of people who loved me and wanted to do everything they could to help me through this. They knew and I knew that there couldn't be a repeat of the previous night.

It was time for me to be honest. It was time to admit: I needed help.

NOWHERE TO HIDE

As the early winter months of 2018 passed, the battle with the drink never really went away. Some days I would be okay, but on other days, I simply couldn't handle the pain of grief and loneliness without it.

It was an almost daily struggle not to stop on the way back from the school run and get something for the evening. If I could get home without stopping at the shop, I knew I had won for that day.

But on other days, the fear of the lonely night ahead was too much. Every time I engaged with it, the pattern was the same – at first, I would feel free from the pain. The numbing effect of alcohol made the loneliness of sitting at home, alone, night after night, with my boy asleep upstairs, almost bearable. But as the night went on, it took me to ever more dark places. Thankfully, there was never a repeat of that New Year's Day night. Every time I drank, I knew just how dangerous it could be, but just knowing that wasn't enough to make me stop. And I didn't have the strength to stop without help.

As spring arrived, I'd had enough. Reluctantly at first, I agreed to go to Alcoholic's Anonymous. Heading to my first ever meeting, with my close friend Dave alongside me for moral support, I felt a total failure. It had only been a few months since I had taken that decision to stop drinking. Back then, I had felt so strong – now I was heading to my first ever AA meeting! What on earth had my life become?

As I walked into the room feeling a sense of trepidation, and not knowing what to expect, I felt nothing but relief as I looked around. I was half-expecting to see a room full of slightly down-trodden, ruddy-faced men and women. I couldn't have been any more ignorant. Here was a group of people just like me. People who, to the outside world, probably looked like they had their life in order; people who knew that alcohol was a fight they couldn't win alone. Instead of feeling judged, I felt accepted. Instead of worrying about what people would think of me being there, I felt nothing but welcomed.

At one meeting, a guy about my age shared his story and as he did, said something that has stuck with me ever since:

'If you have a problem with drink, there is literally nothing in life, no situation, no experience, no relationship, whether good or bad that cannot be made immeasurably worse by drinking.'

I couldn't get those words out of my head. However much I had tried to justify it, drinking was making a bad situation even worse. If I was going to find a reason to live again, if I was going to try and be the best dad for Ethan, then I could not let the booze rule my life.

I've spoken with a number of other widows who are part of the brilliant Widowed and Young charity that was set up to support men and women who are widowed at 50 years and younger. And it has helped me understand my own response to grief. Whenever I asked other members what their relationship had been like with drink after bereavement, most of the responses were the same – it had been a battle for a time; but in time, they knew it was only making their situation even worse.

Grief is incredibly painful. At times it's a physical ache – that knotted stomach of fear that grips you every time you think about what has happened and the fear of what happens next. Alcohol helps mask those symptoms of grief; the problem is that it can only ever give you temporary respite. All it really does is postpone dealing with the unavoidable parts of grief that are still there when you wake up in the morning.

The loneliness was the hardest thing for me. On the nights I didn't drink – and there were more of them as time went on – I had to confront the loneliness head-on. Without the drink to hide behind, I almost had to grit my teeth and find a way through it. Some evenings it felt like a kind of endurance test, my whole body would feel tense.

Unless you've been bereaved it's difficult to understand just how profound the loneliness is when the person you long for isn't there anymore. There is no solution. Life without them feels incomplete.

Some nights, I would just sit on the sofa where I had always sat, and stare at the other sofa where Gemma had always sat. Sometimes a flicker of a memory would make me smile, but mostly I sat there with a heavy heart and wonder why I hadn't sat next to her more often. Why hadn't I held her hand more, as we sat watching the telly? Why hadn't I appreciated much, much more, just how blessed I was to have Gemma in my life?

Grief is a horrible, stark reminder of all the parts of life you take for granted. You yearn for those normal nights, sitting at home together. But the person you thought would be there, side by side with you for years to come, is suddenly gone. And the things that remind you of them are everywhere. Her phone sat silent and unused on the shelf, her latest book lay forever more unread by the bed. Everywhere I looked, it breathed a painful, unsolvable absence.

As my trips to Alcoholics Anonymous became a regular part of my week, my friends started to regularly ask, 'How are things with the drinking?' Most of the time, I felt comfortable talking about it, but there were other times when the question really grated. Alcohol had become a symptom of my loneliness, but no one ever seemed to ask, 'How are you coping with the loneliness?' Maybe it was because that's an altogether more uncomfortable question and if you get an unpalatable answer, it demands a response.

If a friend tells you they're struggling with loneliness, you can't just respond with, 'I'm sorry to hear that' and leave it at that. Like me, my friends must have been struggling with the reality that it wasn't something they could fix. There was no fix. Sometimes though, I wished people had asked me more about the loneliness and less about the drink. It left me wanting to scream at people that it wasn't all about the drink, I was just bloody lonely.

Grief is uncomfortable for everybody. We don't like the way it reminds us of our own mortality, and the fragility of life. But sometimes we need to ask the uncomfortable questions because if we don't, it leaves the bereaved feeling more isolated than ever.

THE BEAUTIFUL GAME

Grief takes life's brightest moments and makes them bittersweet. Even while you're enjoying the sweetness of an experience or a memorable moment, you're still feeling the searing pain and absence of the person who should be sharing in that moment with you. Never did this feel quite as acute as the day Ethan got to be England football mascot for their friendly against Italy at Wembley.

In the days and weeks after Gemma died, the world of football was unstinting in its support for us both. Whether it was online, by post, or messages to my phone, we were inundated with managers, players, and former colleagues offering their sympathy and support. Too often in football we focus on the negatives – the money swishing around the game, the overpaid players, the flashy cars and lifestyles, the theatrical diving – but it's at times such as this that you appreciate that there is a real togetherness within the football community. When the chips in life are down, the beautiful game has an amazing way of gathering around people and helping them back to their feet.

My own club, Norwich City, was unwavering in its support. In February, they invited Ethan to be a mascot, and at the first home game after Gemma's death, they put a message on the big screen at Carrow Road at half-time, paying tribute to her and wishing Ethan and I the very best. A week later I was sent a photo from Loftus Road where Queens Park Rangers had put up a similar message at half-time. At a time when I felt so horribly alone; the comfort I drew from gestures like this meant everything.

One message that really stood out was a letter from the (at time of writing) Tottenham Hotspur manager, Mauricio Pochettino. Although I had covered plenty of Tottenham matches during my time at Sky, I had never really spoken to Mauricio apart from the occasional 'Hello' in the tunnel before a game, but he took the time out to write me a letter. What moved me most was the fact that this wasn't one of those letters written by someone else at the club with a computer-generated signature at the bottom; this was a personal letter from the man himself. A man I had never properly met, a man who before this had almost certainly never heard of Gemma, but a man who took the time out to express how sorry he was. As I read his words, my respect for the Argentinian grew even more:

Dear Simon

I wanted to write to you after hearing the sad news of the passing of your wife Gemma.

I cannot imagine the pain you are experiencing right now, and I wanted to let you know that the thoughts of everyone at the Club are with you and your son Ethan.

I know that she will be sorely missed, and I want to extend my deepest condolences to you on behalf of all the staff and players.

Sending you strength at this difficult time.

Kind regards,

Mauricio Pochettino

Among the messages that poured in during those first few weeks was a touching message from the Football Association, asking if Ethan would like to be a mascot for England for the game against Italy. I was genuinely taken aback by their offer and bowled over by the fact they wanted to do something special for my boy. I replied with an emphatic yes, and a few weeks later, on 27th March, we experienced a moment that will live with us for the rest of our lives.

I stood nervously near the tunnel where the players were due to emerge in a few minutes' time, and word came through that Ethan was going to be walking out first. Moments later, as Wembley roared, there he was, walking out, hand in hand with the England Captain for the night, Eric Dier. I don't think I have ever felt a sense of pride quite like it. As my boy walked past with a look of nervous anticipation on his face and gazed up at the huge crowd surrounding him, I shouted his name as loud as I could. Somehow above the cauldron of noise echoing around the stadium he heard me, looked to his left and gave me the biggest of smiles.

I didn't stop looking at him for a second, and as the anthems rang out, the sweetness and bitterness of that moment hit home. Here was my boy getting to experience something only a handful of kids ever get to experience; a moment that was making me bubble over with fatherly pride. But I couldn't hide the pain of knowing that Gemma wasn't there to see it. I could picture her face, I could see the tears of pride in her boy that would have welled in her eyes. I knew what a moment like this would have meant to her. And that's when then it hit me afresh – whatever Ethan was going to go on to achieve in life, his mum would never be there to enjoy it with him. On an unforgettable night at Wembley, grief was trying to spoil the moment – I refused to let it, and as the anthems reached their final notes, I kept saying to myself, 'Don't let the pain rob me of my joy.'

In many ways, that became my mantra from then on. Tough though it was at times, I had to accept that life was forever more going to be a strange cocktail of opposing emotions. I had to learn to accept that when those special moments came, like that night at Wembley, the joy was always going to be accompanied by a sense of pain. The question was, could I learn to accept that this was an inevitable part of grief, or was I going to allow the pain to forever rob us both of our joy?

As we drove home later that night, with Ethan still dressed from head to toe in his new England kit, I asked him how his night had been. Wearily he turned to me and said, 'It was amazing, Daddy, but I'm just so sad that Mummy wasn't here to see me. She's missed so much that I've done since November. She'd have been so proud.' Here was Ethan expressing his own walk through the bittersweet landscape of loss. He had just experienced one of the most memorable nights of his life, but it had also been a painful reminder of the huge hole that had been ripped in his life. I told him again and again how proud of him I was, and how many messages I'd had from families and friends watching at home, saying how brave and amazing he was. His tired eyes began to close and moments later he was fast asleep. As we sped up the M40 towards home, I said quietly out loud, 'Darl, you'd have loved tonight. We miss you so, so, much, but please know our boy is doing us both so proud. I love you, your boy loves you.'

However difficult this new life was going to be, that night at Wembley showed us both that though the pain of Gemma's absence would accompany us both for the rest of our lives, when those moments of joy came, we could embrace them and rinse them out for all they were worth. Though the cancer that took her never allowed us the time to talk about life without her, I knew that more than anything, she would have wanted us to experience joy again.

STOPPAGE TIME

As time marched on and the weeks turned into months, the question about what was going to happen with my career began to play on my mind more frequently. From the moment Gemma fell ill, Sky had been unstinting in their support and understanding. There was never any pressure from them for me to return to work, or to make a decision on my future; but I knew the day was coming when I would have to decide what I was going to do. Every time I thought about work, I thought back to that first morning after Gemma died, and the conversation with Ethan when he'd asked what was going to happen to him when I went back to work? As I reflected on all that had happened and how totally different life had become, I began to wonder if I'd ever be able to return to what I loved doing. Could I ever really care about the game in the same way when I'd just gone through this? And most importantly of all, what *would* I do with Ethan when I was heading to Manchester for the 10th time that season?

Gemma had been such a huge part of my time with Sky. Just three weeks after I took the job on *Sky Sports News*, we got married, and throughout those 13 years, she was my ever-present. When I had those times of doubt about whether I was good enough, when I had those periods of depression, she was the constant.

She was the one I'd always turn to for reassurance. She was the person I always rang as soon as we came off air, even if it was just to say that my train had been delayed yet again!

Every time I thought back to my last game at Old Trafford and the painful memories of that panic attack in the disabled loo, I heard her reassuring voice and recalled the calming words that helped me get back on my feet and get on air. And every time I thought of doing it without her, my blood ran cold – she would never be on the end of the phone for me again. If I went back to work and had another panic attack, Gemma wouldn't be there to guide me through. How could I ever do my job again without my best friend alongside me?

As the months went by, more people started asking, 'When are we going to see you on our screens again?' I wish the answer had been as simple as the question. I wrestled with the practicalities of it, knowing that all the old routines, the tried-and-tested ways of balancing home life with work had been irrevocably altered.

Friends and family were unstinting in their offers to look after Ethan if I went back to work. But that just took me back to the same question – was that the life I wanted for him?

I couldn't be with Ethan every hour of every day, but was a life of being passed around different friends every time I went to work the kind of life he deserved? No one knew him better than me, and I knew he'd hate that being his new weekly reality. How could I head off for work knowing he was unhappy? The more I thought about it, the more I knew that going back to the job I loved was going to be almost impossible. Ethan was taking his first, tentative steps on an unwanted journey, and, for as long as I possibly could, I wanted to walk with him, side by side.

It wasn't just a question of practicalities; I was also struggling to reconcile work with life's new reality. When something like this happens you often hear people talking about how it changes your perspective on life. In truth, it changes much more than that. When I thought about the game I had loved my entire life, it just didn't seem to matter anymore. No disrespect to them, but when I imagined myself back in the studio, listening to Gary Neville and Jamie Carragher having a heated debate over whether it was a penalty or not, I knew I'd have been thinking, *Who cares?* When you've lost almost everything in your life, who cares if it's a penalty or not? They care. And they should care.

For Gary and Jamie, the fact they care so much, and have an infectious passion for the game makes them the brilliant pundits they are. For the supporters watching at home, it matters. Of course it does. And up until a few months before, it mattered to me too.

But four months on from losing Gemma, football didn't feel like it mattered at all. How could I go back into that studio feeling like that? Maybe for a time, I could have put on an act and pretended to care; but I knew it wouldn't be long before people would have seen through the mask; spending your working life in front of a camera leaves you with nowhere to hide. I didn't want to end up looking like a fraud, I didn't want people to start saying I didn't care – it would have been damaging professionally, it would have been unfair on Sky, and on the brilliant people I had spent so many years working with. With each week that passed, it was becoming ever clearer – I couldn't go back. As April arrived, I knew it was time to decide; Sky was beginning to make plans for the next season.

I talked to my boss, Gary, and felt like I was letting everybody down; I felt guilty that I was turning my back on a company who had stood by me in the hardest of times. But he was never anything less than completely understanding. He never tried to talk me out of it, he never made me feel like I was making a mistake, he just reiterated again and again that the door would always be open for me. If, in a year's time, I felt differently, they would welcome me back with open arms.

A call that could have been so hard left me feeling a huge sense of relief and peace. As we chatted through how we would announce it, I suggested that I write a blog to explain why I had made that decision. I was very aware that many others who suffer the loss of a loved one, simply don't have the financial means to step away from work, they are back behind their desk before they've even begun to really start to grieve. I didn't want people to make the wrong assumptions. I didn't want anyone just assuming that I had been handsomely paid by Sky and thinking, *It's alright for him*. The simple truth was, that had Gemma not had life insurance, I *would* have had to return to work the next season, or we'd have had to sell up and move away from Reading. There seemed precious few blessings in life anymore; but I did feel blessed that I had the freedom to be able to devote the next couple of years to being there for my boy. I only wish it could be the same for other parents who suddenly find themselves walking grief's horrible path.

I finished the blog with these words:

I don't want to turn this into an Oscars speech, but I have to say a few thank yous. I want to thank the late, great Vic Wakeling for having faith in me all those years ago. For being prepared to give me a chance when others had shut the door. I want to say thank you to everyone I've worked with over the past 13 years: the guys at Sky Sports News, the legions of unsung heroes who work behind the scenes on the football, and also to David Jones and Kelly Cates, both of whom have taken on a bigger work load in the months I've not been able to work. Both are class acts and both have been brilliant in their support of me since Gemma went.

But the biggest thank you goes to Sky itself for the unswerving support they have given me over the past few months, not just when Gemma fell ill and in the aftermath of her death, but also in the weeks before when I was suffering from anxiety and depression. When I first became unwell, not only did they give me the time off to get better; they wanted to understand. Initially, I was fearful of talking to them about mental health. I shouldn't have been. Every step of the way, they supported me, gave me the space to try and get better, and wanted to understand what I was going through – and this has carried on through these hugely painful last five months. They have been quite simply amazing and have also been gracious enough not to just accept the decision I've made, but also to tell me that the door will always be open. The love and care they have shown Ethan and myself, has been simply incredible, not least by the boss of football, Gary Hughes, and the head of Sky Sports, Barney Francis.

And a final thank you goes to you guys. Those who have supported me over the years on Sky and those of you who have been so loving and supportive of me over the past few months. And thank you to the world of football whose support has never diminished – it means so very much.

So for now, this is it. A wonderful, unforgettable 13 years comes to an end in a way I could never have foreseen or ever wanted. But what now? Over the next few months I'm going to be writing a book, and I also want to explore some other broadcasting opportunities. Broadcasting is all I've known for the past 20 years, I love it and am not turning my back on it. I also want to plough more time into raising awareness and money for Bloodwise UK. Blood cancer took my wife; I have to do something. But most importantly, I'm going to be giving every ounce of energy I have to helping my boy navigate this strange new chapter of life and as a Christian, I have to trust God in this. This is not blind faith, this is real faith – and sometimes, that means stepping out into the unknown.

Who knows where I may be in a year's time but for now, God Bless, and I hope to see you on a screen near you one day soon.

Simon x

As I hit save, the tears began to well in my eyes. I knew I was making the right decision, but it felt like I was losing everything.

STEALER OF DREAMS

My decision was due to be announced by a Sky press release and my own blog three weeks later. Having felt nothing but a sense of peace about announcing my decision to leave, when the day came, it was harder and far more emotional than I had ever anticipated. I had completely underestimated just how big a moment it was going to be.

I woke at just gone three o'clock that Friday morning with a huge sense of dread. The familiar sicky feeling in my stomach was worse than ever. I sat in the lounge, lit only by a flickering candle, fearing that I was making a massive mistake. I'd been told so many times that you should try to avoid making any big decisions in the early stages of grief, yet here I was bringing down the curtain on a job I had loved for over a decade. The one thing I needed to hear more than anything as I sat in the quiet of that morning was the reassuring voice of Gemma. So many times during our life together she had been my calming voice of wisdom, but now I was making the biggest decision of my life without her. I tried to picture her, sitting beside me, with her arms around me, and wondered what she would have made of all this. I wondered if she would have backed my decision or tried to encourage me to go back? But this is one of the starkest realities of grief – the person you most want to share everything you're feeling with, is the one person you no longer have.

I was still facing up to a future of navigating life without my co-pilot by my side; somehow I had to keep flying without her.

As we arrived at Ethan's school later that morning, those fears and worries began to overwhelm me, and I started to break down in the playground. It felt like I was experiencing loss all over again. Before anyone could come over to see if I was okay, I kicked the railings in front of me in anger and frustration. Not surprisingly people decided I probably wasn't in the mood for a comforting word and kept their distance that day!

Part of me still knew that, under other circumstances, I'd have been getting on a train later that day to cover the weekend game between Liverpool and Stoke. But in this alternative dimension, I was saying goodbye to a job that had filled me with such pride. As the playground babble echoed around me, I wanted to scream. Once I'd kissed Ethan goodbye, I hurried back to the car as fast as I could, avoiding eye contact with anyone I passed.

It was a good day for my weekly counselling session, and as soon I sat in Richard's office half an hour later, he could see I was struggling. He told me, 'This is another huge loss for you; you're now not only grieving for Gemma, you're grieving for the loss of the life you once had, and though the pain you're experiencing is different to the pain of losing Gemma, it's still incredibly painful.' Like he had done countless times, Richard had understood everything I was feeling. Not for the first time, it felt like he was the only person who actually got me; the only person who knew how big a deal this was. The loss of a job is a huge life event to deal with for anybody; but I felt that because of the greater loss of Gemma, my family and friends hadn't fully understood how big a moment this was. Until I woke up that morning, I don't think I had either!

The rest of that day felt like one long countdown to three o'clock. I tried to distract myself by having lunch with a friend, but it was all I could think about. At about a quarter to three, I parked in a road close to school, and read my blog for a final time. As the clock moved ever closer to three, my finger hovered nervously over the publish button. It felt like I was on some kind of bizarre death row, and I was killing my own career.

Three o'clock came and the decision I had wrestled with for so long in private, was made public. There was no turning back. Gemma had gone, and now, for the foreseeable future, my career had gone as well. It felt like grief was beginning to rob me of everything I had ever loved. But that's the inescapable character of grief, it is the ultimate thief – it doesn't just steal lives, it steals hopes and dreams.

Later that night, as I lay next to Ethan at bedtime, he turned to me and said, 'Daddy – you know Children in Need and the rickshaw challenge Matt does? One day when I'm old enough, I want to do it too. I asked him why and he simply said, 'I want to do it to help other children who lose their mummies or daddies.' 'Oh my boy,' I said, 'You really are absolutely amazing. Mummy would be beyond proud of you, and so am I.'

On one of the toughest days I had had since Gemma died, Ethan's words gave me hope for the future. Hearing him speak such words of kindness, in spite of his own sadness, expelled any lingering doubts I had – I knew the decision to devote the next couple of years to him was the right one. To be able to walk the road with him was a blessing and a privilege I was very thankful I had been given.

DADDY'S LITTLE HELPER

Ethan never stopped asking questions about what life was going to look like going forward. And sometimes, those questions would be hard to hear, and even harder to answer. As we lay in the dark one morning, I asked him if there was anything he was worried about that day? For a moment he didn't say anything; but then he looked at me and said, 'Yes – I'm worried that when I grow up and get married and have kids that, Mummy won't be here to meet them, and my children won't have a granny.'

These were such hard words to hear. Here was my eight-year-old boy thinking about life a long way into the future, imagining all those life milestones to come, and yet already painfully aware of how big an absence his mum was going to be. These were questions I had barely begun to think about, but he was already beginning to realise that her absence would be a painful companion for the rest of his life.

A few nights later, as I kissed him good night, he returned to an old question:

'Daddy, if you ever were to get married again would you have a baby with that lady?'

I laughed nervously, and clumsily replied, 'I can't really answer that, my boy. Maybe I would, I don't really know.' I hoped my rather inadequate answer might be enough; it wasn't, Ethan wasn't finished yet. 'But Daddy, if you got married again and that lady didn't have any children of her own and wanted them, would you have another baby then?'

We'd discussed the possibility of me getting married again one day; but he'd never taken the conversation this far. I wanted to pull up the handbreak on the conversation and glibly tell him that he didn't need to worry about these kinds of things for a long, long time. But as always, I knew I had to keep that door open to whatever questions he wanted to ask. Scrabbling around for an answer, I was only able to say that maybe, one day, that might happen.

Ethan was far from done! 'But Daddy, if you did have a baby again one day, would they be my real brother or sister?' I was stumped. Gemma had only been gone a few weeks; why was he thinking about those things? I tried to fob him off by saying I might not even get re-married, so he didn't need to worry about it, but he was having none of it.

'But Daddy – would they actually be my brother or sister?'

Reluctantly and with an exasperated tone to my voice I told him, 'If, and it's a big if, my boy, I do get married again one day and I was to have any more children then of course they'd be your real brother or sister because like you're part of me; they'd be part of me too.'

I tried to make a weak excuse about needing to go back downstairs but the questions kept on coming.

'Daddy, if you did get re-married, would I have to love that lady in the same way I loved Mummy?'

Of all the questions he had asked me since November, this was the one that stopped me in my tracks. It was such an incredibly deep question and showed a level of emotional maturity that I never expected to be coming out of the mouth of an eight-year-old.

As I lay there and reflected on it, I knew that however difficult it was to answer, it was something that at this moment, mattered to him. I knew he was searching for some security; he was trying, in his own way, to discover what his new life might look like. It was never going to be the same again; but could it one day, bear some resemblance to the life he had known before? I looked at his expectant eyes and said, 'Well you know Pompa (Gemma's Dad) and Grannie (Gemma's Mum) aren't together anymore, and Pompa is now married to Nanu (Anne-Catherine)?'

'Yes,' he replied.

'Well we love Nanu, don't we?'

Again he replied, 'Yes.'

'But we don't love her in the same way that we love Grannie, because Grannie is Mummy's mum. So if ...' (and I did put a lot of emphasis on the word "if"') '... I did get married again one day, then I hope you would grow to love that woman lots and lots; but you won't ever love her in the *same* way that you loved Mummy.'

'Okay,' he replied, and with that, he clutched his cuddly monkey to his face and asked what my Mummy memory was that night. I said (not for the first time) that I was going to miss her amazing roast dinners; Ethan said he was going to miss watching *Strictly Come Dancing* with her!

I lay in bed later that night, listening to the sound of Ethan sleeping and wondered (again, not for the first time) how I would have coped without him. On that night I had told him about his mum, I had expected his world to collapse in the same way he had collapsed to the floor. For a time, it had, but all these weeks on, he was showing a strength and maturity that I had never expected. In the same way that Gemma had been that unshakeable rock of reassurance for me, Ethan was now beginning, in his own unique way, to fill part of the void that she had left. Whenever I was struggling, whenever I was feeling sad, and the tears began to well again, he was so often there with an encouraging hug, or wise word. Sometimes he even told me off! If I was getting unnecessarily annoyed with bad drivers on the way to school, he would grab my arm and say, 'Don't get stressed, Daddy!' He was even beginning to sound like his mum!

One afternoon, I was upstairs on the landing sorting through yet another heap of washing while Ethan played downstairs. I glanced out at the garden below – it was a mess. I looked into my office – untouched since she had died, with piles of paper everywhere. It was a mess. I looked at the clock and knew it was nearly time to make Ethan's tea. What could I make him? I couldn't give him Marmite on toast yet again! It all felt overwhelming. I hated this new life as a solo parent. All the parts of home life we had shared now sat squarely, and uncomfortably, on my shoulders. I started to cry yet again. As I was beginning to understand more and more, it's in the mundane and simple parts of life that grief grabs you most often.

As I knelt by the dirty washing, sobbing, I suddenly heard the pitter-patter of feet on the staircase – and there he was: Daddy's little helper was on hand once again to save the day. He wrapped his arms around me and whispered in my ear, 'Don't worry, Daddy, we're going to be okay,' and in an instant, my tears of sadness turned to tears of joy. I had said it before and I would say it again: 'You're amazing, my boy, you really are amazing.'

I only wish I had felt able to help him in the face of his own sadness in the same way that he had helped me. So many times when I kissed him good night, he would tell me again, 'Daddy, I really, really miss Mummy. I miss her saying good night and giving me a cuddle and a kiss.'

And every time, I could only lie down beside him, wrap my arms around him, and say, 'I know, my darling boy. I think about it every day. I love you so much.'

On another night, Ethan woke up complaining that he was feeling sick. His face was pale, and he looked so fragile. I felt almost as sick as him – sick with the realisation that she was no longer there to comfort her boy with her soft reassurance and her warm embrace. Her absence was acute as I held him, and as I put him back into bed he started to cry through his tears – 'I want Mummy, I want Mummy back!'

I have never felt more helpless and hopeless. As Ethan hunched over the sick bowl, we had no one to turn to; no one alongside us to share the burden of these difficult moments. It was just the boy and I, cut adrift in the ocean of grief, and it felt like the loneliness would never end. Those early days of being surrounded by family and friends felt like a distant memory. It felt like the world had carried on without us.

RANDOM ACTS OF KINDNESS

As the house grew quieter and the weeks crawled on it wasn't just the love and courage of my boy that kept me afloat, the thoughtfulness of others gave me new strength.

Life can sometimes feel so cynical, and the news is so often saturated with negativity that instead of looking for the best in people we find ourselves expecting the worst. At times, it feels like we're losing faith in the kindness of others. But then a card arrived from a guy called Dan Ritchie.

I had never met Dan, I hadn't even heard of him, but like so many others, he wanted to get in touch to say how sorry he was, and how much he had been moved by Gemma's story. I didn't know why, but there was something different about Dan's letter. It wasn't just another kind person offering sympathetic words, Dan wanted to do something.

It felt like such a random suggestion at first, but he invited Ethan and I to go and stay with his family on their farm near Ledbury in Herefordshire. I told him that, at some stage, we would love to come and visit. A week or two later, Dan was back in touch. As a father of three children, the story of what had happened to Ethan seemed to have touched him in a very profound way. And he appeared to want to try to understand what it was like to go through something like this.

For anybody trying to support a friend going through the loss of a loved one, it is almost impossible to comprehend what it is truly like, unless you've been through it yourself. Until Gemma died, my only brush with loss was when my grandma died at the age of 80. I was 18 at the time and while I was heartbroken to lose her, she'd had a long life and a good life.

Gemma had had a good life; but she hadn't had a long life. And that changed everything. When she went, all our hopes and dreams for the future went with her. Afterwards, it felt like I was starting life all over again.

But if you haven't been through something like that, how on earth can you even begin to understand what it feels like? Unless you've walked in the uncomfortable, ugly shoes of grief, how can you second-guess just how painful and life changing it is? You can't. But that doesn't mean you can't try to understand.

Dan wanted to do exactly that. Hearing our story caused him to question how he would cope if the same thing happened to him? How would he carry on and be a father to his three children without his wife, Kate, by his side?

As Dan made contact again, he asked what kinds of things Ethan was into; he said his boys wanted to get him "a little something". Even though he had enough of the stuff to fill an Olympic-sized swimming pool, Lego was Ethan's predictable reply. A few days later, a large box arrived. The "little something" turned out to be a Lego train set (as any parent of a Lego-obsessed child will know, a Lego train set doesn't come cheap!) I knew that when the boy arrived home from school later that day, he would be beyond excited, even though it would inevitably be Daddy doing the lion's share of the building! But as I pulled the train set out of the large brown box, I noticed something else in there – a grey, fabric lunch box with a label on it, marked "Simon". I unzipped one side to find a whole array of different snacks – nuts, pretzels, and other goodies; but then, as I unzipped the other side ...

It was a moment I'll never forget. Inside were bundles of small, cream-coloured cards, held together by a bow of green string, and on top of them all was a card that read: *even Dads need snack notes.*

Posting my snack notes to Ethan on Instagram had become a part of our daily routine, and Dan wanted to do the same for me. He had written me a note for every single day of 2018! Some were words of encouragement, others were words of affirmation, and, as a Christian himself, others were motivational words from the Bible.

I sat there with the bundles of snack notes in my lap, utterly astonished. A man who, two weeks ago, was a total stranger, had been so moved by Gemma's story, that he had spent two whole days at his desk painstakingly writing out a year's worth of cards. If ever there was a moment where the light felt like it was breaking through the darkness, this was it.

This random act of incredible kindness moved me to tears. Grief can be such an isolating experience; even when you're surrounded by people you love, you can still feel horribly alone, but moments like this, and the many other random acts of kindness we experienced over the months to come started to infuse me with a fresh hope that somehow, we *would* get through this.

A few days after Dan's gifts arrived, I decided to post one of his snack notes on Instagram instead of Ethan's. The note simply said:

Know that all of heaven is cheering you on Simon.

And below it, I wrote:

Today's #snacknote is a bit different. Since Gemma went, I have been so moved by the support and messages I get from people on here, people I haven't even met, yet people who care about me and what we're going through. A guy called Dan Ritchie who I have yet to meet (but will) had seen my notes for Ethan and felt I needed some help to encourage me and help me keep going when I feel like giving up. So he's written me a daily note too! That's #lightinthedarkness right there.

The reaction to this post was as incredible as it was unexpected. One person wrote in reply:

Oh wow, that is absolutely amazing. Grief can be so isolating but it can also reunite us all. With so much sadness in the world and for all the pain you are going through this is absolutely heart-warming.

Another posted:

This is one of the nicest things I have ever seen somebody do. How thoughtful for this man to do this for somebody he has never met. How wonderful is our generation, truly loving to each other. I'm moved beyond words. Stay strong Simon.

The story of this random act of kindness really resonated with people, and as that day continued, many of the online papers began to report it. But it wasn't just being reported in the UK ... Dan told me that a friend of his had rung him to say that his family, who lived in Australia, had heard a story about this amazing guy called Dan back in the UK who had done a remarkably kind act for a TV presenter who had recently lost his wife. Knowing Dan as well as they did, they assumed it must be him! Understandably, Dan was somewhat bemused – but at a time when so much of what we see in the news is so bereft of hope, this was a story that punched a hole through the pervading mood of cynicism. It hadn't just given me a renewed sense of hope, it had given hope to so many others. Random acts of kindness always have been, and always will be, incredibly powerful.

And with that lunch box of notes began a friendship that became so important then, and is just as important to this day. Dan was forever checking in, forever sending me texts to ask how I was doing. His efforts in trying to understand what I was going through helped him to show a level of empathy that went beyond his own life experiences. And it meant so much.

There were too many times during those early months when I wanted to shout at people, 'Do you know what this feels like?' But I often stayed silent. It wasn't their fault they didn't understand. The truth is that unless you've been through it, you are never going to be able to fully appreciate what their experience feels like, and how it affects them every hour of every day. But I know – and Dan showed me – that *trying* to understand, attempting to think about what that person might be going through is a very powerful way to support them.

When I felt at my lowest, when those days came when I doubted I had the strength to carry on, the generosity and love of friends, and the kindness of complete strangers carried me through.

OUT OF THE ASHES

The random acts of kindness didn't stop. In fact, something rather incredible began to happen ...

In Caversham, there is a wonderful little café called Nomad Bakery. They often say it's the people who make places, and Laura, who ran it, made that place. Laura wasn't just a brilliant and creative cook who poured boundless energy into her café, her warmth drew people back, time after time.

It had been a firm favourite of Gemma's and we had often visited as a family. But in the early days after she went, I just couldn't go back. It was laced with too many reminders of happier times, and it took weeks before we started to venture back in.

At first it felt painfully poignant. Just the simple act of finding a table for two and not three felt like a kick in the teeth. Looking up and seeing groups of young mums, swapping stories of the early weeks of parenthood over a flat white, brought back memories of the times we had sat there as a family, with Gemma effusively praising Laura's poached eggs on sourdough toast and her irresistible dressing! Now we felt like the "odd couple" – the father and son who didn't seem to fit the social norm anymore.

Perhaps it was going to be better to avoid these places, find somewhere new, somewhere that held no reminders of yesterday's life. And had it not been for Laura, I doubt we would have gone back. But Ethan still loved having his Marmite on toast there, and every time we ventured back, there was Laura with her warm, welcoming smile. Rather than pretending life was normal for us, she always asked how we were doing. Even when she had coffee orders coming out of her ears, she would take time to chat with Ethan and make him feel at home. A place I had wanted to avoid became a place I wanted to go to; a place we both felt comfortable at the most uncomfortable of times.

I wanted to show our appreciation to Laura for her kindness. We did run out to the nearest supermarket one day when she ran out of Marmite, and bought her the biggest jar that money can buy, but that didn't feel like enough. So instead, I started to put an occasional picture of Nomad up on Instagram. One thing I would never describe myself as is a social media influencer, but given it was a small business, and Laura had devoted so much time and energy into making it such a special place; I felt that if I could do anything, however small, to help her build the business up, then I should do it. I very much doubt my weekly photos of Nomad's delicious food brought in hordes of new customers but it did something else; something quite unexpected.

Before Gemma's death my Instagram feed was mainly taken up with endless shots from a drone I had treated myself to, a year before. If you weren't into drone photography, then I probably wasn't the Instagrammer for you. Gemma sometimes used to say I had become a drone bore!

On 12th November 2017, I posted a photo of the sun setting behind the chimney pots on the top of the house – two comments and 103 likes.

Two days after Gemma went, I posted a picture I had taken during the floods of 2014. The River Thames had burst its banks, and one afternoon the three of us went down to the end of the garden, with camera in hand. With the help of the shutter timer on the camera, a tripod, and a quick bit of running through the ankle-deep water, I managed to capture a picture of the three of us, hand-in-hand with Ethan in the middle, looking out at the sunset. United by love, huddled on a little sliver of land, surrounded by water and silhouetted against a winter's sky, that photo encapsulated Team Thomas. It still hangs in our lounge to this day.

In contrast to my "artistic" shot of our chimney pots, this post received 349 comments and 2,918 likes. Without intending to, Instagram had started to become a platform where I felt safe to share how I was feeling, to express through photos and words what loss felt like.

Twitter felt like a much harsher place; after finishing a live game for Sky I would deliberately not look at Twitter for 24 hours after coming off air. Even when I felt I'd had the best of days; it would only take one nasty comment to make me feel rubbish about myself. Instagram felt a calmer and altogether more peaceful place. The people who were starting to follow me in ever greater numbers were doing so because they were interested in Gemma's stor, not whether I thought Graeme Souness had been too harsh on Burnley's defending!

As 2018 wore on, I began to post more and more about the journey we were on, and in posting about our regular visits to the Nomad Bakery I hoped to give Laura a tiny bit of publicity, but also show that, however tough life was, we were still finding some moments of happiness and light. And it wasn't long afterwards that it started to happen ... gifts from total strangers began to arrive at the bakery!

As Ethan and I sat there one Sunday morning, Laura came up to us and said, 'I have some packages for you.' I looked at her, somewhat bemused; but a few minutes later she arrived back with about five different parcels and a bundle of cards. And the more times we went, the more gifts arrived. It was both incredibly touching and, at times, a little embarrassing, as Laura appeared at our table, armed yet again with brown parcels instead of food. For the other regulars, it must have been a strange sight – who were this father and son who got to enjoy a mini-Christmas every time they sat down for a flat white and Marmite on toast?

Along with my next picture, I wrote:

One thing I have realised in a new way these past few painful weeks is that there are some incredibly kind people in this world. We live in such cynical times, yet these are all gifts that have arrived @nomadrdguk because people know I come here but don't know my address. #thankyou #blessed

It feels unfair to single out two acts of kindness when there were so many others; but there were two gifts that stopped me in my tracks – both from amazing artists who had seen pictures I had posted of Gemma on Instagram and turned them into amazing black and white drawings.

The first was by a lady who went by the name of Sammy Bird Art, who sent an incredible drawing of Gemma, based on the photo we had used on the order of service at her celebration. We chose that photo because it was so natural and un-posed. It caught her radiant smile, and Sammy's drawing captured it perfectly.

The other picture came from Lucy Ong and it was a drawing from a picture I had taken of Gemma on holiday a few years before. It's the photo of her that I will always treasure the most – Gemma holding Ethan, with Ethan laughing and Gemma smiling back at him. If ever there was a photo that encapsulated the beautiful bond between them both, this was it, and Lucy's drawing captured the moment so wonderfully. These "strangers" had done something as beautiful as the pictures they had drawn. And both pictures now hang proudly at home.

At times, these random acts of kindness from people we had never even met was overwhelming. Ethan was showered with more sets of Lego than even he could believe. I had to remind him, time and time again, that life wouldn't always be like this. I didn't want him to devalue the generosity and kindness in any way, but it was also important for him to understand that out of something horrible, great good can still come.

Countless kids experience loss; but not many get to experience the extraordinary level of kindness we did. I was always very aware of that, and never once did I take it for granted. Very occasionally, someone would post an unpleasant comment online pointing out that if I hadn't worked in the job I had, none of this would have happened. They said it wasn't fair given how many others go through exactly the same thing. In some ways they had a point; but what was I supposed to do – send everything back? Ask people to stop being so kind?

Rather than feel embarrassed, I tried to see it for what it was. Out of the ashes of something hideous, something very beautiful was emerging. Something that did so much to restore my faith in people, and something that in many ways restored some of my faith in God.

There were plenty of times over that first year when I questioned my faith. Many moments when I wondered where God had gone, and doubted whether he even cared. Why did he sound so silent when I needed him most? But my faith tells me he never went anywhere; and it was through the extraordinary kindness of people like Dan, Sammy, Lucy, Laura, and so many others that God showed his presence. The light I had been searching for shone out of the darkness in the most unexpected ways.

NO TO "PLAN B"

When you hear people talking about the first year after losing a loved one, you'll often hear them talking about "firsts". And in the first few months after she left us these firsts felt relentless. Our first Christmas without her came just a month after she died. A month later, I had my first birthday without her, and before I knew it, the shops were starting to fill with Valentine's Day and Mothering Sunday cards.

But there was a bigger first coming ...

Sunday 20th May. That day should have been Gemma's 41st birthday. I started to feel sick at the very thought of it. It felt like we'd been celebrating her 40th just a few weeks ago; now we were thinking about a day when we'd be remembering her, not celebrating with her.

The memories of that beautiful evening came flooding back. The rain of that Saturday morning had cleared, and the sun had shone. The music played, the Prosecco flowed, and Gemma had looked radiantly happy. She was in her element – surrounded by the family and friends she loved; her smile never left her face that night. She celebrated what turned out to be her final birthday with a bang, and I'm so glad she did.

On an evening round at Dave and Debs', we reminisced about that night, and how to mark her birthday. And then it hit me – I turned to them and said, 'Why don't I do it again? Why don't I flip a negative into a positive? Instead of moping around that weekend feeling sorry for ourselves, why don't we celebrate her life in the style she loved?'

As we talked more, I could feel a surge of excitement and optimism growing within me. One of the things I had talked about with Ethan in the early days was planting a tree close to the house in memory of his mum. I had never wanted her to have a grave; I wanted something that felt more hopeful; somewhere that we could think back to the times we had enjoyed as a family. 'Why don't I get the tree planted before the party?' I said to Dave and Debs. 'And then we can have a moment when we gather everyone around the tree and bury some of her ashes ... and then party.' By lunchtime the next day, I had been in touch with every family member and friend I could think of to save the date – Saturday 19th May 2018, the day before her birthday.

The replies flooded in, and when the number of people coming tipped past 150, I began to panic. I had sorted out the catering and had asked our friend Beccy Kean, who had sung at Gemma's funeral, to provide the music but that was as far as I had got. More and more, I asked myself why I had taken it on. It was still less than six months after she'd died, and there was so much to do, so much to organise; I had barely begun.

I should have known that I could always rely on the help of my friends.

As I stood at the school gate one afternoon waiting to pick Ethan up, one of the mums I had got to know over the past few months, Jane Wing-King, came over to ask how I was doing. When I told her what was going on and how overwhelmed I felt, she just grabbed me by the arm and said, 'Si, let me help.'

Jane was an absolute life-saver, and over the next few weeks she became my official party planner – my "Winkings-Wonders" as

I liked to call her. Working in fashion design, she was full of ideas and took the idea of a celebration party to remember Gemma and just ran with it. Without her generosity and creativity, it would never have ended up being the day it was.

With about a month to go, Jane asked me something that I hadn't even considered – 'Si what happens if it rains? Have you got something sorted?' Given that I was hosting a garden party during an English summer, this was a pretty obvious question; but amid everything else going on in life; it was one thing I hadn't even thought about. Panic set in again. The money I had put aside for the celebration was already spent. But as things stood, if it chucked it down, we would be stuffed, or more to the point – soaked! I sat in our garden imagining nearly 200 people trying to shelter from the rain and knew I had no choice but to try to find a marquee.

As I perused the marquee companies in our local area, my eyes began to water as I discovered how much even the most modest of white tents was going to cost, and I couldn't really afford it. I knew I wasn't going to be earning for the foreseeable future, and this wasn't the ideal time to be forking out for a wedding reception style party. But the party was just weeks away, the RSVPs were in, hotel rooms were booked, the food, drink, and decorations were paid for; cancelling wasn't an option.

I started to wish I had never had the idea to host a party. What was the point? It was a party for Gemma, but she wasn't even going to be there to enjoy it. I felt so desperate that I ended up doing something that, normally, I would have been too embarrassed to write, let alone send: I put out a message on Twitter in the vague hope that someone might be able to help:

I apologise for this blatant tweet but I've run out of options. Next month, on what would have been Gemma's 41st birthday I'm having a party to remember her and scatter her ashes. Am trying to find a marquee but am running out of time. Can anyone help?

I never expected the response I got. Within an hour, a company called the Brighton Marquee Company got in touch to say they wanted to help, and didn't want any money or publicity in return.

I could scarcely believe it, I had only sent the tweet in the vague hope someone might give me a bit of a deal; I had never expected this. As I read their email again and again in the April sunshine, a tear welled in my eye, and I felt incredibly blessed. All the anxieties and questions about hosting the party began to dissipate – for one of the few times in those first few months, I was now starting to actually look forward to something with a sense of excitement and hope.

So, on a weekend in May that would have marked her 41st birthday, we turned what could have been a hard and terribly sad day into a day of joy, and it was everything I could have hoped for. The sun shone, there was warmth in the air and the garden and marquee looked beautiful. I knew that however hard it was going to be to celebrate a life no longer with us, it would have been everything Gemma would have wanted. Jane's vision and generosity had turned our garden into something very special. From the flowers, to the bales of hay for people to sit on, to the wooden pallets turned into tables, she made it everything that Gemma would have loved.

That morning, I recorded a short video diary in the May sunshine:

This weekend I just wanted to embrace her life and celebrate with family and friends in the same kind of way we celebrated her 40th here in the garden 10 months ago. It was a day that was filled with love, laughter and happiness, and I think today is also going to be another day of love and laughter, and happiness, but underpinned by a huge sadness that she's not here to enjoy it with us. But I'm really glad we're doing this; I'm really glad I took that decision a couple of months ago to turn a negative into a positive. It's been a lot of work, there have been many times when I've thought, what on earth am I doing? But I'm so glad I'm doing it.

The day was a bit of a blur. One moment, everyone was arriving, the next, darkness had fallen and the day had come and gone. In some ways, I felt a bit cheated. After all those hours of preparation and all that worry, I hadn't felt like I got to truly appreciate and drink the day in. But ultimately, what mattered most – and the moment that I will forever remember most fondly – came just after four o'clock, when we gathered round the tree we had planted in her memory. Beneath the tree sat the plaque I had had made with the simple words:

Gemma Rachel Thomas – 20 May 1977 – 24 November 2017.
A wonderful mother, beautiful wife and beloved sister.
Loving, compassionate, missed.

Our vicar, David, said a few words. Gemma's mum, Wendy, and her dad, David, made their own emotional tributes, and I said a few words. I reflected on grief being a path that everyone has to walk alone; that Ethan's walk was different to mine but at the heart of our unique journeys was the same thing – missing Gemma, as a mum and a wife. I apologised for the times in the last six months when I'd got some things wrong and thanked people for their incessant love and support, for not giving up on me, for not giving up on Ethan. And I said, 'Gemma hasn't just left a huge gap in our lives; she's left a huge gap in all of our lives.'

Then, as our friend Pete Wilmott sang, Ethan and I knelt in front of the tree and poured some of her ashes into a small hole. It was a moment no child should ever have to experience at such a young age, but when I'd explained what we were going to be doing, he told me he wanted to be a part of it. I'm so glad he was.

Afterwards, I picked him up into my arms, and the music continued to play, we released a load of white balloons with the words – *You are loved. You are missed. You are remembered.*

In so many ways, that day and that moment felt like the *real* farewell to Gemma. While the funeral in December had been everything I had wanted it to be, it came when the storm of emotions was so intense and, at times, so bewildering, that it had really been about just getting through it. But this party that I never wanted to host became not just a special day of celebration and remembrance, it marked a significant milestone on the road of grief. A milestone that marked a new sense of optimism for the future. A weekend that could have been such a negative time turned into something hugely positive.

The next day, standing close to Gemma's tree, I recorded another video diary reflecting on what I had learnt about grief in the first six months and how I had come to understand it in a different way:

Until now, I had thought that grief was something that time would heal, but I don't think it does. What I think time actually does, is change things. The gap that Gemma has left in my life is huge. It has felt like a hole so big that it almost encompasses every part of my life. For a long time, people have believed in the idea that over time that hole begins to shrink. But the truth is, it doesn't. Because if that hole does get smaller then it means that day by day week by week I'm going to miss Gemma less. Even after only half a year without her, I already know that it's simply not going to happen. I'm never going to miss her less. Ethan is never going to miss her less. Her mum, Wendy, and her sister, Rebecca, are never going to miss her less, her dad and closest friends are never going to miss her less – that is never going to change. What changes, I think, is that a new life begins to grow around that hole and what you're going through. That hole is never filled, but slowly, life begins to change, new people come into your life, experiences change, you start to do new things, bit by bit life does begin to change.

And then I said something that, as I look back now, feels more than ever like a turning point – the moment of realisation that however unwanted and different this new life was; it could perhaps, one day, be as good again:

For so many months all I have been able to think about when it comes to the future is that life is never going to be as good again. It can never be the same again, but as the weeks have turned into months, I've come to realise that life could, perhaps, be as good again. It doesn't have to feel like a Plan B because Plan B, by its very definition, is second best. It's the plan you put in place in case Plan A doesn't work out; but it's never the intended plan.

But my relationship with Ethan is better than ever before, it's stronger than ever before, it's more profound than it has ever been. The love and the bond between us has more depth to it than ever before because of what's happened – that's not a Plan B relationship, that's not second best, that's Plan A. So why can't experiences, why can't holidays, why can't everything else be as good again? If I was to meet someone in the future – totally different though it's going to be – why can't it be a Plan A relationship? It might not be, those parts of life we enjoyed as a three might never be quite as good again, I might be being way too optimistic; but that's what I'm going to aim for. I'm going to chase down Plan A again. It's never, ever, ever, going to be the same; but maybe, just maybe it could be as good and that does give me hope.

John Polo who is now a hope and empowerment coach, lost his own wife, Michelle, to cancer and out of his own loss has become a beacon of hope to so many others. He said that, in the early weeks after he lost her, 'The thought of hope that I could survive without her did nothing but fill me with rage.' I too had been that man who thought life would never be good again, who thought everything would always look and feel grey. The very idea of feeling hope again had been an affront to how I was feeling. But on that beautiful, love-filled day in May, I felt a surge of hope like never before.

THE ODD COUPLE

In the weeks that followed, I reflected many times on that thought: *could* life ever be as good again, or was I trying to chase down the impossible? There were plenty of occasions when grief continued to weigh so heavily that it felt like this life-long burden would never allow me to experience true happiness ever again.

Ethan's summer holidays were beginning to loom on the horizon. For the first time ever, it was going to be just the boy and me. What on earth were we going to do? For all of Ethan's life, this was something I had never had to worry about. I'd be around for the first couple of weeks after he broke up; but then the football season would begin, and Gemma would make sure the rest of his holiday diary was full of activities, days out, and time away with friends or family. (Another one of those aspects of life that I had taken for granted.)

Six weeks without the structure and routine of school can feel overwhelming for parents at the best of times; I felt totally overpowered. As I pored over my diary, and all the weeks yet to be filled, I once again experienced one of bereavement's many familiar feelings – dread. What on earth were we going to do? Going abroad would be too hard and too poignant. How could I handle the idea of lying by the hotel pool, surrounded by happy families when, less than a year before we had been the happy family? But I also knew that being at home would be just as hard. What would we do every day? Being stuck at home for days on end, surrounded by the memories of our old life, knowing that friends were heading off on their family holidays, would be too much to take.

I stared at the empty diary, sadly. Maybe I'd been wrong. Maybe life couldn't be as good again.

A few days later, I had lunch with Katy Hill. Our paths had first crossed on *Blue Peter* back in 1999, and although she had remained a friend, we had lost touch over time as life and careers took us in different directions. But one of the many blessings that came out of something so horrible was how many old friendships were restored. Lots of people I hadn't heard from in years got in touch, and reached out in a really meaningful way – Katy was one of them. Barring the occasional *Blue Peter* reunion, we hadn't really talked in years; but over the course of 2018, our friendship was renewed. Katy and her sister, Naomi, were hugely supportive. If we weren't meeting up for coffee, they would both come over on some evenings and bring dinner with them. And as the weeks turned into months, their love and support never waned – they were the kind of friends I would come to refer to as the "stayers"; they were there for the long haul.

As we ate, I told Katy how much I was fearing the holidays, and wondering what on earth we would do. I told her, 'I know it's going to be different, I just want it to be memorable for Ethan. I want him to be able to say at the end of the holidays that he had a really good time.' Katy was a mother too; she knew why this felt like such a big deal.

'Why don't you go on some kind of road tour?' She asked.

Katy told me the story of Sarah, a woman she knew, whose husband had had a cancer scare. Afterwards, she had quit her role on the BBC's *Dragons' Den*, taken her children out of school for a year, and gone on a tour around the world. And if anyone asked her why, she told them, 'Life is short. You've got to grab it and live it, and create memories that matter to you.'

As Katy told me all about Sarah, I began to feel that same excitement I'd felt when the idea of holding a celebration on Gemma's birthday weekend had come to me. I knew holidays could never, ever be the same again, but like Sarah had said, here was a chance to make new memories. Rather than seeing those six weeks as some kind of parenting endurance test, here was an amazing opportunity to do something different, to try to experience some joy together despite the ever-present pain of missing Gemma.

So it was decided: Ethan's summer holiday was going to be a UK road tour – in a camper van! Just one small problem … I didn't have a camper van!

A few weeks later, after much deliberating, number crunching, and endless conversations with van dealers, I took the plunge, sold our car and bought a camper van. There were plenty of times when I questioned the wisdom of spending that sort of money, while my career was on hold, but every time, I reminded myself that life *is* short, and creating memories, especially with your children, is priceless.

On the day we brought it home, I stood there, just looking at it on our drive – feeling a whole array of emotions, but not the kind of ones that normally accompany the arrival of a new vehicle. In so many ways this van, this lump of German-crafted metal, was a physical representation of just how much life had changed in the past eight months and I wondered what Gemma would have made of it. Gemma had never been a huge fan of camping. In truth, she hated it, always preferring the comfort of a hotel over a night under canvas. On one trip to a family festival in Hampshire a few summers before, she had lasted just one night before taking the comfier and quieter option of a night at her sister's nearby flat! If someone had told me a year before that we'd spend next summer in a camper van, I'd have laughed in their face. But now, we were about to embark on a summer holiday, going from campsite to campsite – Team Thomas on Tour!

In so many ways, those six weeks with Ethan were everything I wanted them to be. There was lots of fun and laughter, plenty of new experiences to try, and precious opportunities for us to talk about everything that had happened.

There were challenging times as well. Whether we were on the campsite or on a beach, we were still surrounded by families – and the constant reminder of how much our lives had changed. We were the odd couple. Could we even be described as a "family" anymore? In those moments, I had to remind myself that there was (hopefully) nothing odd about us, and although it was just the two of us, we were still a family.

The evenings, like at home, were often a struggle. When Ethan was tucked up in bed in the campervan pop-up roof (to this day he's never let me sleep up there despite my endless requests to try it), I had a lot of time alone with my thoughts. On some nights, I was able to read a book or watch a film; but on others, I could only reflect on the lives we were now living. As I sat in my deckchair by the van, I looked on as the lights flickered in the nearby caravans, as couples and families enjoyed cosy evenings, and I felt so utterly lonely and different. Often, I would sit there, looking up at the stars, wondering … ˙

Is Gemma really in heaven? Does heaven actually exist? What if it doesn't? What if it's just the crutch we've invented to soften the devastating blow of death?

Could she still see us? If she could, what would she make of how we were doing? She'd probably have laughed at me becoming a member of the Caravan and Motorhome Club!

That question of whether she could still see us was something I confronted many times over the first year. Whenever I posted anything about her online, I would regularly receive comments saying things like, 'She's still with you,' or 'She's watching over you,' or 'She hasn't really left you.'

Some people sincerely believe in the idea that the departed are still, somehow, alongside us, but I really struggled with that. In some ways I *wanted* to believe that Gemma was still with us in some kind of spirit form, but in so many more ways, I didn't want to entertain the idea at all. If she *was* somehow still with us, then she would have witnessed everything. She would have watched on helplessly as her boy crumpled in a heap of tears on the night I told him she had gone. She would have seen the times I was close to giving up, and the nights I'd found solace in a bottle. If she was somehow watching over us, it wouldn't have been a very pleasant watch.

Whenever I found myself wrestling with the notion of the dead still being with us, I would sometimes think about the film *Ghost* with Patrick Swayze and Demi Moore. In the opening scenes, Swayze's character, Sam Wheat, is murdered as he walks home with his wife Molly. Suddenly Sam finds himself watching Molly crying over his body – to his horror he realises he's dead and has now become a ghost. Despite the unforgettable Righteous Brother's "potter's wheel moment", it's a painful watch. Here is a dead man who has to watch his wife break down in despair and for the first half of the film, he is helpless to do anything about it. The idea that Gemma was still somehow alongside us, watching helplessly on was too painful to entertain.

When I wrestled with those questions about life after death, all I could do was try to hold on to my faith, and the belief that one day, we would be reunited in heaven. For some of you, I know this will sound like something out of a fairy tale; a story made up to soften death's sting. But for me, that belief remained.

There were many times when I was holding onto my faith by my fingernails; but I never quite let go. In the same way I wanted people to respect what I believed about life beyond the grave, I had to learn to respect the fact that everyone deals with death in different ways. While it was of no help to me to believe that Gemma was still with us in some way, I know it's a belief that helps others through their own grief. And it's not for me, or any of us, to judge them or belittle them. At a time when we seek comfort, we need to be allowed to draw that comfort from wherever and whatever gives us a sense of hope and peace.

We spent the final few days of the school holidays down in the south of France, visiting Gemma's dad in the beautiful Rhone Valley – a place Gemma had loved so much. On the final day, Ethan and I sat together in a beautiful town, Grignan, eating ice cream in the glorious sunshine. As he sat there, managing to get more of it over his face than in his mouth, I asked him how the last few months had been. Had he been able to enjoy life despite missing Mummy? Was Daddy doing an okay job? His reply was predictably short, so I decided to ask him to name the five things Dad had done best over the past few months and this is what he told me:

1. *Keeping me entertained.*

2. *Treating me well.*

3. *Making nice food for me.* (Massively proud of this one!)

4. *Giving me lots of thumbs-up when you're proud of me.*

5. *Being the best dad ever.*

I felt it was only fair that I said something about him in return, so I told him the five things he had done best:

1. *Being brave.*

2. *Being kind and thoughtful.*

3. *Making me laugh.*

4. *Comforting me when I'm sad.*

5. *Loving me unconditionally.*

'So how many marks out of 10 would you give the holidays?' I asked him.

'I give the holidays a nine out of ten. I've missed Mummy a lot but I loved being with you.' Those words meant absolutely everything. We'd both missed Mummy hugely, it hadn't been the same, it couldn't possibly have been; but it had been good. Really good. We had created new memories and done things that will live with me, and hopefully Ethan, for the rest of our lives.

It might not have been the summer either of us would have ever wanted; but it never felt second best. It had been a Plan A holiday.

THE LAST FIRST

The last of the "firsts" came in November 2018 – the first anniversary of Gemma's death.

Even though she had been gone so long, there had been a strange comfort in still being able to say that we'd seen her within the last year. It somehow made her feel closer to me. I didn't want that day to come where I'd be saying to Ethan that we hadn't seen her for more than a year, especially in the knowledge that the passage of time from the last moments we spent with her was only ever going to get longer. I wanted the time since we last saw her to carry on being measured in months, not years!

I knew more than ever that this was not a time to be at home wallowing in self-pity, surrounded by potent reminders of yesterday's life. But what else could we do? How could we mark the weekend, take time to reflect, and still find moments of happiness and joy despite the sadness?

On a trip to Blakeney in North Norfolk back in the February half term, I had bumped into a guy called Rob while out on a walk. Rob also worked for Sky, but our paths had never crossed. As we chatted in the bracing North Sea wind, Rob spoke about how much he had been moved by Gemma's story, and talked about how much Ethan and I were loved by everyone at Sky. A few days later, I got this email from him:

Hi Simon,

It's Rob, the random Sky bloke who stopped to chat in Blakeney.

I thought about our chat and decided I should get in touch – there are too many coincidences not to: I was brought up in Cromer, my family and I are mad Canaries fans; you and I both work at Sky, and Blakeney is simply the place where I feel at one with the world.

I simply cannot imagine what you, and your son Ethan, are going through as you try to make sense of what has happened, and contemplate what lies ahead. I'm not in a position to offer you any words of wisdom. Nor can I say something like "it will get easier over time". I suspect that is true, but I don't know that. It would feel like those words were somehow cheap, particularly coming from someone you don't know.

But what I can do is extend an arm of friendship, and support. My place in Blakeney is a walk to the quay, has four bedrooms and four bathrooms, and lies empty for long stretches of the year. If you ever fancy getting away from it all and spending more time up there, and saving a few quid, I will happily chuck you the keys – for free. You'd be doing me the favour, it's good for the place to be used.

Zero offence will be taken if you don't reply – just add my thoughts and best wishes to the swell of support which builds around you.

All the best

Rob

Not for the first time, I was taken aback by the kindness of a virtual stranger – it didn't take me long to pen a reply and tell him I'd love to take him up on his generous offer. As the anniversary moved ever closer and the question of what to do remained unresolved, I remembered Rob and his offer and what he had said about Blakeney being that place where you feel "at one with the world." We'd holidayed as a family in Blakeney lots of times and Gemma had loved it; I knew it was the right place to remember her that weekend. It was decided. We would head to North Norfolk with Gemma's mum and sister, and spend time with them and my family, remembering Gemma, sharing stories about her, and scattering some of her ashes. I knew there'd be plenty of tears, but I hoped that there'd be lots of laughter too.

Sadly Gemma's sister, Rebecca, never made it to Blakeney.

Nine years earlier, her father, David, had been diagnosed with myeloma, but with ongoing treatment had been able to carry on living a full and good life. Only months after Gemma's death from acute myeloid leukaemia, David's ongoing treatment stopped having any positive effect. Despite exploring other avenues and new treatments, David's body failed to respond, and by the time Gemma's anniversary arrived, his health had deteriorated so much that Rebecca had no choice but to go and be with her dad. Life for her at that moment must have felt so very tough. In the space of just 12 months she was facing the very real possibility of losing half of her family to blood cancer. All we could do was hope and pray that he held on; I couldn't face having to tell Ethan that his beloved Pompa had gone as well.

While Ethan was fully aware what this weekend marked, he was mostly thinking about seeing his cousins, especially Thomas, the next day. But on the night before the first anniversary, as we settled into Rob's beautiful house in Blakeney, he said something to me that, even by his standards, took me by surprise. 'Daddy, I know this weekend is going to be difficult and sad for you, but if you ever need a hug, just come and find me.' Not for the last time that weekend, a tear began to trickle down my cheek, and as I hugged him tightly I whispered again, 'My boy, you are amazing, you really are. I don't know what I'd do without you.'

While he slept that night, I wrote this to mark the anniversary, to try and encapsulate what we had lost; but also to sound a note of hope for the future:

A year since ...

Your last breath was taken and cancer took a life half lived.

You flashed that smile and said 'hello darl.'

You last kissed your boy goodnight.

I last got to kiss you goodnight.

You pulled that trademark roll of your eyes.

That infectious laugh was heard.

Our boy cried Mummy and heard a reply.

We enjoyed another of your amazing dishes.

I waved you goodbye at the garden gate.

Your Mum could ring her Gems and say 'hi' and lovely Becs could say 'hello Sis.'

The Prosecco fizzed on a Friday night with friends round the table.

You bought another blue jumper that looked like the last.

One year on ...

A year when everything changed, and all our dreams were rearranged.

A year when life's certainties fell away, twelve months of pain almost every day.

A year when at times the darkness closed in; but somehow we never quite let it win.

A year when hope felt short in supply, times when we had no will left to try.

A year sometimes God felt so distant; but He never left our side for an instant.

But somehow with time comes the will to carry on, times when the light really felt like it shone.

The fight from my boy that kept me trying, always stood by with a hug when I was crying.

The love of friends and our family's support has meant when we were falling, we were always caught.

Grief never ends it has no final destination, it's the price we pay for love's saturation.

Gems we love you. Yesterday, today and forever. Xx

My family arrived the next day. It was a day of fun and endless games of hide-and-seek for Ethan and his cousins. For the rest of us, there were the expected tears and laughter, and times when we just sat in silence, lost in our own thoughts, remembering Gemma.

Later that afternoon, after a brisk walk by the Blakeney marshes, we gathered on a rickety wooden jetty close to the harbour. I placed a small speaker down on the ground and played one of the songs I had played in her hospital room as she neared the end. As the November light faded, each of us took a moment to reflect and remember. The place we had loved visiting as a family would now forever be a place of remembrance as well. A place where I wouldn't just feel at one with the world, but at one with Gemma also.

An hour later, I was back at the house, staring intently at my watch. And at a quarter to six, I looked up and said, 'There it is, Gemma's been gone a year.' In the weeks building up to that moment, I had often wondered what it would be like. Would it be as bad as I feared? I thought I would feel a profound moment of horror, but really, it was nothing more than a quiet moment of calm realisation. A marker in time.

In a strange way, it felt like the day was actually harder for our family and friends. For me, it was a day that ultimately didn't change anything. It was another day when, like the 364 days before, I thought about Gemma almost constantly. I relived the uncomfortable hours of that Friday in the Churchill Hospital like I had done most days. That wasn't going to change. And that night, like every other, I would be going to sleep knowing I would wake up to the same disquieting truth – she was gone, and never coming back. Even a year on, that grim realisation was only just beginning to lessen in its intensity.

For her wider family and friends, it was different. They hadn't forgotten her, far from it, but her loss hadn't fundamentally changed their lives in the way it had ours. They missed her hugely, of course they did, but the nightmare of her absence didn't confront them every day.

My friends who were married still had their husbands and wives. They didn't wake in a half-empty bed; they didn't have to comfort a child who missed their other parent. No doubt their lives felt different, but they went on the same, nonetheless. When the anniversary came, and the posts on social media started appearing, it felt like people were re-engaged with the horror of it with a renewed shock at the speed at which it all unfolded. But for us, it had never gone away.

For a little while, we were back in the bubble of love, support, and protection of a year ago; but this time, the support mostly came in the form of words, not presence. As we headed home on the Sunday evening, the dread of returning to our empty house filled me with a renewed fear, and I braced myself for another one of those nights where our home felt like an enemy. After a weekend remembering Gems, I was in no mood to enter the place that spoke of her absence the loudest.

As Reading drew closer, I received a text from our neighbours, Emma and Rich. Right from the start, they had been an incredible support for Ethan and I. In the early days Rich even offered to knock a hole in the wall that divided our houses and build a hatch, so if ever I needed anything or was feeling lonely, I could open the hatch and say, 'Hello!' To this day he still maintains it was a serious offer!

Despite Emma's own pain at the loss of a friend she had grown to love in the six years we'd been neighbours, she never stopped popping round almost every day to see if we were okay – and she didn't just do that for the first few weeks, she has continued doing it to this day. We were stuck at the traffic lights (honestly!) when I read Emma's text:

I know you're on your way back which I know is going to be hard. Would you like Rich to pop in and light a fire so it's nice and warm when you get back? xx

Before the lights turned green (really!) I fired a quick text back:

Emma that's so, so kind. That would be amazing xx

A simple act of kindness made such a difference. Instead of returning to a dark, cold house, it was full of light and warmth. What could have been a tough, horrible moment after the emotions of the weekend felt just that bit better thanks to the kindness of our thoughtful neighbours.

Too often, when people are struggling to know how to support the bereaved, they get lost in concern about doing and saying "the right thing". But the little, practical things, like offering to cook a meal, baby-sitting, or even lighting a fire, can feel so meaningful.

*

Sadly, on 23rd January 2019, just 14 months after Gemma, her father, David, succumbed to myeloma, and died at the age of 71. For Gemma's sister, Rebecca, who lost her beloved sister and father in the space of just over a year, life seemed unbelievably cruel. She told me it felt like her family was disappearing in front of her.

It was impossibly hard telling Ethan that Pompa had gone. They'd had such a special relationship. And it was another huge loss to bear in such a short space of time. The boy his Pompa had called "Itsy" felt like he was losing everything he loved. But he dealt with it so bravely.

In some ways, it was a comfort to know that David was free from the disease that had turned him into a pale shadow of his former self, but in the immediate aftermath, that was small consolation for Rebecca and Ethan. Two huge figures in their lives had now left life's stage, leaving such a sense of emptiness in their absence. Life for them must have felt so unfair.

NOTHING BUT TIME

One year down the rocky road of grief, the one part of the journey that we have never got used to – and perhaps never will – is the loneliness – and it comes in many forms.

As amazingly as Ethan dealt with the maelstrom of emotions that he had to cope with in that first year, he also had to learn to live with his own sense of loneliness. Even a year on, he still couldn't get used to the pain of seeing his friends with their mums. Whether it was at the school gate, at church, or during visits to friends, everyone else's mum was always there, reminding him of what he has lost. I know that at times that made him feel impossibly lonely, and sometimes, as we've headed home from visiting friends, his tears have flowed. For his friends, life carries on as it always has done, but his life had been changed almost beyond recognition.

There was a sense of that in my own loneliness too.

Spending time with the friends you've known for so long should help, but sometimes, they're among the loneliest times of all. It's not a physical loneliness; it's an emotional and psychological one. You don't just feel as if you've been separated from the person you loved; grief feels like it separates you from everyone else. They're not suddenly ignoring you, but sitting with friends who still have each other, and whose children still have a mum to give them a hug or a word of reassurance, accentuates the agony of all that you have lost.

In November 2017, I fell into that parallel universe, and many months later, I was still trying to find my way back to some kind of reality. You carry on as best you can with the routines and rhythms of life, but no longer really feeling like part of the world. That's the loneliness of feeling so different, so set apart from the life you once had ...

Fourteen months on, I was sitting in church one Sunday, when a couple came up to the front to talk about the marriage preparation course that was beginning in a few weeks' time. As I watched the video and listened to a newly married couple being interviewed about why the course had been such a help to them, I felt about as far away from their experience of life as it was possible to feel. Yet just over a year ago, I'd enjoyed 12 years of the journey they were now embarking on. I knew I wasn't the only one – there would have been others who had been hurt by marriage, and others who had never had the opportunity to marry, but in that moment, I felt totally alone, set apart from the 300 or so people around me.

Not for the first time, I rose to my feet and quietly headed for the nearest coffee shop. It wasn't anyone's fault, a church service can't be tailored to suit everybody's needs and reflect where they're at in their lives, but in a place where I should have felt most at home, I felt anything but. And for the first time in my life, I understood that for many people, church can feel like a very lonely place. Being surrounded by families when you're struggling to even feel like a family is sometimes just too much to bear. Exchanging strained smiles across the aisles as people struggled to know what to say only exacerbated this sense of being set apart. Far too often, the church that was built on the life of Jesus struggles to reflect who he truly was. The figure of Jesus who I had come to know was someone who loved the marginalised, the social misfits, and the people others didn't associate with. Sometimes, it feels like too many churches have become places where those very people can feel the most marginalised and alone.

*

It was the physical loneliness that I never got used to, and I still struggle with it to this day. It's not as relentless and claustrophobic as it felt in the early months, but it's still a presence in so much of life. All those nights after Ethan had gone to bed, and I was alone, downstairs, in an empty lounge, that never got much easier.

The bereaved feel that bitter intensity of loneliness so acutely because what we yearn for more than anything is the one thing we can no longer have. The person we have loved for so long is no longer beside us.

Until she went, Gemma's life was so intertwined with mine that, when those cords were broken, the void was impossible to fill. The life I had led for so long had vanished, and left me with a broken heart and a life that feels forever incomplete. This is a loneliness with no easy solution.

There were plenty of times when I wanted to sell up and move away, make a fresh start somewhere, far away from the reminders of yesteryear. But it would only ever have given us a temporary respite. You can't escape grief. Whether we were in Caversham or Cromer, a change in location was never going to address the hole Gemma's absence had left. Loneliness was going to remain a painful part of our lives.

Loneliness felt like it came and went as it pleased. There were days when it felt bearable, others when it felt overbearing. The need for companionship and company felt like hunger pangs – once Ethan was fast asleep, I craved that presence of someone alongside me. Some nights it felt like I was in some kind of mental battle. *Is this one of those nights when I can grit my teeth, clench my fists and get through it? Or is this a night when I give in; when I find solace in drink?*

I tried catching up with box sets of series we had watched together, but every five minutes I would be hitting rewind as the latest plot twist passed me by – I just couldn't concentrate. And it was these simple things that really served to accentuate the loneliness. Part of the fun of watching shows together is being able to enjoy them with someone else, to talk about them, to laugh together. Without her beside me, it felt like so much of the fun had been extracted from life.

In *A Grief Observed*, CS Lewis talks about how time changed following the loss of his wife, Joy:

"Up till this I always had too little time. Now there is nothing but time. Almost pure time, empty successiveness."

That was so true for me. Without Gemma, there suddenly seemed to be so much time to fill. The evenings felt like days, and the weekends often felt like weeks, especially if I had failed for the umpteenth time to plan anything to do. When Gemma was with us, I never had to concern myself with filling the diary with social engagements, or worry about what to do in between school finishing and Ethan's bedtime.

That responsibility for Ethan's time worried me hugely at first. The post-school hours had been theirs – spending time together, taking him to play dates, or just enjoying being together and making tea. If I was working from home, I'd pop down for a bit, and enjoy some time with my boy; but after we lost her, that part of the day suddenly rested squarely on my shoulders. What *could* I do with him in those four hours? For so long it had been another aspect of life I had taken for granted.

I felt so hopelessly inadequate taking on everything Gemma had done with such ease and grace. So many times, I felt like a failure. Too many times I believed I was falling a long way short in the single parenting test. All too often, I struggled to know what to do with him in the hours before bed. The wonderful array of delicious teas Gemma had made for him were replaced with too many rounds of Marmite on toast, as I struggled to find the motivation or imagination to cook him a proper meal.

On the afternoons I was struggling, the temptation to just let him sit, staring at a screen for the rest of the day was never far away. So often I just wanted to say yes to everything – 'Yes you can have another chocolate snack, yes you can watch yet another episode of DanTDM on YouTube, yes you can have another half an hour on the Playstation, yes you can stay a up a bit later tonight.' He was going through so much – why not give him what he wants if it helps him feel a bit better? Some days I was able to structure his afternoon and be firm over screen time and snacks, others I was just too exhausted and gave in.

Becoming a single parent is a huge challenge for anyone, regardless of their circumstances, but when it's accompanied by grief, it feels even harder. You're dealing with so many different emotions, trying to find the answers to a multitude of questions about the future, and all while attempting to become mum and dad to a child who has their own grief and loneliness to deal with.

CS Lewis was right; without Gemma, and without my career, there was nothing but time, and when that time wasn't filled, the loneliness would crowd in. Instead of time feeling like a precious gift to be savoured and enjoyed, it felt like something to be endured. Sometimes I would find myself looking back at the family planners from years gone by with Gemma's elegant handwriting filling almost every day. The planner from just one year ago looked so vibrant, so full of life. A year on, the days in the diary stretched out with an uncomfortable emptiness.

As time went on, I began to realise that, ultimately, the only way to deal with this feeling of acute loneliness was to try to come to a place of acceptance. A place where, however reluctant you feel, you begin to slowly embrace your new reality. In the early months of grief that is almost impossible; you're still experiencing those moments of denial when you still half believe that your loved one is going to walk back in through the front door. But as denial begins to subside, you grudgingly start to accept that, for the foreseeable future, loneliness is a part of your life. Eventually, I did come to accept that on my terms – in the firm hope and belief that it wouldn't always be like that, and that one day things would change.

WIDOWED AND YOUNG

In the months spent writing this book about our journey through that first year, I spent many hours deliberating on whether or not to write this next chapter. But having spoken to so many people who have been through a similar experience, it's a subject that I don't feel I can ignore – grief doesn't just change you, it also changes relationships.

The second Saturday after Gemma died, a lovely lady called Yvonne came to visit our home, and spent the morning with Rebecca, Wendy, and myself. Yvonne had suffered her own tragedy a few years before, when her husband Simon died very suddenly, leaving Yvonne and their three children behind. In her desire to give everybody a better understanding of grief, and to help others going through bereavement, she set up her own charity (ataloss. org). Knowing that Yvonne understood our journey, I hung on her every word. But there was one thing she said that struck me more than anything – 'Your relationships are going to change. There will be some that will deepen, you will find that new people will come into your life because of what's happened, and sadly, you will experience other friendships falling away.'

Those words played on my mind long after she left. I couldn't get my head around the idea that losing your wife would cause some of your friendships to fall away. At a time when you're going to need to lean on your friends more than ever, why would any of them fall by the wayside? When everything felt like it was changing, this was one area I did not want to change and didn't believe *would* change – I was wrong.

In those early weeks after we lost Gemma, the support of our family and friends was amazing, even unrelenting. The front door became a revolving door, and the kitchen was a hive of activity. At a time when worries and fears about the future were crashing in like a tsunami; the practical challenges of day-to-day life and all the necessary things you have to do following a death were looked after by this amazing army of people around us. Team Thomas delivered when it mattered most.

For the first 16 weeks, Ethan and I never spent a night on our own in the house – not until we were in a place to go it alone. And I will remember and cherish that support for the rest of my life. When life's darkest and most bewildering hour came, the constant support of our family and friends carried us through on a wave of love.

But as those weeks turned into months, something started to happen that I wasn't expecting. Some of that support began to slowly ebb away. The knocks on the door started to grow less frequent. The texts asking how we were doing dried up. And, week by week, I began to feel ever more isolated and ever more alone.

Some of the people who had sat alongside me in some of my lowest moments now looked uncomfortable around me, not knowing what to say, or where to look. A few stopped contacting me altogether, and I never heard from them again. There were times when I wondered if it was just me, maybe this was what I should have expected; perhaps I was being over-sensitive to the smallest of changes. But, as time went on and I spoke to more and more people who had lost a loved one, I realised it *wasn't* just me, this was something that a lot of bereaved people go through.

The Widowed and Young charity was a great resource for many of my questions. In the early days, I asked people what *they* thought about going to see Gemma's body before the funeral. In the three weeks between her leaving us and the funeral there had been many days when I had wanted to go and see her in the chapel of rest. Deep down, I knew it was probably not the best idea. I knew it wasn't Gemma lying there; she had long gone. But it remained a dilemma. Eventually I went onto the Widowed and Young page and asked people what they thought – should I go, or were my last memories of her best left in that hospital room in Oxford?

Within a couple of hours, around 30 people had replied. There were some for whom a final visit had been a real help, giving them a sense of closure. But for the vast majority, the same sage advice was expressed again and again – don't give yourself a memory you don't need. My dilemma was over. The last time I had seen her, she still looked like Gemma; I didn't want to spoil that memory by giving myself an altogether *different* memory.

Being able to talk to people who had gone through the same thing, or were further down the road of grief made a big difference. And when it came to supporting the bereaved long-term, the Widowed and Young community was equally insightful. Most of them made the same observation – they felt a huge amount of support in the early weeks, but as time went on, most of them experienced that support falling away. Their friendship dynamics changed, and they felt an increased sense of loneliness and isolation. The more I read, the more I came to realise that there is a big question mark over how we support the bereaved long-term.

Part of the problem is that so much of grief, is hidden. If it was a physical illness, then those first few days and weeks would be like being in intensive care. For a time, the bereaved would need round-the-clock care and attention. The visits to see them in hospital would be almost constant, and the calls to check in and see how they're doing would be daily. But as the intensity of those first few weeks of grief relent, they would be moved out of intensive care and onto the ward. As the weeks of recuperation continued, the visits would lessen in frequency, but they wouldn't stop, and the calls to see how they were doing would continue until, one day, they would finally be discharged.

The problem with grief and knowing how to support people long-term is that it isn't always obvious, months after a death. In the early weeks I was a complete mess. The traumatic grief I was suffering expressed itself in very obvious symptoms. I was emotional, I was confused, I was prone to panic attacks, and at times, I was angry. There were plenty of times when no one knew how to help me. But as time goes on, the intensity of grief does begin to lessen, and the symptoms become less pronounced. There might have been days at the school gate, or out socially, when I appeared to be okay on the outside, but the truth is that, more often than not I was in unbearable pain on the inside. The trouble is that unless your face is etched with sorrow, or you're breaking down in tears, people can't easily see how you might be feeling. It would have been easy to assume that I was okay, or that I was being strong and stoical. In reality, I was just trying to survive each day. If I was that grief victim in intensive care, I'd have been a long way off coming home.

But an unexpected and untimely death also challenges us in other ways – it confronts us in a very direct and uncomfortable way with our own mortality. When we first become aware that we are mortal beings, we quickly learn that none of us are getting out of here alive! And no matter how long and happy our lives are, we know that at some stage, we're going to have to deal with the loss of a loved one. But until death actually stares us in the face, we try not to think about it, and we certainly don't talk about our fears with anyone.

Gemma's death was so quick, so sudden, and so untimely that it felt like a bomb going off. We might have been the ones at the epicentre, but the shock waves reverberated out way beyond us. People said things like, 'How could this happen so fast?' and 'I can't believe she's gone.' Gemma's story is a painful and very direct reminder of just how fragile and precious life is. But it's a story that people can only stomach for so long. It was an unwelcome reminder that very little is certain in life, and that if it could happen to *her*, it could happen to anyone.

I wonder if it was just too hard for some people – seeing us now as a two, not a three, and feeling her absence so acutely. Perhaps that's why they stopped visiting. It wasn't about us. It wasn't that they didn't love us anymore. Perhaps it was just too painful for them to be around us. Maybe that's why they stayed away.

Let's face it, trying to support the bereaved takes people way outside their comfort zone. It means spending time with someone who is in the most vulnerable place they have ever been; a place where all of their emotions are laid completely bare. The world they once knew has disappeared, all of their "certainties" have been torn away, and their *new* world doesn't feel safe.

Knocking on their door, or making that call is scary. Maybe they're coping with it that day, or maybe they're lost in grief. But it's hard to have to wallow in someone else's grief again and again. Shouldn't they be "getting over it" and getting on with life again?

There aren't any linear stages to grief; most of the time those emotions of pain, anger, confusion, denial, and fear come and go like the wind, and though they may lessen in intensity and frequency, they can last a lifetime. For some of those standing on the sidelines cheering *me* on, it must have felt like trying to stare at the sun. Eventually, you have to turn away because it's too painful.

I know that, on many occasions, I was a very difficult person to be around. I know there were too many times when I lashed out in frustration at people for not being able to understand, or I reacted by saying the wrong thing. But how *could* anyone else truly understand? None of us (thankfully) had ever been through something like this before – no one had lost their life partner at half-time in life, and no one had seen one of their friends' children suddenly left motherless. Of all the people who were there for us over that first year, no one had a reference point or instruction manual to work from, they were all trying to do the best they could, faced with an almost impossible situation.

In trying to help some of my friends understand more, I would sometimes ask them, 'Have you thought about what you would do if this happened to you?' More often than not, this question was met with a look of real fear. You could see it in their eyes, it was something they'd thought about, but it was not a thought they could dwell on for very long. One friend told me, 'Mate, I can't even go there; it's too frightening a thought.' Death is frightening, it confronts us in uncomfortable ways, it asks questions of us that we'd rather not contemplate, and sometimes, it's easier to put our fingers in our ears, hum loudly, and carry on like nothing has happened.

If you're trying to support the bereaved, particularly if loss has come to them very suddenly, the simplest advice I can give you is: cut them some slack. Grief is not an excuse to behave like an idiot, but it is going to make people behave in ways they don't recognise. And they are going to make plenty of mistakes along the way.

As my counsellor, Richard, said on many a Friday morning, I was experiencing traumatic grief. In many ways, I was displaying the signs of post-traumatic stress disorder (PTSD), the kind of condition that has affected men and women returning from areas of conflict. So many of the symptoms of PTSD were now part of my every day – panic attacks, being easily moved to tears, irrational fear, trouble concentrating, outbursts of anger, and difficulty staying asleep. I had seen something far worse than any nightmare I'd ever experienced: my wife had died in front of me, having only been diagnosed three days earlier. Like Richard said, it was like being involved in a car crash – it was only weeks after the impact that I began to emerge from the wreckage and learn to walk again.

In the immediate aftermath of that "car crash" in November, I became a very difficult person to be around, I felt like no one understood. All they were trying to do was help; but there must have been many moments when they wondered if it was worth it! As the intensity of those first few weeks died down, it was hard to hear what it had been like, trying to support me. The recurring term people used to describe me was: "a mess". There were undoubtedly times when I was too far gone to help, and I know that, at times, it left my friends feeling helpless and hurt. Perhaps that's why, consciously or subconsciously, they distanced themselves. And in many ways, I don't blame them.

But there was also something at play that I just couldn't appreciate at the time – they were also dealing with their own grief. They too were missing Gemma terribly. They, like me, were in pain, and dealing with the myriad of questions about life, death, and faith that an event like this throws up. They had lost a friend, and while their lives hadn't fundamentally changed in the ways ours had, they were hurting, and all the while, trying to love and support an unpredictable me!

Now, more than ever, I realise how big a challenge supporting the bereaved is. Sometimes it does feel too much. The pain and unpredictability of the person you're trying to support can leave you feeling more of a hindrance than a help, and frustrated that nothing you say or do makes any difference. But I think sometimes, part of the problem is that's it all too easy to take it personally, to feel like it's an attack on you, when really, it's someone in huge pain lashing out.

It *is* disconcerting, it *is* hard to hear, but at a time when that person's world feels so unstable – try to hang in there. If, for your own sanity, you need to step away for a while then do it; but don't stop reaching out. Try not to walk away. Even a regular text asking how they are can make a big difference, and don't take offence if you hear nothing back. Too many times, I heard via friends that someone had messaged me or left a voicemail, and because they hadn't heard back, they'd assumed I wanted to be left alone. But I didn't want to be left alone. I was having to deal with so much, not least being a single parent, that I would often forget to get back to people. Most of the time in that first year, I could barely remember what I was doing later that same day, let alone anything else. I never wanted friends to stop reaching out.

But ultimately, the biggest problem with trying to get alongside and support the bereaved is this one unpalatable truth – you cannot give them the one thing they crave the most. No one can give them back the person they've lost. And that is the *one* thing that could make it better. I just needed my wife, my best friend, my rock; I needed Gemma back. I was crying out for the impossible, and perhaps knowing that made it feel impossible for others to know how to support me. Grief is a horribly messy path. To stand alongside those in pain means you're going to need to get your hands dirty.

In the same way Yvonne had been right about some relationships changing, she was right about something else – new people did come into my life. My friendship with Dan Ritchie grew and deepened over that first year, as we got to spend more time with him and his family. In my lowest moments Dan was always on the end of the phone. On more than one occasion, he just dropped what he was doing and made the two-hour journey down to Reading to spend time with me.

I had the joy of getting to know Ruth and Tony, a couple I'd met at a Christian festival in the summer. They had four lovely children, but had suffered their own tragedy when just two years before, they lost their two-year-old boy, Jethro, very suddenly. As I got to know them better, they were able to support me in ways that others perhaps couldn't, because they understood what loss felt like. Like me, they too had wrestled with those big questions about life and faith. They knew what it felt like when people were awkward around you, or didn't know what to say. And despite having four kids, and each other, they also understood how lonely a path grief can be. As our friendship deepened, they were always checking in and asking how I was doing, and if I was having a bad day, they were always on hand to offer a word of encouragement.

These new friendships weren't replacing the ones I already had, but I think the reason why they became so important and grew so quickly was this – they had never met Gemma. They were full of sadness and empathy for the huge blow life had dealt us, but they were able to support us in a different way, because they weren't grieving for Gemma like so many of my family and friends were. They wanted to hear stories about her, they wanted to get to know the person we had lost; but they were able to draw alongside us without having to navigate their own pain. Spending time in our house was different for them. They could see the pictures of Gemma around the house, they could no doubt imagine her in our kitchen, creating her culinary magic; but those moments didn't evoke poignant memories of times spent with her in that place.

There was another friend too. And on 26th January 2019, quite unbeknown to me, they arranged a surprise birthday lunch for me at the nearby Thames Lido – a lovely old Edwardian Ladies bath that had been restored to a stunning pool, spa, and restaurant. It opened just one month before Gemma died (she'd have loved it) and over that first year, it became a place where I found peace and tranquillity. I thought I was just going for a massage and lunch with Ethan and a friend; but as I rounded the corner of the restaurant, there, quite unexpectedly, were 14 of my friends laughing at the look of shock on my face. They were some of my oldest friends and some of my newest – but all of them had played a huge part in standing alongside us in our toughest year. I was surprised, I was touched, but above all, I felt something tangible had changed. Ethan knew what it was. As I drove him to school on the Monday morning, I asked him what the two best bits of the weekend were. He said, 'Your birthday and seeing you happy again, Daddy.'

BRAND NEW MORNING

At a quarter to six on a bright, cold November evening, after what had felt like the longest day of my life, my world fell apart. Over the course of that next year, my boy and I had to try to put our world back together again.

At first, it was a battle just to breathe, a struggle just to stay alive. The waves of grief were so big and so relentless, I felt like I was drowning in those dark waters of fear and confusion. It took every ounce of my strength to drag myself back to the surface and draw breath.

There were moments when tiny shards of light would pierce the darkness and give me the briefest moments of hope, but for so long, the gloom of grief felt so oppressive. Slowly, as the weeks became months, the storm began to relent, and the light began to shine brighter and for longer. The periods of relative calm stretched out and, bit by bit, I stopped treading water, just trying to survive, and slowly began to swim. There were many times when this journey felt so rudderless; there are times when it still does. And I wonder, *Where am I heading? Will this journey ever end? Will the darkness ever relent? What is the point?*

But as the march of time continued, and we kept each other going down the road of grief, we homed in on that speck of light and new lands beyond. There were times when the land and the light never seemed to get any nearer; there were times when I wanted to give up, but something kept driving me on. The will to keep going grew stronger.

Then, almost without realising it, that land turned from being a distant form on the horizon to something you could almost reach out and touch. The light was now burning brighter and for longer. Suddenly, for the first time, our feet could feel the seabed below. Bit by bit, we discovered what it felt like to walk again. As we pulled our legs through the water to reach the shore, waves would still hit us from behind and knock us off our feet, the currents would try to drag us back out to sea again; but the desire to reach shore drove us on – and then finally, somehow, we were on land once again. So much was familiar and bore the hallmarks of the life we knew before. So many things reminded us of the beauty of life. Yet this new land, this existence without Gemma, felt so utterly different. Life is still beautiful, but it feels and smells so utterly different.

I will never stop missing the land and the life we knew before; the gaping hole that Gemma's death has left in our lives will never be filled. This journey through grief will never truly end. This first year has been but the opening chapter of life's new story. My grief is no longer my persecutor; it is my constant companion as I begin to find life again in this new, unfamiliar place.

I know that life can never be the same again. But I have boundless hope that it can be as good again, and for that, I will always thank my boy's incredible strength and unconditional love. He kept me swimming towards the light on the most desperate of days. I will always cherish the support of the family, friends, and strangers who stood by us in the darkest of times. And I believe that, even when he felt so distant and quiet, God never once left my side.

I know now that however desperate life can feel, however hopeless the situation may seem, there is always light to be found in the darkest of places and a reason and hope to live again.

Whatever life has thrown at us so far, and whatever may come next, I am determined to keep seeking the light and searching for joy. My heart will forever be broken that Gemma and I never got to enjoy a long marriage together, that our love was interrupted, and that Ethan's mum never got to see him grow into a man. But I am forever thankful for the years we had, and in trying to honour her life and memory, I know that I have to continue to find hope, enjoy new experiences, and savour life again. I owe it to Gemma. And I owe it to Ethan.

Team Thomas will never give up.

12 MONTHS –
12 THINGS I LEARNT ABOUT GRIEF

1. It does slowly get a bit easier.

This was a phrase I heard time and time again in the early weeks after Gemma went, mostly from people who knew what they were talking about; people who had suffered loss themselves. At first, I would look at them with an expression of incredulity. How on earth could something this painful, this life-changing ever get easier? But very slowly, it does. For most of those early weeks, the storm of grief felt so intense that it seemed like there was no way out. It was almost impossible to imagine that the sun would ever shine again; but it did, and the waves began to calm. In the early days those moments were fleeting, but over time they became longer and came more often.

Part of this process is about learning to accept that the loss of someone you love is not something you are ever going to get over. The gap they have left in your life is never going to be filled, the love you feel for them will never diminish. You have to come to a place of acceptance that grief is going to be a lifelong companion. That sounds hard, but why would you want it any other way? If grief, by its very definition, is an expression of love, you don't ever want that love to end. If it does, it means your love for that person has died. As the weeks and months went on, I learnt to enjoy parts of life again, savour new experiences and new relationships in the knowledge that however much joy they brought me, that joy would forever co-exist with the pain of Gemma's absence – only then did grief begin to feel a bit easier.

2. Children are incredibly resilient.

On that night I sat in front of Ethan and told him his mum had gone and he sobbed uncontrollably on the floor, I feared the pain would be too much for him to bear; but in so many ways he bore it better than me. His response to the biggest loss any child can suffer never failed to surprise me, humble me, and inspire me. During the many times I have reflected on that first year without Gemma, I have often wondered what life would have looked like without Ethan – the honest answer is, I'm not sure I would still be here. During the most hopeless of days when the darkness felt at its most oppressive, he gave me a purpose and a reason to live. Whenever I felt like throwing the towel in, his words: 'Team Thomas never gives up' became our motto. He wasn't going to give up, and thanks to him, neither was I. The strength of an eight-year-old boy strengthened his dad in ways he has yet to fully understand.

On his 9th birthday, his first without his mum, I posted this message on social media:

With family, friends – old and new, and God, I have got through the hardest ten months of my life, but my boy is the single biggest reason I am where I am today. In among his own pain and sadness, he has inspired me and given me the will to find life again. No child should ever have to suffer the loss of a parent so young, but he has navigated his strange new world with courage, grace, kindness, compassion and a strength beyond his years. Everything his mum poured into his life over those eight short years now radiates out of him and that is surely Gemma's biggest legacy. I am beyond blessed to have him. Happy Birthday my precious boy.

3. Nobody's journey through grief is the same.

At the heart of grief is the same thing – loss. But how we react to that, and how we deal with it, will be as unique as the person we have lost. While we may experience similar feelings: pain, denial, confusion, hopelessness, loneliness, and desperation, the ways we respond will vary hugely.

Some people will find that withdrawing from the world for a time and drawing the curtains will help. Others – like me – will want to surround themselves with people and try to embrace life again, however hard it might be. Some people will find that it will be too hard to go on living in the house they shared with the person who has gone, and they will choose to move away and start again. But for others, leaving a place that holds so many memories is almost unthinkable. Some people will want to talk about the person they've lost; for others, it's too painful and they'll talk about anything but.

Some may long to find love again; while others will rail against the idea of meeting anyone else. What may feel totally right for one person may feel completely wrong for the other, and for all of us, whether we've experienced loss or not, it is not our place to judge. All we can ever do is try to understand and carry on loving them. Grief is a deeply personal experience; we need to let people grieve in whatever way they need to.

4. Grief can at times feel like a tormentor.

It can torment you when you least expect it. One moment you're having a good day, the next, out of nowhere, it grabs you and knocks you down again. One minute, you're enjoying a rare moment of joy, the next, you're in floods of tears, with no obvious trigger for the sudden swing in emotions. One morning, you wake up and feel able to embrace the day ahead, other mornings you just want to hide under the duvet.

Nowhere did grief torment me more than in our home. There were days when being in the house we had shared with Gemma was bearable, even when Ethan was at school and I was alone.

The quietness and calm of the area we lived in was a source of comfort and peace. I could look at the pictures of Gemma on the mantelpiece, or see her jewellery hanging on the stand in our bedroom and remember the happy times with fondness. But on other days, that place felt like my enemy. The quietness felt oppressive rather than peaceful, the memories of her that shone out of every room were too painful to even look at.

In his book, *Memoirs of a Geisha*, Arthur Golden wrote this about grief:

"Grief is a most peculiar thing, we're so helpless in the face of it. It's like a window that will simply open of its own accord. The room grows cold, and we can do nothing but shiver."

One minute, life can feel okay, and you can feel the warmth of the sun on your back; the next, that window swings open and the tormenting chill of loss hits you all over again.

5. Grief is so often lurking in the mundane.

When you "do life" with someone, they become such an integral part of your everyday life. So much of what they do and what they bring to the relationship goes almost unnoticed; it's only when they've gone that you realise just how intertwined your lives were, and how much you relied and leant on each other. Without them, everything is suddenly on your shoulders, and even the most menial of tasks can serve as a painful reminder of everything that's been lost. Gemma was such a wonderful cook, and everywhere I look in our kitchen, there are reminders of her. Even the simple act of opening a drawer and seeing all of her baking ingredients lying there would be enough to set me off.

There are all the obvious triggers of grief – hearing a piece of music she loved, or seeing an old picture of her. But more often than not, a glance into the kitchen cupboard to grab a can of tomatoes, or hanging out another pile of washing, would bring on the tears.

6. It's okay to laugh.

In the early days, I felt bad for laughing. What on earth was there to smile or laugh about when you've just lost someone you loved so much? I remember going for a walk with a couple of friends from Sky only a few weeks after she went, and as we began to reminisce about our years working together and regaled each other with amusing anecdotes, I began to laugh properly again for the first time. But it didn't feel right laughing, I felt guilty. I felt like I was somehow disrespecting Gemma. In truth I was doing nothing of the sort. She would never have wanted me to spend the rest of my life stuck in a pit of sorrow, she wouldn't have wanted me to go through the rest of my life with a face permanently etched with self-pity. Gemma would have wanted me to find joy again. Laughter is a big part of finding that joy again and healing some of the hurt.

7. Most people are incredibly kind.

So much of the year that followed Gemma's death restored my faith in people. From the kindness of family and friends to the random acts of kindness from total strangers. At a time when life felt so alien to what we had known before, it was a powerful reminder of just how many good people we had around us. In a period of life that felt relentlessly hard, the time people spent with us, the messages they sent us online, the practical help they gave us, and the gifts they sent to our favourite coffee shop, sent us a wave of love that helped to keep us afloat.

8. Life is too short – live it to the full.

We hear it so often, we say it to others – but how often do we fully appreciate what it really means? It's not a throwaway line; life *is* very short. Even if we get to enjoy a long and fulfilling life, the years fly by, fast.

The events of November 2017 taught me so much about life, and perhaps the biggest lesson was: don't take anything for granted. Enjoy the here-and-now, let tomorrow worry about itself. As I said towards the end of my eulogy to Gemma at her celebration, I would have given up almost everything I had for one more hour with her. I had taken so much for granted, I thought we were going to have many, many, more years together. Perhaps if

I'd appreciated just how brief life can be, I'd have appreciated her even more than I did.

9. Even when you think you can't find them, there are always words ... but not emojis!

One of the most common refrains received by the bereaved from otherwise well-meaning people is, 'There are no words.' The truth is there are always words, plenty of them – approximately 170,000 of them in the Oxford English Dictionary! The problem is that many of them feel so hopelessly inadequate, especially when death comes at the wrong time in life, or tragedy strikes. We want to try and say something comforting, perhaps we want to try to make some kind of sense out of what has happened. Or maybe we just feel the need to say something profound. But every time we try to think of something to say or write, it all sounds so utterly trite, and so in the end, we say nothing, or we respond with, 'There are no words.'

For anyone suffering the pain of loss, neither option is of much comfort. If we choose to say nothing out of a fear of getting it wrong, we end up leaving that person feeling even more isolated. But if we decide that there aren't any words, it can leave the bereaved feeling frustrated that people aren't able to fully acknowledge what has happened. Even those three simple words – 'I'm so sorry' – are better than silence. They may appear horribly insufficient, but acknowledging what has happened, in however small a way, is always better than saying nothing. And if you really can't find the words, then a comforting hand on the shoulder, or a hug, can still mean so much.

Sometimes, when death interrupts the expected order of life, we've got to be bold enough to call it what it is. Of all the things said to me in the wake of Gemma's death, that mum in the coffee shop said it best when she said, 'I'm so, so, sorry ... it's just fucking shit.' While I'm not advocating turning the air blue when supporting the bereaved, this reaction encapsulated everything that had happened, and everything I was feeling. What had happened to Gemma and what happens to countless others is just horrible and brutal, and it makes trite platitudes about the deceased being in a better place, or no longer being in pain, redundant. I know it's hard, but if we're struggling for words, we should maybe just call it what it is.

As for emojis ... they're an easy option; but for the bereaved a cartoon image of a face with a tear, or a pair of praying hands, feels, well, just inadequate.

10. Grief has no timeline.

A few years ago, Chris, a family friend from our days living in Norfolk, lost his wife Ruth after a long illness. A bit like me, Chris was very open about his grief, particularly online. His regular Facebook posts over the first year after he lost her were often moving and, at times, painful to read. But as one year became two years, and two became three, Chris was still posting about Ruth. The posts weren't as frequent; but I can remember thinking to myself, *Come on, Chris, isn't it time to move on?* As I know now, this was a thought borne out of complete ignorance. I had no idea what it felt like to lose the love of your life; I didn't know how it reshapes every aspect of your life. All too often, after a year or so has passed, we think the bereaved should be getting back to normal and getting on with life. Except nothing feels remotely normal about life anymore. There is no moving on. Getting over it is equally ridiculous. The pain and grief of losing a loved one is something that might lessen in intensity, but will live with you for the rest of your life. Grief is not constrained by time.

11. It's so important to be able to talk about the person you've lost.

All too often, we avoid talking about the person who's gone in the company of the bereaved because we worry that it will be too painful for them. While it's important we acknowledge that everyone deals with loss differently, and some people *will* find it too painful, I can only talk from my own experience. I found those times when people avoided mentioning Gemma really hard. They weren't doing it deliberately, or out of some kind of disrespect, they probably believed that talking about something else would be a positive distraction. The reality was, I wanted to talk about her. I didn't want Gemma's name to become taboo, I wanted to share happy and amusing stories about her – I wanted to keep her part of the conversation. In talking about the person, you help keep their memory alive. Embrace the memories, it may bring a tear to the eye; but as time passes it will almost certainly bring a smile as well.

12. Getting older is a blessing!

We've become almost obsessed by worries about getting older. We hit a stage in life where we start to feel almost embarrassed to say our age, and wish we were 10 years younger. Whenever another birthday arrives, it's all too often accompanied by people taking an intake of breath and saying things like, 'Ooh, 46, won't be long before you're 50!' I used to be like that. I didn't want to be in my forties, let alone hit 50; but now I see it differently. Gemma died at 40. At the time of writing, the average life expectancy for a woman in the UK is 82.9 years, so she lost out on over half of her life. Like so many others, cancer robbed Gemma of so many years of life ahead.

As I celebrated my 46th birthday in January 2019, I didn't worry about being another year closer to my half century, I saw it as another year I had got to enjoy seeing my boy grow and develop, another year (albeit a hard one) that I got to enjoy more of this thing called life.

Being another year older isn't something to moan about, it is a blessing.

ACKNOWLEDGEMENTS

They often say everyone has a book in them – for a long time I wasn't convinced I did. This is the story I never wanted to write; but it's the story I wanted to tell. Nearly all of us are going to face loss at some stage in our lives; it's the inescapable part of life's rich journey. Sadly, Gemma's story is not unique. Thousands in this country are still affected by cancer every year and for far too many wives, husbands, partners, children, and friends, it continues to cruelly steal the lives of the people they love the most.

This isn't an A–Z on how to cope with grief, it's simply our story. The story of Gemma, the heartbreaking story of a life cut so short and the story of how my boy and I journeyed together down grief's bumpy road and began to find a reason to live again. Hopefully this story will show that however much the darkness closes in, however bereft of hope life can sometimes feel, there is always light and life to be found.

I hope this is a book that honours Gemma – the wife, mother, daughter, sister, and friend who is missed so much. A book that gives hope to those who find themselves on a similar path to ours and helps those who are yet to walk it understand more about something all of us will face; but too many still find too hard to talk about.

I want to thank from the bottom of my heart my family, Gemma's family and my friends who have steadfastly stood by me over that first year. While they navigated their own grief for Gemma; their love for us never waned even when I was at my very worst. A big thanks also goes to my agent, Luke Sutton, who has been an incredible support to me since the day she left us. Always full of wisdom, always on the end of a phone when I was full of doubt, and always having my back.

And thank you too to my friends at Sky, whose support for us never once wavered. When I was struggling with depression and anxiety they showed nothing but understanding, and when Gemma left us they held us as a family and never let go.

Thanks too to Trigger, who had the faith in me to give me the chance to write this book, and my editor, Chris Lomas, who gave me the freedom to write it in the way I wanted. Trigger have done so much to make it the book it is.

And a big thank you goes to Derrina. An amazing woman who has stood shoulder to shoulder with me in some of my darkest hours and has become a rock not just for me, but for my boy too. Out of something so very painful has come someone very special. A woman of understanding, compassion, and boundless kindness who has shown me it is possible to love again in a way I could have never quite believed. Standing alongside the bereaved takes a very special person and she is just that. She has found a place in her huge heart for not just Ethan and myself, but Gemma too. She is one in a million and I feel incredibly blessed to have her in my life.

She has also been a fount of wisdom over the six months it took me to write this book. Always ready to read my words, challenge me and keep on encouraging me. It wouldn't be the book it is without her. She's a very private person so out of respect for her I have left this part of the story out. All I can say is thank you from the bottom of my heart for helping me to smile once again, embrace life again, and feel love again. I love you very much.

Finally I want to thank the most important person of all – my boy. When his world collapsed in November 2017, I feared this would be too much for an eight–year-old to bear. At times it felt like it was. But so many times he's been the one who has picked me up off the floor when the burden of grief felt too much. His love, kindness, and incredible wisdom has dragged me back to my feet again. One day I hope he comes to realise that in the same way I was there for him, he was there for me in an even bigger and more profound way. His mum's love, compassion, patience, and kindness live on in him. I am biased (of course) but, my boy, you are incredible, and I love you to the moon and back!

Cancer and cancer care charities

Bloodwise https://bloodwise.org.uk

Marie Curie https://www.mariecurie.org.uk

Maggie's https://www.maggiescentres.org

Bereavement charities

Widowed and Young https://www.widowedandyoung.org.uk

Child Bereavement UK https://childbereavementuk.org

Daisy's Dream https://www.daisysdream.org.uk

Grief Encounter https://www.griefencounter.org.uk

Cruise Bereavement Care https://www.cruse.org.uk

The Good Grief Trust https://www.thegoodgrieftrust.org

At a Loss https://www.ataloss.org

Winston's Wish https://www.winstonswish.org

**If you found this book interesting ...
why not read these next?**

Man Up Man Down

Standing up to Suicide

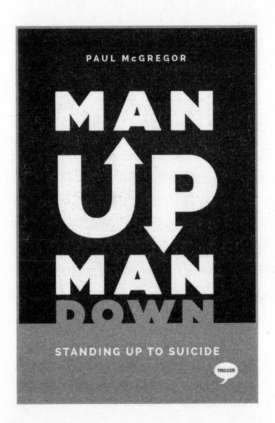

When his dad died suddenly by suicide, Paul was devastated.
Now he's on a mission to change how we think about men's
mental health and what it really means to "man up".

Daddy Blues

Postnatal Depression and Fatherhood

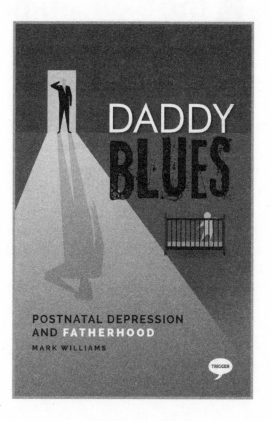

Mark knew of baby blues for mothers, but never thought it might happen to him. And then it did. *Daddy Blues* explores a story we all know, from a different perspective.

the *Shaw* mind
FOUNDATION

Creating hope for children,
adults and families

Sign up to our charity, The Shaw Mind Foundation
www.shawmindfoundation.org
and keep in touch with us; we would love to
hear from you.

*We aim to bring to an end the suffering and despair caused
by mental health issues. Our goal is to make help and support
available for every single person in society, from all walks of
life. We will never stop offering hope. These are our promises.*

TRIGGER™

The mental health & wellbeing publisher

www.triggerpublishing.com

Trigger is a publishing house devoted to opening conversations about mental health. We tell the stories of people who have suffered from mental illnesses and recovered, so that others may learn from them.

Adam Shaw is a worldwide mental health advocate and philanthropist. Now in recovery from mental health issues, he is committed to helping others suffering from debilitating mental health issues through the global charity he co-founded, The Shaw Mind Foundation. www.shawmindfoundation.org

Lauren Callaghan (CPsychol, PGDipClinPsych, PgCert, MA (hons), LLB (hons), BA), born and educated in New Zealand, is an innovative industry-leading psychologist based in London, United Kingdom. Lauren has worked with children and young people, and their families, in a number of clinical settings providing evidence-based treatments for a range of illnesses, including anxiety and obsessional problems. She was a psychologist at the specialist national treatment centres for severe obsessional problems in the UK and is renowned as an expert in the field of mental health, recognised for diagnosing and successfully treating OCD and anxiety-related illnesses in particular. In addition to appearing as a treating clinician in the critically acclaimed and BAFTA award-winning documentary *Bedlam*, Lauren is a frequent guest speaker on mental health conditions in the media and at academic conferences. Lauren also acts as a guest lecturer and honorary researcher at the Institute of Psychiatry King's College, UCL.